Bachelors and Bunnies

Bachelors AND Bunnies

THE SEXUAL POLITICS OF *Playboy*

CARRIE PITZULO

THE UNIVERSITY OF CHICAGO PRESS

CHICAGO AND LONDON

Carrie Pitzulo is assistant professor of history at the University of West Georgia.

The University of Chicago Press, Chicago 60637
The University of Chicago Press, Ltd., London
© 2011 by The University of Chicago
All rights reserved. Published 2011
Printed in the United States of America

Chapters 5 and 6 were first published as "The Battle in Every Man's Bed: *Playboy* and the Fiery Feminists," in the *Journal of the History of Sexuality* 17, no. 2 (2008): 259–89.

20 19 18 17 16 15 14 13 12 11   1 2 3 4 5

ISBN-13: 978-0-226-67006-5 (cloth)
ISBN-10: 0-226-67006-6 (cloth)

Library of Congress Cataloging-in-Publication Data

Pitzulo, Carrie.
  Bachelors and bunnies : the sexual politics of Playboy / Carrie Pitzulo.
    p. cm.
  Includes bibliographical references and index.
  ISBN-13: 978-0-226-67006-5 (cloth : alk. paper)
  ISBN-10: 0-226-67006-6 (cloth : alk. paper) 1. Playboy (Chicago, Ill.) 2. Men's magazines—United States—20th century—History. 3. Sex role—United States—History—20th century. 4. Sex role—Press coverage—United States—History—20th century. 5. Sex—United States—History—20th century. 6. Hefner, Hugh M. (Hugh Marston), 1926– 7. Sex role in mass media—History. 8. Sex in mass media—History. I. Title.
  PN4900 .P5P54 2011
  051—dc22

                                                          2010044987

Contents

Acknowledgments

Anyone who has ever endured the writing of a first book knows that it is an arduous process, and one that would hardly be possible without the support and contributions of many people. I am intellectually indebted to Barbara Ehrenreich and Beth Bailey, whose works introduced me to the notion of masculine crisis and *Playboy*'s possible relationship to it. Many thanks to my editor, Douglas Mitchell, for his enthusiasm and guidance. From our initial conversation, before my book was even complete, Doug assured me that my work was worthy and important. Thank you as well to Tim McGovern, Katherine Frentzel, and Levi Stahl at Chicago for all of your hard work on my behalf, and to the anonymous reviewers of the manuscript and of an article that came out of this project, as well as to Matt Kuefler, who edited that article for the *Journal of the History of Sexuality*.

During the numerous incarnations of this project, many people provided me with support, intellectual insight, and friendship. Thank you to Gerald Markowitz, whose incredible generosity and good-heartedness were so appreciated through these many years. Likewise to Carol Groneman, who was always honest and who believed in my work, and Katherine Jellison, who brought me to women's history. Thank you to Dagmar Herzog, David Nasaw, and Randolph Trumbach, and Thomas Kessner, who all pushed me to do good work and have looked out for me intellectually and professionally. Thanks as well to various friends and colleagues who commented on the first drafts of this work, and to Mike Wallace and Suzanne Wasserman, who were helpful in the earlier stages. During a casual conversation at a department party, Marta Petrusewicz convinced me of the necessity of telling the Playmates' stories when I thought I was just writing about men.

Kurt Conklin contributed information on archival holdings of media, Barbara Winslow kindly shared her memories, and an utterly fortuitous meeting with Julia Akoury Thiel at an American Historical Association conference provided me with an important interview connection. This research was presented at various conferences over the years, and feedback from commentators, panelists, and audience members contributed to the evolution of my work, especially at the Berkshire Conference on the History of Women, the Popular Culture and American Culture Association, the American Historical Association, and the Organization of American Historians. Many thanks to Neena Kumar, Lennard Thal, and to my high school teacher Joseph Dercoli, who always knew I would be a writer.

At Playboy Enterprises, Inc., I cannot thank enough Lee Froelich and Jessica Riddle for their support and generosity over the years, and particularly for granting me access to the archive and guiding me through it. This project opened up in so many unexpected ways, and much of that was attributable to the friendly network of Playboy contacts who generously sat for interviews and put me in touch with other subjects, including Hugh M. Hefner and Christie Hefner, as well as Arlene Bouras, Nat Lehrman, Barbara Nellis, James Petersen, and Dick Rosenzweig. Likewise, profound thanks to Playmates Marilyn Cole, Dolores Del Monte, Alice Denham, Jennifer Jackson, Gale Morin, Joyce Nizzari, Martha Smith, Victoria Valentino, and would-be Playmate Carole Waite. Thanks as well to company associates Jill Boysen, Mark Duran, Gretchen Edgren, Rob Hilburger, Elizabeth Kanski, Steve Martinez, Lauren Melone, Mary O'Connor, Marcia Terrones, and Teri Thomerson. Everyone I met who was affiliated with Playboy was so kind and supportive.

I cannot imagine what this process would have been like without the many wonderful friends with whom I have commiserated, complained, and laughed so often. Thanks to Gregory Emch, and to Amit Vaidya, as well as to Debra Michaud and Michelle Roman, who put roofs over my head during several research trips to Chicago, and Dave Cuthbert, who arranged lodging during my trip to Los Angeles. Thank you to Kristopher Burrell, Melvin Coston, Anthony deJesus, Carla DuBose, and Kevin McGruder, all great friends and colleagues. They made me laugh more than anyone, at times even turning my tears of misery into tears of hilarity. Thank you as well to my co-conspirators at Medgar Evers College—Esin Egit, Jennifer Griffith, Steven

Nardi, and Antonio Pastrana. Their endless humor and intellectual and professional insights were a treasure. Tremendous thanks to Mara Drogan, Kate Hallgren, and Carolyn Herbst Lewis for their intellectual contributions to my work, and most especially for their friendship. Mara and Kate keep this work fun and exciting, even worthy of weekend pilgrimage, and Carolyn has been there since the beginning. I am so happy to have you all as peers, colleagues, and friends.

Finally, I am forever indebted to my family, especially my mother, Jacqueline, and my father, John. My mom gave me feminism, and my dad is the reason I am a historian. They have both given me nothing less than unconditional love and support, never asking the dreaded question, "Aren't you done yet?" Thank you to Jonathan and Sandra Bensky, who have been so enthusiastic about my work. And deepest gratitude to my personal cheerleader, my unofficial publicist, and my intellectual and emotional sounding board, my husband Brian Bensky, whose support never waivers. Thank you for everything. Last but not least, love to our cats—Scully, our constant distraction, and Phoebe, who lets me use her as a bookstand while she sleeps on my desk.

Introduction

Playboy: The Sassy Newcomer

One of these days, I'm going to do an editorial on the subject.[1]

UNIVERSITY OF ILLINOIS STUDENT JOURNALIST HUGH
HEFNER ON AMERICAN SEXUAL MORES, 1948

In 1970, feminist leader Gloria Steinem interviewed the founder of *Playboy*, Hugh Hefner, for *McCall's* magazine. The confrontational exchange read like a showdown. Hefner was defensive. Instead of emphasizing the support he and *Playboy* had given to liberal feminism, he focused on militants, calling them "foolish." He predicted that in the future women would have no complaints about their status in society.[2] Hefner wondered why feminists were not "grateful" to his philosophy for liberating women, charging, "I didn't pick them out as special enemies, you know. They picked me out first."[3] For her part, Steinem argued that Hefner was stuck in the 1950s, and accused *Playboy* of objectifying women and of exploiting men's insecurities in the name of capitalism. The face-off suggested that Hefner's world might not survive the era's sexual and political revolutions, no matter the role his libertine philosophy may have played in helping them along.

If Steinem thought Hefner was irrelevant in 1970, her claim could not be made today. In recent years, the Playboy empire has experienced a resurgence with the top-rated E! television program *The Girls Next Door*. The smash reality hit, which premiered in 2005, focuses on the lives of Hefner's three blonde girlfriends and is one of the most successful shows in the network's history.

It is particularly popular with women. A woman moderates the "Playboy Mailing List," an important web-based clearinghouse for all things Playboy.[4] Likewise, the ultimate expression of hip, contemporary womanhood at the turn of the millennium was HBO's *Sex and the City*. For an entire season protagonist Carrie Bradshaw wore a Playboy rabbit-logo charm around her neck, and in one episode, the friends made a trip to the Playboy Mansion—which Hefner told me indicated that he "had won some kind of war" with American culture. The rock band Weezer filmed the video for their 2005 hit song, "Beverly Hills," at the mansion. Brian Grazer is producing the upcoming biopic *Playboy*, a film based on Hefner's life; Columbia TriStar released the comedy *The House Bunny* in the summer of 2008. Furthermore, Playboy Clubs have sprung up once again in Las Vegas and other cities. The rabbit logo is more internationally recognizable than ever before, as Playboy's brand continues to expand to include a variety of consumer products such as t-shirts, jewelry, and the like. Women are the target audience for the rabbit-branded items that fill Playboy specialty shops and department stores around the world. How did Hefner's ode to male hedonism become a modern icon for women?

That was not the initial question that motivated this research. Inspired by Barbara Ehrenreich's work on Playboy in *The Hearts of Men: American Dreams and the Flight from Commitment*, I assumed that all fruitful inquiry into the history of the magazine necessarily pertained to masculinity, and that a consideration of femininity in *Playboy* would be redundant. Much has already been said about objectification in the centerfolds; why restate the obvious? As a feminist, I was aware of the traditional critique of *Playboy*, and expected to find rampant sexism in the magazine. Indeed, I found the most hostile gender bias was not located in *Playboy*'s centerfolds, but rather in its antiwoman and antimarriage diatribes of the 1950s and early 1960s. But upon close examination, I realized that the story of *Playboy* was much more complicated than I had presumed.

Nonetheless, it is the magazine's early gender hostility that initially catches the attention. But Hefner's antagonistic attitude was a product of the cultural climate of 1950s America and not unique to his magazine. Historian James Gilbert writes that most postwar social critics "used a vocabulary of gender invective, with a deep antifemale cultural bias and a scurrilous assessment of the role of women in culture."[5] This hostility arose from the well-founded sense that traditional power relations were being upset. Competition with the Soviet Union appeared to threaten not only American global dominance, but also the very lives of citizens. By the mid-1950s, the civil rights movement solidified its challenge to white supremacy, while the changing needs of American capitalism had given rise to an increasingly corporate workplace in which men had little need to flex muscles and express traditional manliness. Instead, some perceived the desk jobs of middle managers as emasculating and degrading to American manhood. And in spite of an intense postwar emphasis on domesticity, women were working outside the home in unprecedented numbers.

When Hugh Hefner founded *Playboy* in 1953, America was in the grip of what many observers considered a "crisis" of masculinity. These broad social tensions provoked pervasive anxiety over what it meant to be a man in a changing world. This translated into a cultural angst over the ability of middle-class men to maintain their traditional authority in the home, workplace, and the world. The issue was widely recognized in the postwar years. In 1958, noted historian Arthur Schlesinger, Jr., contributed an article to *Esquire* magazine entitled "The Crisis of American Masculinity." That same year, *Look* magazine published "The Decline of the American Male," which situated the middle-class man's "collapse" within a "pit of subjection, where even his masculinity is in doubt."[6]

Reflecting and amplifying these concerns was the spotlight shown on American sexuality. Various factors combined to make the sex lives of the middle class endlessly fascinating—and anxiety-producing—to many social critics. Alfred Kinsey's demonstration that private sexual practice was far more varied than social prescription dictated, as well as the popularity of Freudian psychology and rampant homophobia made sexuality a cultural topic of conversation. Calling sex a "national obsession" for postwar Americans, historian Elaine Tyler May has shown that massive societal pressures placed heterosexuality under scrutiny. Cold war domestic politics tied the strength of the nation to the strength of the American family. If men and women, the contemporary logic decreed, did not fulfill their traditional duties as husbands and wives, father and mothers, providers and nurturers, the very fabric of society would be weakened, and the country would lack the stability necessary to battle the Soviets. To this end, the traditional double standard that rigidly controlled feminine sexuality strengthened. Yet a modern emphasis on sexual health and fulfillment contributed to complex demands of heterosexuality, and in particular on women's behavior. The result was a confusing world in which sex was considered both taboo and a crucial part of one's happiness—as long as one pursued it within the confines of heterosexual monogamy.[7]

As Ehrenreich has demonstrated, *Playboy* reacted to this stultifying pressure to domesticate in part by celebrating unencumbered bachelorhood, and it sometimes denigrated women in the process. But even amidst *Playboy's* early juvenile, no-girls-allowed rants, there were surprising pearls of enlightened compassion and liberal politics in the magazine. Thus, after my initial skepticism of *Playboy's* gender politics, I soon discovered that mature, progressive morsels hinted at a broader political agenda, one that I would find illuminated in the next decade.

Although the bachelor lifestyle remained a central focus for the magazine, the sophomoric chauvinism of *Playboy's* early years was for the most part abandoned in its second decade, by which time the publication began to take itself more seriously. The shift was largely the consequence of editorial director Auguste Comte Spectorsky's attempt to raise the level of sophistication in the magazine. In 1957, Hefner lured Spectorsky away from the New York literary scene to *Playboy's* headquarters in Chicago. Spectorsky had made a name for himself with his bestselling take on the postwar middle class, *The Exurbanites*. Influenced by the larger cultural critiques of the day, Spectorsky brought with him an intense anxiety over the plight of the modern American male. Though Spectorsky's perspective somewhat reinforced the gender antagonism of *Playboy's* early years, the overall seriousness with which he approached the magazine, combined with increasingly liberal social trends, moved *Playboy* away from puerile tirades against women.

By the early 1960s, the magazine expanded its focus on literature and serious journalism, reflecting the sweeping changes taking place in the country itself. As politics became central to many American's lives, issues of civil rights and individual freedom gained more attention in *Playboy*. In the process, the magazine revealed a surprising degree of fair and sympathetic gender politics, as we will see. But even in an era of liberal reform, both in and outside of the magazine, *Playboy*—like the culture itself—was fraught with contradiction as it grew from the 1950s into the '60s. The centerfold Playmates exemplified this contradiction. Many feminists have criticized the Playmates for their objectification, presumed submissiveness, and, according to writer Ariel Levy, lack of individuality. But in order to decipher their historical meaning, the centerfolds must be considered in the context of postwar America.

figure 1.   April 1968. Reproduced by special permission of *Playboy* magazine.
Copyright 1968 by Playboy.

After World War II, middle-class women's sexuality was policed by a
strict double standard. Media critic Susan Douglas argues, "The legacy of
the 1950s was that no 'nice' girl ever, *ever*, went all the way before marriage,
and no nice woman ever really liked sex."[8] Women who rejected this sexual

standard were often denigrated or in some way punished.[9] This was not the concept of femininity embodied by the Playmates. In the years before the modern feminist movement challenged women's domestic assignment as well as the sexual double standard, the Playmates joyously celebrated feminine sexuality. The images in the centerfolds suggested that women—even the nice ones, even the single ones—enjoyed sex. Indeed, *Playboy* declared, the girl-next-door had the *right* to enjoy sex. This was a subversive claim in the postwar years.

Like its version of femininity, *Playboy* presented a conflicted picture of ideal masculinity. Clearly, the magazine known as "entertainment for men" was a salute to straight manhood. But *Playboy*'s relationship to masculinity was complicated. Rather than strictly promoting traditional male authority, or even confidence, the magazine also served to objectify masculinity through its incessant emphasis on that quintessentially American pastime, consumer self-improvement. From its founding, *Playboy* included regular advice columns on fashion and cooking, with frequent features on interior design, entertaining, travel, and the like. Men were instructed on how to live like swinging bachelors, regardless of how realistic that goal may or may not have been for many readers. Challenging the heterosexual positioning of the magazine, men were encouraged to turn their roving gaze from the centerfolds to the myriad images of other men showcased in the magazine, and ultimately to their own mirrors. In an era of expanding consumption and shifting gender standards, *Playboy* prodded male readers to scrutinize themselves, and potentially each other, with a self-consciousness usually reserved for women.

The contradictory nature of the magazine's gender politics was brought into sharp relief with the confrontation between *Playboy* and the women's movement in the early 1970s. The magazine became more explicitly political during the sixties, espousing liberal positions on civil rights, the war in Vietnam, free speech, and the like. But Hefner and his editors found themselves in a dilemma regarding feminism. The political slant of the magazine dictated support for women's rights as a natural outgrowth of its overall philosophy, which stood unwavering for individual liberty. But the emergence of some radical factions of feminism, which challenged not only the brand of femininity promoted by the Playmates but also critiqued heterosexuality itself, was more than Hefner and many of his editors could bear—and more than his publication could have withstood, had the radical view truly taken hold in the culture. Editorial comment in the magazine, charitable donations of the company, and archival evidence demonstrated Hefner's consistent support for liberal feminism, but he chose to foreground his aversion to militant activism and thus helped to solidify a misplaced legacy of antifeminism.

Exploring these contradictions, this book traces the winding path the magazine forged in its construction of gender, and ultimately considers the ways in which *Playboy* confronted—and contributed to—changing notions of heterosexuality. My work reevaluates the magazine's treatment of womanhood, feminism, monogamy, and romance, and its idealization of straight masculinity through consumerism. As one of the most popular and influential magazines in the country, I argue that *Playboy*'s renegotiation of postwar heterosexuality was more pro-woman, even quasi-feminist, than previously acknowledged. The magazine promoted more than male libertinism, it expanded upon traditional definitions of sexual privilege to include women's liberation as well. But, perhaps counterintuitively, *Playboy* was not solely focused on hedonism. It also contributed to an ongoing romanticization of heterosexual monogamy by insisting upon mutual respect for and within relationships. Putting its own twist on commitment, however, *Playboy* advocated not the avoidance of marriage, but delayed marriage for men and for women as a means to personal growth. Thus the magazine acted as a bridge between the traditionalism of the previous era and the modern celebration of personal freedom and fulfillment.

Bachelors and Bunnies follows the narrative arc of *Playboy*'s evolving gender universe from its founding in 1953 through 1973, when the magazine's formula was established, institutionalized, and ultimately tested. This book begins with *Playboy*'s earliest and most obvious constructions of gender—the sophomoric antagonism that reflected the pervasive misogyny of the postwar period, the centerfolds that defined *Playboy* and made it famous, and the ubiquitous lifestyle columns that carved out a central role for men in the expanding consumer culture of the 1950s. In the second half of the book, attention shifts to the politicization of *Playboy* in the 1960s and early '70s by examining the *Playboy* Philosophy and the attendant expansion of readers' letter columns, to Hefner's confrontation with the women's movement, and finally to his philanthropic commitment to liberal feminism through the work of the Playboy Foundation.

In short, *Bachelors and Bunnies* traces the evolution of *Playboy*'s politics from what it called "womanization" to feminism, and from gender exclusion to mutual respect, while acknowledging the contradiction that always marked Hefner's thinking on issues of sex and romance. This book, however, is not an exhaustive look at *Playboy*'s first twenty years, nor is it a study of pornography. Indeed it is debatable, based on one's own political persuasion, whether *Playboy* was ever pornographic. *Bachelors and Bunnies* positions the magazine within the context of the eroticization of postwar popular culture, rather than the underground pornographic fringe. My work joins in the conversation started by scholars like Bill Osgerby, who see *Playboy* as moving commercial sexuality away from the "cultural margins to the mainstream."[10] Therefore, this project does not formally engage the important discussions of porn studies. However, questions of obscenity and legal regulation, as well as feminist antiporn critique, are historically relevant to the narrative and so I address these issues where appropriate.

My focus is on the editorial voice of the publication as it pertained to gender and sexuality. *Playboy* was first and foremost considered a provocative magazine, and there is much regarding its construction of heterosexuality that has been overlooked by the previous literature. As a recent *New York Times* article noted, Hefner and his inner circle lament that this part of *Playboy*'s history has been "lost."[11] And like the fabled reader who claimed to have read *Playboy* only for its articles, but no doubt appreciated the centerfold each month, I also discuss the Playmates because they were essential to the magazine's sexual worldview and because I believe a revisionist interpretation of them is possible.

None of this is meant to downplay the messages that can be found in other parts of the magazine, such as its important fiction or popular cartoons. Indeed, my argument rests on the premise that an adequate understanding of *Playboy* can come only by considering the whole product. However, I focused on the intellectual and political views of *Playboy* as expressed through the words of Hefner and his editors, not those of writers and personalities who appeared briefly in the magazine. Finally, primary source evidence on the editorial stance of the magazine and on its centerfolds was especially rich and illuminating. I had full access to the company's archive in Chicago, some of which had not been perused even by *Playboy* staff for decades, and is therefore new to the historical record.

Those archival sources included company memos, correspondence, reader letters, and the like. The memos in particular provided a fascinating look at the behind-the-scenes evolution of the magazine. For many years

Hefner had isolated himself and worked exclusively from his nearby Chicago mansion, thus long, detailed memos were his primary means of communication with his editors and staff. I have also relied on interviews I conducted with Hefner, as well as Playmates and editors from the era, to construct this history. While I am aware of the problems inherent to oral history, faulty memory among them, I have considered the interview material in the context of other accounts to affirm their accuracy. Thus, they have been situated in conversation with archival documents as the basis of this work.

Hugh Hefner has always been obsessed with his history and legacy, a fixation that began long before the first issue of *Playboy*. He started to document his life in scrapbooks as a teenager, and there are now over two thousand volumes in his personal archive. Additionally, many of the editors from the early years of the magazine spent decades with the magazine. They were not only important contributors to and creators of *Playboy* in its formative years, but also knew by heart the "story" of Hefner and *Playboy*, and had almost as much at stake in the magazine as did the man himself. Although that fact makes these recollections vulnerable to exaggeration or self-interested distortion at times, it also makes them coherent and the overarching narrative of *Playboy* consistent. And since the oral histories tend to reinforce the archival documents, they are used here in conjunction. I have noted where the hyperbole or faulty memory is obvious or essentially at odds with the historical record.

This research locates *Playboy* within the evolving meanings of heterosexuality in the twentieth century. Although it may seem obvious that *Playboy* promoted straight sex, its formulation was a reflection of a new, more inclusive heterosexuality. The magazine's version of sexuality elaborated on emerging cultural trends that celebrated hedonistic pleasure and nonreproductive sex, which by the 1960s became important priorities within the dominant society. John D'Emilio and Estelle Freedman and others have demonstrated the media's crucial role in mediating twentieth-century sexual standards.[12] *Playboy* joined in this conversation and became one of the leading postwar arbiters of heterosexual expression.

But while *Playboy* unapologetically celebrated heterosexuality, it did not do so to the exclusion of alternatives like homosexuality. Instead, Hefner was greatly influenced by the work of Alfred Kinsey, and embraced Kinsey's notion of a sexual continuum in which most people exhibit some degree of sexual desire for both the same and the opposite sex. In the pages of *Playboy*'s prominent advice column, the Advisor, Hefner and his editors reassured readers who perceived themselves as less than thoroughly straight by repeatedly citing Kinsey and his theoretical spectrum. So Hefner was aware of sexuality as an often fluid, changing experience and did not uncritically present his magazine's agenda for straight masculinity, but rather he acknowledged a range of human expression. Undoubtedly, *Playboy* championed heterosexuality as the most desirable option, especially in its centerfolds. But in the context of the pre-Stonewall American media, compassion for gays and lesbians was a welcome relief for some of *Playboy*'s gay readers, as we will see in chapter 4.

Playboy's role in the negotiation of postwar heterosexuality was an important step in a century-long project wherein understandings of sexuality evolved according to the needs of society. As Jonathan Ned Katz and others have demonstrated, modern dichotomous notions of heterosexuality and homosexuality emerged from the turn-of-the-twentieth-century medical field as a way of classifying and codifying sexual norms, and reflected broader middle-class renegotiations of sex. This was in contrast to previous generations that conceived of sex as a repertoire of behavior, ideally focused on procreation, not an immutable component of an individual's identity. Additionally, George Chauncey has shown that early twentieth-century men, especially those of the urban working class, were often able to pass back and forth between hetero- and homosexual experience with relative ease. As long as a man performed appropriate masculinity—in which his strength, aggression, and power were not in question—he could use more effeminate men for sexual release, just as he might use a female prostitute, and otherwise lead a "normal" heterosexual life.

By the middle of the century, though, blurry working-class sexual distinctions had given way to exacting middle-class categories of gay and straight. Men were still expected to uphold standards of traditional masculinity in dress and manner, but now manhood was proven by one's choice of sex partner. With this new categorization came an emphasis on pleasure and personal fulfillment. Fleeting same-sex desire or affection between men, let alone a homosexual encounter, became associated with an overall nature. Men were pressured to demonstrate complete devotion to heterosexuality, or risk being labeled a fag or queer.[13]

Playboy emerged as a cultural phenomenon precisely when the new heterosexuality—and the pleasure principle Katz talks about—were becoming engrained as social standards. But Hefner put his own twist on the rules: *Playboy* told its readers that straight sex was best; however, the magazine insisted that *both* men and women should be free to explore its expanding postwar terrain. Since men's sexual freedom depended upon liberated women, *Playboy* upheld the increasingly modern emphasis on heterosexual pleasure as a worthy goal for personal fulfillment regardless of gender, in and outside of committed relationships.

Playboy's contribution to the heterosexual project can be seen clearly not just in its centerfolds, but also in its articles and editorials, as well as in its extensive reader letters columns. There were many components to the playboy lifestyle, and not all of them were of a sexual nature. From the early years of the magazine, *Playboy* earned a reputation, and many publishing awards, for its smart design and layout; it was noted for its popular cartoons; and it attracted some of the best writers in the country with its high circulation and compensation rates. Its literary heyday included writers like Vladimir Nabokov, James Baldwin, and Ernest Hemingway. Likewise, starting in 1962, *Playboy* included interviews with some of the most influential and controversial people in the world, such as Martin Luther King, Jr., Ayn Rand, the Beatles, Jawaharlal Nehru, Jean-Paul Sartre, and Joan Baez. Major journalistic pieces on war, economy, government, and the like became regular elements of the magazine. Additionally, Hefner's empire variously spanned television, book publishing, film production, jazz festivals, travel, and many other leisure, entertainment, and consumer industries. One of the most important manifestations of *Playboy* outside the pages of the magazine were the Playboy Clubs, which began in Chicago in 1960 and soon spread across the country and the world with their sexy "bunny" waitresses.[14]

By the mid-sixties, Hefner's empire had become an institution. For instance in 1962, a final exam in a Harvard business course focused on the entrepreneurial practices of Hefner, while the *Playboy* Philosophy found its way into Sunday morning sermons.[15] One church's weekly service program asked, "What is the contemporary moral incarnation of The *Playboy* Philosophy—and of the Christian gospel?"[16] The mainstream media acknowledged the breadth of Hefner's influence. William F. Buckley, Jr., noted that *Playboy* and its hedonistic credo were a "movement" that included "professors and ministers and sociologists." Writing for the *Los Angeles Times* in 1972, Digby Diehl called *Playboy* a "major instrument of social and moral change in the mid-20th century."[17]

But by the late 1960s, changes were sweeping the country, and many critics lamented what they considered to be *Playboy*'s outmoded brand of sexuality. A *Time* cover story on Hefner in 1967 implied that his unrelenting attack on American morals "might just possibly make sex go out of style."[18] Another journalist wondered if the magazine "had run out of new techniques that titillate [since] it has become sort of an institution."[19] Hefner admitted as much in 1973. He said of the social changes affecting *Playboy*'s position in American culture, "[*Playboy*] is not nearly as avant-garde, or on the forefront of the fight for sexual freedom in terms of content, as it was. [S]ociety has moved so far."[20] Maybe the sex in *Playboy* stopped being cutting edge, but such statements spoke to how far the magazine had traveled from 1953 into the mid-1970s. Indeed, biographer Steven Watts argues, "Hefner has played a key role in changing American values, ideas, and attitudes. From the beginning, his enterprise was about more than dirty pictures, more than a girlie magazine . . . It was a historical force of significant proportions." Hefner was "a cultural bellwether in postwar America."[21]

The institutionalization of *Playboy* demonstrated the vast cultural reach of Hefner and his philosophy, and provides an appropriate end point for this study. By 1973, *Playboy* reached an apex as a cultural icon. Its paid circulation hit a peak of seven million per month in the early seventies.[22] Competition from more explicit magazines like *Penthouse*, brought to the U.S. from Britain in 1969, was heightened by *Hustler* in 1974. Furthermore, the long 1960s, with which *Playboy* had been so intellectually engaged, were finally coming to a close.

Sexy girls-next-door and all-American consumer abundance came to define, at least for Hugh Hefner, the good life. Although *Playboy* trumpeted its status as "entertainment for men," this book reveals the foundation from which the magazine justifies its current appeal to women in the twenty-first century. In fact, that appeal was not unheard of in the postwar years. Though *Playboy* was at times antagonistic toward women, and it unquestionably prioritized straight masculinity, its overall vision of sexuality was more modern and equitable than the cultural tradition of male privilege from which it was born. So while that early era of Hefner's empire, with its swinging bachelors and Bunnies, may seem long gone, *Playboy* has a legacy of inclusive heterosexuality—for men and for women—on which to base its latest incarnation.

1

The Womanization of *Playboy*

There is a new spirit on the land . . . the sexes . . . may acquire a
mutuality . . . which does not entail the obliteration of differences.

PLAYBOY, 1962

*H*ugh Hefner, the world's ultimate playboy, was the deliberate invention of Hugh Marston Hefner, born in 1926, to what he calls a
"typical Midwestern, Methodist home with a lot of repression."[1] The young
Hefner was quiet and mild mannered, a far cry from the adult man that the
world would come to recognize in his ubiquitous red silk smoking jacket,
surrounded by beautiful young women, and partying in his mansion with
five decades worth of celebrities. Today, Hefner says he always had the passions that were expressed in his magazine, from the sex to the politics.[2]

His battle for sexual liberation, he claims, did not evolve from the creation of *Playboy* in 1953, but rather was always a focus for him. In a recent
interview, he described an emotionally difficult childhood, "at an unconscious level, in a home in which . . . there was no demonstration of affection,
I associated that [at the time] with repression and censorship."[3] Likewise, in
his brief stint as a graduate student at Northwestern University after serving
stateside during the Second World War, Hefner wrote a paper entitled "Sex
Behavior and the U.S. Law," in which he concluded that almost every American would be in jail if all the laws against various sex acts were enforced.[4]

Finally, through his magazine, Hefner found a way to champion his particular version of sexual freedom.

Hefner accomplished this by not only pushing the boundaries of acceptable sexuality in American popular culture, but by doing it with panache. Fashion, cutting-edge stereos, jazz records, and martinis were as important to the *Playboy* lifestyle as promiscuous heterosexuality. Unafraid of cliché, Hefner sums up his personal philosophy, "We do need more love on this planet, we *should* make love, not war . . . And then in the process, maybe you can also do it with a little style . . . that's where I come in."[5]

Indeed, Hefner came in at a point when America was teetering between two eras, two contrasting ways of understanding itself. For the older generation, having lived through economic depression and war, traditional values of family, thrift, and hard work were the rule. Pivoting on the axis of World War II, the younger generation would soon embrace a culture of liberation, consumption, and luxury. The same was true of Hefner. Before he started *Playboy*, he was an average man living a life of traditional trappings. But the comfort and stability of middle-class suburbia left him restless, and he soon transformed himself into the "Czar of the Bunny Empire."[6]

Hefner claims that it was romantic travail that motivated his first personal re-creation: "I first reinvented myself when I was in high school, after being rejected by a girl. [I] started referring to myself as 'Hef,' instead of Hugh, and started changing my wardrobe, and wrote a record column for the high school newspaper" with the byline, "'Hep Hef.'"[7] Hefner says that *Playboy* was another manifestation of his urge to reformulate his identity, "[I] did the same thing with the magazine, [I] came out from behind the desk in the end of the '50s and early '60s and . . . became Mr. Playboy."[8] Friend and colleague Jim Petersen says that part of Hefner's genius was in understanding that millions of American men were questioning their lives and identities in the same way.[9]

Those questions produced tensions and anxieties that found their way into *Playboy*, sometimes with American women as the target. The result was an intense chauvinism separate from the oft-criticized centerfolds. *Playboy* published various articles, particularly in its first decade, that were belittling and sometimes downright hostile to women, making it easy to brand *Playboy* as a sexist magazine. But that attitude was not unique to *Playboy*, and was a product of the cultural climate of postwar America, when such gender antagonism was common.

After the triumph of World War II, the United States experienced unprecedented prosperity and international influence. Yet the sunny world of American confidence and optimism was haunted by a dark anxiety. Fears of nuclear annihilation, homosexuality, and a breakdown of white hegemony stalked many Americans. Cold war tensions played out not only on the world stage but also at home. In the midst of domestic change and international instability, conservatives urged Americans to reject the new versions of gender that were being helped along by Alfred Kinsey's revelations and Elvis Presley's sexual display. Instead they cautioned men and women to batten down the hatches and return to traditional values.

With change looming on the horizon, however, people began to doubt the familiar expectations of marriage, as well as traditional sexual assumptions. But the path toward a new way of ordering sexual relations, and their attendant economic, political, and social implications, would not be easy. As women increasingly challenged their conventional roles as wives and mothers in the 1950s and early 1960s, American culture grappled with new definitions of gender. One symptom of those changes was what contemporaries and historians alike have referred to as a "crisis" of masculinity.[10]

Just as Hugh became "Hef" because he could not get the girl he wanted in high school, postwar American men were forced to adjust their identities because of a cultural, and in many cases actual, tension over sex and changing femininities. Women entered the workforce throughout the 1950s in unprecedented numbers, or in various other ways defied traditional stereotypes.[11] Their efforts were often met with hostility as the insecurities of American gender politics became apparent. Contradictory prescriptions offered by magazines, newspapers, films, psychology, and sociology said that while a good woman was expected to settle down and raise a family, she must beware of succumbing to the dreaded "momism."[12] Mothers were expected to give their family love and devotion, but avoid becoming overprotective and dominating, or risk turning their sons into weak sissies, or worse, homosexuals.

Some men felt pressured or disappointed by many postwar women's rush to domesticate, while liberated women were often seen as castrating feminists. In 1947, psychologist Marynia Farnham and sociologist Ferdinand Lundberg published their best-selling *The Modern Woman: The Lost Sex*, which argued that feminists were " 'neurotically disturbed women . . . [with] . . . a deep illness.' "[13] Contributing to the gender anxiety of the age, historian Beth

Bailey notes that after World War II, American women outnumbered men for the first time. Agitated by the media, women fretted over a perceived "scarcity of men."[14] She notes that while men returned from war and the marriage rate began to skyrocket, books and magazines nonetheless "seized upon the 'man shortage.'"[15] Articles in newspapers and magazines like the *New York Times*, *Good Housekeeping*, and *Esquire* fanned the flames of domestic angst. Women were told that many who wanted to marry never would, and were warned by psychiatrists that "these women would become 'neurotic and frustrated . . . and '[damaged].'"[16] "We're short 1 million bachelors!" "Male shortage . . . It's worse than ever," and "one girl in every seven will have to live alone, whether she likes it or not," were just some of the doomsday predictions being leveled at women in the postwar years.[17]

Bailey argues that many men responded to this pressure from women with resentment and hostility. She writes, "Returning servicemen launched a full-scale public condemnation of the American woman." A July 1945 article in *Esquire* magazine argued that men "had been released from the domination of American women by discovering that they were romantic heroes to the rest of the world's women." A *New York Times Magazine* article entitled "The American Woman? Not for this G.I." complained that American women whined more "over the lack of nylons than . . . European women over the destruction of their homes and the deaths of their men."[18]

Women were not the only ones confronting change, and intense scrutiny, at this time. Men grappled with questions and anxieties over how to act as husbands, fathers, lovers, and citizens in a changing world. Strong, fearless warriors were needed to battle the communists, but those same manly men were also needed to stabilize a rapidly changing domestic front. However, many social observers felt that white, middle-class men—the established leaders of society—were losing their traditional power and virility. David Savran argues, "The reconfiguration of workplace and home . . . signaled a feminization and domestication of normative, white, middle class masculinity. This . . . was perceived by many as being the sign of a male identity crisis."[19]

Arthur Schlesinger, Jr., provided a prominent articulation of the era's gender tensions in "The Crisis of American Masculinity." Writing for *Esquire* in 1958, he argued, "the male role [has] plainly lost its rugged clarity of outline. Today men are more and more conscious of maleness not as a fact but as a problem." Schlesinger admitted that women's equality threatened traditional manhood, but he found the conformity of modern society in general the cause of men's weakened status.[20] He argued that the "American male is left, finally, unsure of 'what sex he is.'"[21]

Likewise in 1958, *Look* magazine published *The Decline of the American Male*. Writer J. Robert Moskin asked of the American man, "Why Do Women Dominate Him?" Moskin blamed the rise of women's economic power and growing sexual liberation for the supposed weakening status of men, arguing, "as women grow even more numerous and more dominant, we will have to invent new meanings and myths for maleness."[22] The book repeated the common refrain: female dominance at home, in the bedroom, and increasingly in the workplace was undermining male authority.

Some critics held American culture, with its emphasis on consumerism and economic striving, responsible for beating down overworked husbands struggling to keep up. David Reisman's influential book *The Lonely Crowd* critiqued the notion of the modern "other-directed" man who lived for peer approval, as opposed to the autonomous nineteenth-century man who found fulfillment within himself.[23] Likewise, *The Organization Man*, by William H. Whyte, Jr., decried the conformity and group-think of the contemporary suburban middle class that squashed individualism and created "the tyranny of the majority."[24]

A love of the supposedly feminine leisurely life, a submergence of professional individuality in favor of corporatization, undue female influence, and a decline in rugged manhood topped the list of emerging, undesirable male characteristics.[25] The cold war, and its corresponding gender anxieties, played out not only in the halls of government and the military, but also in American homes and offices, on television and movie screens, in fashion, and within romantic relationships.[26] In a statement made on the thirtieth anniversary of the founding of the Foreign Policy Association, even President Truman pressed Americans to "maintain the 'virility' of their democratic heritage if they are to protect themselves against hazards from abroad," noting that "international problems have moved into the front yard of every American home."[27]

Fueled by the feeling that male homosexuality was on the rise, growing fears of sexual chaos contributed to the gender and political anxieties of the age. The Kinsey report of 1948, which argued for high rates of homosexual experience among men, unwittingly encouraged the paranoia, as did Max Lerner's *America as a Civilization* (1957), which noted an "uneasy sense" that homosexuality was increasing, and an actual rise in visibility of gays and lesbians after World War II.[28] Many social arbiters argued for the traditional family by connecting homosexuality to communism through a supposed common weakness of character.[29]

While apprehension gripped much of postwar American culture, there were challenges to the gender status quo. For instance, David Savran posits that the male rebels of the 1950s, in the form of the Beats and others, "were the symptoms of this crisis, offering both a solution to this 'problem' and a significant challenge to the rigors of normative masculinity . . . and [offering] a set of alternatives to the nuclear family."[30] Likewise, James Gilbert has shown that postwar culture in fact offered American men a variety of masculine options. He argues, "[T]he 1950s were unusual . . . for their relentless and self-conscious preoccupation with masculinity. . . . The absurdity of growing up in the 1950s was heightened by the reluctance—the downright opposition—of a great many cultural spokesmen to accept the changes occurring in American society. Often they interpreted such developments as a threat to masculinity. But at the same time there were dissenting, clear voices, proposing alternative constructions of gender."[31] Gilbert suggests that even portrayals of manhood so often associated with the era's traditional and conformist impulse, as in *The Adventures of Ozzie and Harriet*, revealed the complexity of postwar society.[32]

Similarly, *Playboy* reflected the anxiety of the era while simultaneously defying the postwar status quo—not merely by trumpeting promiscuous heterosexuality, but by taking the brand of manhood so reviled by many midcentury observers and making it useable and acceptable to a mass audience.[33] Like Hefner's rejected teenager, postwar American society awkwardly renegotiated the romantic landscape. Many people found comfort and guidance in the pages of *Playboy*. While not overtly political in the 1950s, the magazine engaged contemporary cultural conversations about gender and reflected widespread anxieties over changing relations between the sexes. The attitude, look, and lifestyle of the playboy included urbanity, liberal politics, style, love of leisure, and lack of familial commitment. Historian K. A. Cuordileone argues that these were precisely the characteristics that many postwar critics lambasted as leading to "the decline of traditional small-town American values, the advent of secularism, juvenile delinquency, sexual immorality, divorce, pornography . . . the corrosive effects of commercialism, popular entertainment."[34] The solution, according to some observers, was to resurrect a supposedly lost American manhood.

As critics from various points on the social spectrum offered ideas on where such a man might be found, one voice amid the cacophony registered its own comment on contemporary masculinity. It came from a swinging single Lothario, a man who rejected the stultifying responsibilities of postwar married manhood in favor of self-indulgence, materialism, and promiscuous bachelorhood. Conceived by Hugh Hefner in 1953, the hedonistic playboy bachelor denied the cold war tensions that consumed so much of American culture. The image was so self-consciously contrived that in the inaugural issue, Hefner penned an article describing his flight from the quick pace of New York to sunny California, "You know me, fellows—I'm an eastern boy. Have been all my life. Just moved out here to Southern California . . . to try and soothe . . . some jangled, city-type nerves."[35] Never mind that Hefner was from the Midwest and would not move to LA until after his eventual transformation into the world-class rake years later.

Before establishing himself as the ultimate Casanova, Hefner was a fairly typical American man. Of middle class, Midwestern origin, he enlisted in the service after high school graduation in 1944. After the war, he took advantage of the GI Bill and enrolled in college. In 1949, he married his sweetheart, Millie, and they had their first child, Christie, in 1953.[36] Biographer Steven Watts says that in the months preceding the founding of *Playboy*, Hefner's "life seemed at low ebb as he strained against the bonds of an unsatisfying marriage, flinched at the unsettling prospect of parenthood, and balked at the thought of returning to an unfulfilling job."[37] It was a time in which he was "really lost."[38] With the publication of *Playboy*, Hefner rejected the domestic life that so many Americans had embraced and began living the exciting, liberated life about which he had fantasized.

In the inaugural issue in December 1953, Hefner laid out some of the motivations behind the magazine. Offering a "diversion from the anxieties of the Atomic Age," Hefner told his readers that the *Playboy* man liked "mixing up cocktails and an hors d'oeuvre or two, putting a little mood music on the phonograph, and inviting in a female acquaintance for a quiet discussion on Picasso, Nietzsche, jazz, sex."[39] This version of masculinity, personified by their mascot, the *Playboy* rabbit, was a far cry from the normative masculinity of the "organization man" and the cold warrior as prescribed by social

figure 2.   A young Hefner working at his kitchen table in South Chicago. Reproduced
by special permission of *Playboy* magazine. Copyright by Playboy.

arbiters of the day. The playboy was a man who lived for himself and his next
date, he drove fast cars, and was an aspiring intellectual. This image of manhood was hardly suited for battling communists and burping babies.

But these were not the goals of *Playboy*. The objectives of Hefner and his
magazine were, quite simply, to get American men to lighten up and have
fun, whether through sex, shopping, or fine dining. As biographer Russell
Miller notes, "Hefner views himself as . . . a man who, through the power of
his unique magazine, liberated the world from the shackles of Puritanism
and reintroduced *fun* into our lives."[40] Initially shunning political comment,
Hefner's opening editorial disarmingly noted, "We don't expect to solve
any world problems or prove any great moral truths. If we are able to give

the American male a few extra laughs and a little [distraction] . . . we'll feel we've justified our existence."[41] Such entertainment was presented in various forms in the magazine, and many of them unrelated to naked women. Regular columns on food and drink, entertainment, cartoons, and party jokes filled *Playboy*'s pages from its inception.

Hefner intended to create a lifestyle magazine, complete with fashion and decorating tips, for the sophisticated urban man. Of course, promiscuous heterosexuality, as punctuated by the ubiquitous Playmate centerfold, was promoted as a right to "be enjoyed right along with nasty pleasures like drinking and gambling."[42] While much of 1950s America was still reeling from the shocking results of Dr. Kinsey's study, also published in 1953, *Playboy* was presenting sexuality as a lighthearted game to be played over and over, with as many teammates as possible.

When *Playboy* arrived, it was not the only magazine to include photos of naked women. Such literature had been available for decades, but was typically considered to be sleazy and disreputable.[43] But Hefner hoped to do something new by aiming his magazine at middle-class males. It would, he hoped, lift consumer sexuality out of the gutter and onto the coffee tables of men across the country. Regarding the majority of existing men's magazines, historian Bill Osgerby says that they offered a "world of swaggering machismo, prurient voyeurism and sexual violence."[44] Likewise, Russell Miller notes, "Conventional men's magazines rarely strayed into the dangerous area of sex. Mostly they subsisted on a diet of hairy-chested prose ('One-Man Marine Army Who Conquered Bloody Batu') and hollow-chested advertising ('Amazing Invention Quickly Helps to Give You a *Strong Manly Voice*'). Women rarely made an appearance in the editorial columns, except perhaps to be rescued from a giant octopus or grizzly bear. Hefner was bored by these endless tales of the great outdoors. His idea of a good men's magazine . . . would be one that directed its attention toward the great *indoors*."[45] In contrast, *Playboy* centered on living the "good life," and was based on consumer indulgence. While a large portion of the magazine's readership were college-age men who could not yet live up to such a high standard, they could look to *Playboy* as a guide to their future ambitions and imagine that somewhere, men were living such a life.

The overall lifestyle that Hefner prescribed was a new take on American manhood, shunning marriage, family, and stoic responsibility. The playboy was a corporate drone but did not resent the position, for it supplied him

figure 3.   August 1961. Reproduced by special permission of *Playboy* magazine.
Copyright 1961 by Playboy.

with the mindless work that allowed him time to plan that evening's date, and the income to woo that date into bed with dinner and drinks. He obsessively kept up on fashion trends, as well as the proper way to serve an oyster. He knew all the best burlesque shows in Paris, and was conversant in foreign films—if for no other reason than they offered more nudity than American films. Of course, the sexy pictures were an easy sell, but even they played a particular role in Hefner's brand of manhood. They told American men that sexually willing and available women were all around them. Postwar culture was offered a new version of heterosexuality that promoted male satisfaction, but also insisted that women—even the nice ones—were sexual creatures, thereby contradicting waves of proscriptive literature that dictated female sexual expression only within the matrimonial bed.

But the magazine's portrayal of femininity was complicated, and not always flattering. The anxiety with which both liberals and conservatives regarded contemporary manhood found expression in *Playboy* through articles that criticized modern womanhood as emasculating and lamented the downtrodden American male. But even the most antagonistic pieces revealed ambivalence over evolving gender roles, demonstrating the complexity inherent in the dynamics of postwar gender politics. In *Playboy*'s inaugural issue, an article on alimony entitled "Miss Gold-Digger of 1953" painted women as conniving wenches only out for money. Characterizing wives as "mercenary" legal prostitutes, the article advocated that men abandon their marriages and "beat it out of town." Calling for reform of alimony laws throughout the country, readers were warned, "the modern gold-digger comes in a variety of shapes and sizes. She's after the wealthy playboys, but she may also be after you."[46] So, in the earliest days of the magazine, an anti-marriage, and often an antiwoman, tone was adopted, giving fodder to *Playboy* critics for decades.

In a similar article entitled "Open Season on Bachelors," *Playboy* columnist Burt Zollo cautioned men against getting trapped into marriage. Reflecting real postwar trends, Zollo argued that many young women used their college years to focus on finding a mate rather than a career. However, he asserted that many women planned out-of-wedlock pregnancies to trick men into marrying them, or sexually teased them until they submitted to the altar. He noted that women's "uses and abuses of sex are endless." Zollo told his readers to "take a good look at the sorry, regimented husbands trudging down every woman-dominated street in this woman-dominated land." They were men who had "already fallen into the pit" of marriage. Insisting that men need not live as asexual hermits, "the true playboy can enjoy the pleasures the female has to offer without becoming emotionally involved."[47] Thus women might be mere objects of the playboy's sexual gratification.

The articles "Miss Gold-Digger of 1953" and "Open Season on Bachelors" sparked a response in the letters-to-the-editor column. One reader admitted to being "one of the victims of *Miss Gold-Digger*," while another praised the article's timeliness saying it "really hit the nail on the head." A woman wrote in calling "That *Miss Gold-Digger* article . . . the most biased piece of tripe I've ever read."[48] "Open Season" caused one female reader to write, "men are not afraid of marriage. To the contrary, they welcome it." She went on to list instances of female acquaintances who turned down desperate marriage proposals from men, while insisting that it is "weak-minded little idiot boys, not yet grown up, who are afraid of getting 'hooked,'" and blamed "facetious articles" for swaying "these infants" into thinking marriage is a trap. Reflecting the alliterative style of the magazine, a male reader supposedly called the article "straight-from-the-shoulders expose of these cunning cuties and their suave schemes."[49]

Reader letters like these were an increasingly important component of the magazine, growing from one to three lengthy columns by the early 1960s. Like *Playboy* itself, they reflected the tensions surrounding the shifting gender politics of the postwar years, and they served to make *Playboy* more accessible to readers. Thus, with the marriage rate on the rise, articles and letters spoke to reader anxieties created by an era obsessed with domesticity. As Americans were encouraged to marry and a baby boom fueled a greater emphasis on home and hearth, *Playboy* reacted to the pressure placed on men to settle down. By telling them that they need not become emotionally involved with their lovers, or even take responsibility for premarital pregnancies, articles like "Open Season" offered a fantasy-driven escape from the demands of postwar adulthood.

However, reaction from readers—men and women alike—complicated any easy answer to the postwar battle of the sexes. A later article on marriage and sexuality sparked even more controversy in the letters pages of *Playboy*. In "Don't Hate Yourself in the Morning," *Playboy*'s Jules Archer wrote that a woman was just as willing as a man to partake in premarital sex, but that she "wants to go on record as protesting and regretting. She needs to assuage whatever shreds of conscience may still be irritating her."[50] Reiterating what Burt Zollo argued in the earlier piece on marriage, Archer said that many single women planned on premarital pregnancy, "They are secretly pleased by their pregnancy, as shown by the refusal of most to even consider abortion, unlike a great many married women who are 'caught.' That they enjoy their pregnancy is indicated by the fact that most don't even have 'morning sickness,' which affects many pregnant wives." Moreover, he wrote that "breaking-in" a woman before she got married actually rendered a "service to society," making a better lover to her future husband.[51] Archer's article portrayed women as manipulators, and he told men that they need not invest in their partners' well being. Nor was a man supposed to take responsibility for unplanned pregnancy, because the woman probably planned it to fulfill her own emotional vacuum.

Beyond this vitriol, the article did more. It reflected a subtle, budding attitude within the magazine that encouraged sexual autonomy, expression, and pleasure for men *and* for women. Archer's article, while misinformed and crude, also argued that women were aware of their own desire, and often appropriately allowed themselves the freedom to have a full sexual life before marriage. Archer wrote, "Girls trained through their studies . . . choose sexual freedom as well as freedom to think out their own choice of profession or life style." He continued, "most of the fair sex gets the same pleasure from amatory acrobatics that [men] do. There is evidence on every hand that large numbers of women anticipate seduction with unabashed pleasure." Archer also cited sociologist Herbert Lamson of Boston University: "In the past men have underestimated the sex desires of women . . . There seem to be plenty of business girls who have their own apartments and who are willing to pay for an evening out with sex at the end."[52] These claims suggested a fairly progressive image of autonomous female sexuality. In the context of this piece, this attitude clearly served the self-centered desires of the playboy, and while it was shrouded in an unhealthy assumption that women are deceitful and manipulative, there was at least the claim that women, like men, have a right to be sexual creatures outside of marriage. This was a subversive claim in the 1950s, and one on which *Playboy* would expound in the coming years.

But in the meantime, Archer's article sparked a heated debate in the letters pages. One male reader responded, "Mr. Archer should be presented some sort of medal good for a free case of beer for having the guts to bring the truth [about women's manipulation] out in the open." Another wrote, "If more American men would educate themselves to these facts [about women], I wholeheartedly believe we would all live in a better world. I know the girls would." A woman wrote that the article was "the most vilest [*sic*] piece of anti-individualist propaganda . . . full of broad generalizations" she had ever read. One man suggested that perhaps Archer had married a woman of low morals, and that is why he had "[torn] down all women." Still another woman agreed with the commentary, "I was a very moral young lady who met a very persuasive fellow, but once convinced, I shed no tears and neither of us hated ourselves in the morning."[53]

Response to articles like "Don't Hate Yourself" provided an opportunity to glimpse the sexual attitudes of the readership, as well as a more detailed commentary by the magazine's editors in response. The magazine reflected the conflicted ways in which these issues were coming to the forefront of social dialogue, just as the wave of middle-class female discontent would soon explode in 1963 with Betty Friedan's *The Feminine Mystique*. In the 1950s, *Playboy* was not concerned with the economic and social ramifications of "the problem that has no name," as Friedan would call it, but women's voices were represented in the magazine's pages, and sometimes they even turned the tables on gender anxiety.

Since the early issues of the magazine, a significant minority of letters to the editor were credited to the pens of women. Historian Joanne Meyerowitz has established the utility of such letters in deciphering the audience reception of magazines like *Playboy* in the postwar years.[54] She argues that the "vociferous" responses of women to *Playboy* and other similar magazines, "demonstrates that commodified sexual representation was a 'woman's issue' well before the contemporary feminist movement."[55] Many letters in *Playboy* in the 1950s were from coeds who claimed to enjoy the publication on their own, and a few were from women who were simply offended and angered by the magazine. Women reacted to the pictures as well as the articles, with some offering photos of themselves and asking how they might become Playmates.

One woman wrote, "*Playboy* is wonderful. My husband and I discovered your magazine . . . and have become avid fans. . . . I'm an ex-PTA President and a Sunday school teacher, but I think you publish one of the best, most entertaining magazines around." Another thought that the magazine was "the greatest thing since diaper service." Other women bemoaned *Playboy*'s lack of respect for womanhood, and one asked, "Do you folks really feel you are doing any good, any service to anyone, including yourselves, publishing a magazine like *Playboy*?"[56] To such questions Hefner and his editors repeated their mission, which was to give men their own publication not "suitable for small children . . . adolescent school girls or maiden aunts, either."[57] In other words, *Playboy* did not shun women readers, only those the magazine would have considered too uptight or prudish to appreciate its frisky joie de vie.

While *Playboy* was officially a men's magazine, a female readership signaled many women's desire for an outlet to express a sophisticated, adult sexuality. Women could read their husband's *Playboy* and enjoy adult humor and topics. Moreover, it demonstrated that some women found the magazine—even with its blatant sexism—useful and interesting, or at least entertaining and mostly inoffensive.

In February 1957, *Playboy* gave a young woman its literary stage when it published "a controversial indictment of the American male" by nineteen-year-old Pamela Moore.[58] In "Love in the Dark," Moore asked, "Are American Men Ashamed of Sex?" She argued, "[T]he one sphere in which the American male flounders, the one sphere in which he is a dismal failure both as a father responsible for the emotional well-being of his children and as a husband responsible for the emotional well-being of his wife, is the sphere in which he must express his maleness . . . the American man tries to hide and repress every manifestation of sex." Driven by an "incredible, perverted, puritanical attitude toward sex," Moore wrote that men's inability to express healthy affection toward their daughters damaged females sexually in their adult years. She argued that women of her generation were much more open about sex than men, and that women were "exploding all kinds of myths behind which men have hidden for generations." Moore insisted that it be acceptable for women to be sexual pursuers and that sex need not be considered evil and shameful.[59]

In a magazine that offered its own challenge to puritanical attitudes toward sex, the article sparked controversy, reflecting the broader sexual questions being bandied about across the country. One woman said that Moore "echoed [her] long-suppressed feelings and opinions perfectly," while another asked that the magazine "confine your articles on sex to those by male authors, since they usually write objectively about this much abused subject, and are without the frustrations of father complexes." Men's views on the article were just as varied. One reader argued, "The sooner the American male wakes up to the fact that he is a sexual failure the better off everyone will be." Another admitted, "It's enlightening to find a top man's magazine with guts enough to print a feminine viewpoint like Miss Moore's." Others felt she needed psychological counseling.[60] This article and its ensuing controversy pointed to the ways in which serious discussions of gender, beyond titillating photos and cynical cartoons, were introduced in the magazine, and indeed the larger society, in the years leading up to the upheavals of the 1960s. The piece's inclusion also showed that in its early years, *Playboy* chose to represent the voice of a woman that played on the gender tensions and anxieties of the day.

As a men's magazine, most discussions of femininity were from the perspective of men. In October 1957, *Playboy* explored the discussion of sexuality found in women's magazines, with "The Pious Pornographers: Sex and Sanctimony in the Ladies' Home Jungle," by Ivor Williams, a pseudonym for regular contributor William Iversen. Williams argued that not only was sex not taboo in women's magazines, but that it was an obsession, particularly while under the guise of medical discussions of the subject. He wrote that women's magazines took a hypocritical attitude toward sexuality by decrying frank discussions on the part of "certain men's magazines," while at the same time fixating on the sexual dysfunction of women and modern marriage.[61] The notion that popular women's magazines were at least as salacious as some critics claimed *Playboy* to be was an idea that Hefner and his editors repeatedly celebrated.[62] The term "pious pornographers" became shorthand at *Playboy*—in company memos, correspondence, and the like— for the sexual hypocrisy of American culture and especially of women.

In September 1963, Iversen expounded on his views of contemporary marriage with "Love, Death and the Hubby Image." The article was a perfect articulation of the postwar crisis of masculinity and anxiety about women's expanding participation in the economy and society at large. Iversen argued that contemporary marriage offered women complete security, luxurious consumption, and total dominance over their husbands.[63] The piece sparked reader response for several months. Various men agreed with the "mental castration and emotional spine breaking of the American man by his mate."[64] Texan James Gardner, apparently facetiously, joked that he "dropped" his wife "with a hard left hook" after reading Iversen's piece.[65] Various women, and a few men, took issue with the article. Cynthia Kolb Whitney's letter described her two-income family, and said her husband did his share of housework, "Why not? Why should either marriage partner be totally the drudge of the other one?"[66]

Mrs. Elayne B. Nord of New Jersey, a self-described feminist, challenged Iversen's take on marriage. For a more "[enlightened]" view, Nord recommended the newly published *The Feminine Mystique*, and argued that *Playboy* encouraged an unhealthy "Battle of the Sexes." *Playboy*'s editors disagreed, saying that in fact, what they promoted was a "positive, quite optimistic view of society—a happy, healthful, heterosexual view—in which the roles of men and women compliment one another."[67] They clarified their view in response to another reader, "We're not opposed to the institution of marriage . . . only to certain negative aspects of it," which they characterized as "suffocating antisexuality and competitive hostility."[68]

Such gender anxiety was not unique to *Playboy*. Historian Kenon Breazeale demonstrates that Hefner's model magazine and main competitor, *Esquire*, had published similar diatribes against contemporary womanhood since its founding in the 1930s.[69] In the postwar years, sexual antagonism in American culture had intensified, and *Esquire* included articles like "The Entrenchment of the American Witch," by *Boston Herald* columnist George Frazier. The 1962 piece described the unfortunate dominance of women who were independent and ambitious, or in other words, "masculine." Such "witches" supposedly lost sight of their natural roles, which were "to love and look up to their men—and . . . to bear their children too." Like so much contemporary commentary, mothers were blamed for creating witches, who, according to Frazier, often turned out to be lesbians because of their "innate dislike and disrespect for men."[70] The battle of the sexes was not one-sided, though. In 1963, Phyllis Battelle contributed an article to *Cosmopolitan* on "The Corruptible Male." Battelle argued that modern American men had become cowardly, dishonest, and immoral. While the piece was a critique of postwar masculinity, Battelle, like the writers in *Playboy* and *Esquire*, implicated women. She wrote that gender equality contributed to the weakened status of masculinity. Furthermore, Battelle argued, women failed to maintain high expectations of men, causing a decline in male virtue.[71] So in the years leading up to the women's movement, there was a palpable anxiety over changing gender roles not just in *Playboy*, but in other established magazines as well.

Without a doubt, *Playboy*'s courting of writer Philip Wylie was the most antagonistic expression of the magazine's gender politics in the fifties and early sixties. Wylie made a name for himself in 1942 with *Generation of Vipers*. The book was particularly famous for Wylie's characterization of a peculiar plague known as "momism." This supposed epidemic of domineering motherhood was, according to Wylie, responsible for all manner of national deprivation, but especially the emasculation of modern husbands and sons.

The book was a bestseller, and today Hefner admits that it had an impact on his own thinking about womanhood.[72]

In September 1958, Wylie contributed an article to *Playboy* entitled "The Womanization of America."[73] Wylie claimed that women had thoroughly usurped most of the power that had traditionally, and rightfully, belonged to men. He warned against the "deadly distaff encroachment of what started as feminism and matured into wanton womanization."[74] Wylie insisted that it was men who accomplished virtually every scientific, economic, and artistic advance in history, and that it was male technological innovations that freed women from traditional domestic labor with washing machines, refrigerators, and the like. Indeed women had supposedly demanded so much luxury in their homes that their harried husbands worked themselves to death trying to provide the income necessary to keep their pampered wives in materialistic indulgence.[75]

Reader John Quinn of Philadelphia loved it: "Mr. Wylie has bravely lashed out at the social sickness that is all too prevalent in our 'utterly dreamy' and 'celestial mauve' society today." Another man preferred Wylie's views to the "puke-inducing Togetherness we are continually having thrown at us." Referring to Wylie's celebration of philandering, however, Mrs. Rose Marie Shelley of Emporia, Kansas, was furious: "A woman who 'accepts' her husband's 'celebrating the appeal of other women' becomes . . . nothing more than his legal bitch . . . You playboys will have to earn woman's respect before you ever establish your male supremacy!"[76]

Wylie's notion of womanization proved useful for Hefner and *Playboy*. Its critique of American society was predicated on a supposed decline of gender difference between men and women. Womanization meant not only a rise of female domination, but a swapping or blurring of gender identity. Hefner was fixated on this trend, and remained so for years. He argued that the breakdown of gender difference and womanization of America had resulted in an "asexual society,"[77] certainly not a welcome outcome for a man like Hefner. Today, Hefner says that Wylie's theories resonated with him because he related "the womanization of America [to] prohibition, antisexuality, censorship, and," he admits with an uncomfortable laugh, "it probably had to do with . . . my own mother. She was such a bright and wonderful woman, but she didn't have a clue in terms of sex."[78] Like so many other postwar Americans, Hefner was influenced by midcentury Freudianism, which located the formation of the adult psyche in childhood, and Hefner blamed the country's ills—and his own—on faulty childrearing.[79]

The magazine continued its obsession with womanization in another format. It published a panel discussion on the topic in 1962. *Playboy* panels began in the early 1960s to address contemporary national topics. They focused on issues such as drugs in jazz music, comedy, and censorship. The womanization panel included writer Norman Mailer, comedian Mort Sahl, Dr. Ashley Montagu, author of *The Natural Superiority of Women*, psychoanalyst Theodor Reik, and others. There were no women on the panel. The conversation touched upon important issues like economics and birth control, but primarily fixated on inane debates such as whether or not men should feel comfortable wearing aprons and washing dishes.

Panel views on womanhood ran the gamut from hateful and ridiculing to occasionally thoughtful and sensitive. Norman Mailer, a *Playboy* regular, exhibited his usual bombastic machismo when he declared, "the womanization of America comes not only because women are becoming more selfish, more greedy, less romantic, less warm, more lusty, and also more filled with hate—but because men have collaborated with them." Writer Alexander King unequivocally felt that total equality between the sexes was "a great mistake and in violation of all natural laws."[80] But not every panelist held antiwoman views. Public relations guru Edward Bernays defended women: "A lot of this so-called feminization is a direct result of a very healthy trend in society: simply that nobody wants to be anybody's servant anymore."[81] Ashley Montagu went farther: "Instead of [men] saying to women, 'We will assist you to develop your qualities and potentialities . . .' they went ahead and said, 'Sink or swim,' just as we did to the Negro in the Reconstruction period."[82] Ultimately, the *Playboy* editors leading the discussion closed on this ambiguous note: "There is a new spirit on the land, evident among our own readership, which would suggest that the younger, urban people of this country are coming to a new awareness of both masculinity and femininity. . . . As our nation becomes emancipated from the notion of associating sex with sin . . . so the attitudes of the sexes may well become more healthy toward each other, may acquire a mutuality and mutual appreciativeness which does not entail the obliteration of differences."[83]

As a best-selling author and "international authority" on the topic of womanization, Philip Wylie was invited to be on the panel, but he declined.[84]

Archival material illuminates an exchange between Wylie and *Playboy*'s editorial director, A. C. Spectorsky, in which Wylie insisted he was too busy to participate in the panel, that the remuneration was too little, and that he felt, despite his appearances in the magazine, that *Playboy* was a "major exponent of disease."[85] Spectorsky "urgently [begged]" Wylie to participate, and upon hearing of his objections, wrote a personal response to Wylie. Spectorsky asserted that the magazine was "extraordinarily healthy and anti-disease." He continued, "*Playboy* is frankly and openly frisky and romantic—as opposed to the prurient morbidity and pious pornography that characterize the bulk of mass media which regularly associate sex with vice, crime, sin and the exposé. . . . *Playboy* believes that there is not an invariable alternative between a matriarchy and a 'he-man' society . . . *Playboy* [believes] that it is perhaps the only voice of the young, urban male . . . [offered] without the taboos and stresses on togetherness."[86]

Wylie was moved to offer a lengthy explanation. In an ironic turn, given Hefner's own critique of womanization, Wylie argued, "*Playboy* serves to abet the 'disease' I consider part of the womanization-of-USA syndrome." Wylie explained that he was "pro-sex to a degree." He believed that all married couples should allow each other outside affairs as long as they were conducted with discretion. Indeed, he felt that values of chastity and marital fidelity were "insane, sinful . . . and criminal."[87] So it was not *Playboy*'s eroticism that bothered Wylie, quite the contrary.

Wylie felt that *Playboy* in fact stifled sexuality. He argued, "*Playboy*, whatever its good intent (of promoting men, to bed, with women) is *used* for a different purpose by the majority and tends, thus . . . to *limit* and *divert* honest libido to inferior ends" (emphasis in the original). He went on, "it has seemed to me that the (admittedly-to-some-extent-woman-dominated) American male has . . . tended to allow mere symbols, images, artifacts, substitutes, portraitures and even women, but at a remove—to become love objects and the goal of his phallic veneration . . . substitutes for any actual sex relationship . . . [I]f they have any emotional impact on any normal male, it will be . . . toward the precise act of nailing some doll."[88] To clarify, Wylie worried that *Playboy* served to sexually arouse men without offering them an actual sexual outlet other than "millions of homemade, solo orgasms," which were apparently unacceptable. He wrote, "Any use of the female in any form that conveys sexual stimulus . . . *must* lead to desire for the real woman and that, in turn to satisfaction of said desire with a real, satisfying and satisfiable woman." Wylie went on to criticize capitalism and especially the advertising industry, for using images of extraordinarily beautiful women to sell products, thus ruining men's expectations of average women.[89]

Wylie blamed most of these dilemmas on women. "Only very sick men, and only in a society where women had them by the short hair . . . would put up with so much, so unclad, so abandoned, a flaunting-of-the-image . . . If sex teasing is sex, then, *Playboy* is a boon."[90] Spectorsky responded by pointing out that one could have a healthy sex life and look at sexy pictures, too.[91] He must have been persuasive, because Wylie later admitted that he had changed his mind about *Playboy*. A psychiatrist friend told Wylie it was none of his business if a man, having been turned on by pictures in *Playboy*, "made love to his wife, or took a doll home and made love, or masturbated." Wylie acknowledged, "After long studying that view I decided he was right."[92]

Hefner remained fascinated with the theory of womanization as he wrote "The *Playboy* Philosophy," a sprawling editorial series, in the mid-1960s. He and his editors conducted extensive research on topics ranging from literature to modern psychology and anthropology for the series.[93] Archival documents show an emphasis on questions regarding patriarchy versus matriarchy as social structures. Though Hefner said he believed in sexual liberation for all, he qualified his version of emancipation by touting conventional gender difference, particularly in terms of appearance and seduction. He supported female sexual expression outside of marriage, but wanted women to look like women and men to have the traditional thrill of the chase.

Ironically, given his paranoia over womanization, Hefner expressed support for what he believed to be the defining characteristics of matriarchy, as opposed to patriarchy, which he associated with sexual restrictiveness, denigration of women, homophobia, and political authoritarianism, among other things. At times he even said he understood why modern women reached for the "social status and other desirables [that] have been the masculine prerogative . . . it is natural for women to strive for comparable status."[94] In a company memo, editor and Philosophy researcher Nat Lehrman articulated Hefner's support for what they called a "matrist society,"[95] because for them such a social organization included "fundamental characteristics . . . we believe in . . . 'permissive attitude to sex; welfare valued over chastity; politically democratic; progressive.'" Lehrman went on to warn, "However, concomitant with these desirable characteristics is the ugly spectre of the womanization of society, which we oppose. Now, if Hef has a theory that gets us off the hook on the second side of the coin, I'd appreciate knowing it."[96]

At the time, Hefner did not have a theory to get *Playboy* "off the hook" for the slippery slope of support for what he supposed a matriarchal society to be—one more sexually tolerant—versus his opposition to womanization. Today, Hefner offers a simple explanation for the contradiction, "A lot of it has to do with semantics, and it also has to do with not having really worked out my own thoughts."[97] So in spite of his contemporary critiques of womanization, Hefner actually embraced social characteristics that might have been associated with femininity. Nonetheless, in the early years of his empire, Hefner grasped for an intellectual justification for his magazine. Regarding female sexual liberation, he often fell short.

Hefner's anxiety was born of a culture of gender apprehension in the 1950s, making his magazine's relationship to femininity problematic. Looking back, longtime editor Jim Petersen denies any sense of anxiety in *Playboy*. In fact, he says that the magazine was so popular precisely because it denied the angst that defined so much of the postwar American experience.[98] As Hefner said in his inaugural issue, the purpose of *Playboy* was to offer men a "diversion from the anxieties of the Atomic Age," it was not to reinforce them.

But given the editorial fixation on womanization, there can be no doubt that those anxieties found their way onto the pages of *Playboy*. Hefner dealt with such concerns in various ways. Unique to *Playboy* was Hefner's embrace of what so many others criticized. He told his readers that the hedonistic masculinity targeted by postwar critics was not only acceptable, it was laudable. When much of American culture was denigrating the effete, urban male as a weak sissy, Hefner joyfully exclaimed that he was actually the manliest man of all. The playboy was so confident in his promiscuous heterosexuality that few doubted his manhood. Simultaneously, Hefner resorted to some of the common postwar defenses against a declining hetero-male hegemony. The hysteria over growing female influence in society found a home in *Playboy* in the form of Philip Wylie's "womanization." While most criticism of *Playboy*'s gender politics has focused on the centerfolds, the magazine expressed antagonism toward women in more direct ways, particularly in the 1950s and early 1960s. Articles denouncing marriage and the supposed rising influence of women challenged sexual harmony and equality far more than did the nude photos. But it was those photos—the centerfold Playmates—that caught the attention of fans and detractors alike.

2

Inventing the Girl-Next-Door: The Pulchritudinous Playmates

Being a Playmate is a natural thing for any girl to do.[1]

PLAYMATE OF THE YEAR 1967, LISA BAKER

Since the early days of the magazine, critics have lambasted Playboy for objectifying women. Indeed, it fetishized busty, young bodies for straight male consumption. Like the rest of the *Playboy* lifestyle, femininity was constructed in the image of Hefner's fantasies. Says Hefner biographer Russell Miller, "He made no secret of the fact that he produced the magazine for himself . . . He wanted to be a suave, sophisticated man-about-town, sexually liberated, irresistible to women, and a masterful lover."[2] The *Playboy* bachelor lifestyle was built on fine living and luxurious consumption. It was a lifestyle that most men could not realistically emulate, whether for financial reasons or otherwise; but Hefner wanted his readers to *think* the lifestyle was in the realm of possibility. Part of a complete lifestyle, the famous Playmate centerfolds cannot be considered outside the larger context of masculinity that was created in the pages of *Playboy*. Like so much of the postwar consumer culture, the Playmate was packaged as part of a lifestyle any man with the will to do so could acquire.

Almost as famous as the centerfolds themselves is the traditional feminist critique of the Playmates as the dehumanized products of patriarchy. These claims are not necessarily wrong, but rather they are too simplistic. *Playboy*'s version of femininity was more complicated and contradictory than that. But since the start of the women's movement, feminists have decried *Playboy's* use of centerfolds. Protesters at the 1968 Miss America Pageant threw copies of *Playboy* into a "freedom trashcan" and declared, "To win approval, we must be both sexy and wholesome, delicate but able to cope, demure yet titillatingly bitchy. Deviation of any sort brings, we are told, disaster."[3] Women's liberationists infiltrated Hefner's Chicago mansion in February 1969, when he held an open house for aspiring Playboy Club Bunnies. Activists handed out leaflets to applicants that read, "Sisters, know your enemy! Hefner has made us into lapdog-female-playthings to be sold on the market along with cuff links, shaving lotion and the latest stereo."[4]

Feminist art historian Maria Elena Buszek offers a typical critique of the Playmates. She attributes them to "casual misogyny"[5] and argues that *Playboy* promoted "women's sexual simplicity, and even humiliation."[6] To critics like Buszek, of whom there are many, the Playmate was nothing more than a pliable toy meant for male gratification.[7] But is it possible to reclaim the Playmate as a positive image of postwar feminine sexuality? When conservative social prescription dictated female sexual expression only within the bounds of marriage, was there potential for empowerment by directly engaging feminine sexuality in the form of the Playmate?

Playboy offered its own contemporary answer to these questions. In 1965, Reverend William R. Moors accused *Playboy* of misrepresenting sex and ruining men's expectations of "real" women. *Playboy* responded, "There is something strange, antisexual and sad in the view that a beautiful woman isn't as 'human' as one who is average in appearance or less. We know that a body sweats, emits, has odors, pubic hair, pimples and breasts that sag; our readers know it, too."[8] Likewise, to Reverend J. Benton White of San Jose, *Playboy* argued that the Playmates were not evidence that the magazine's "approach to sex is 'dehumanizing' and that we 'put down' women." *Playboy* asked, "Did Goya's nude painting of the Duchess of Alba dehumanize her— or glorify her?"[9] According to *Playboy*, the Playmates were "glorified," or offered as "romantic, erotic images for straight men,"[10] in a way that spoke to larger cultural assumptions about gender and sexuality. To the question of objectification, *Playboy* repeated, "we can't agree . . . that photographs turn people into objects and that the appeal such photos may have derives from or perpetuates a desire to possess. A desire to enjoy—perhaps. But we've always opposed the idea that enjoyment of another person . . . can be properly based on ownership or domination."[11]

An exchange in the April 1968 Forum between *Playboy* and Marilyn Kiss of Columbia University clearly illustrated both sides of this issue. Kiss recognized the ways in which the magazine was a potential ally to women, but she could not justify the centerfolds: "Isn't the notion that women are objects what the *Playboy Philosophy* is supposedly fighting? No legislator who regards a woman as a person will support anachronistic abortion laws, red-tape divorce procedures or censorship of the so-called obscene. . . . Supposedly fighting dehumanization in its *Philosophy*, *Playboy* endorses it in the rest of its pages." Calling her accusation "the old and discredited cliché," *Playboy* replied, "Apparently you react to the pictures in *Playboy* like someone taking a Rorschach test: You see what you want to see. Whereas each Playmate-of-the-Month feature . . . [portrays] her in detail as the living person she is, you . . . see 'not a person but a provocative object.'"[12]

Kiss's critique of the Playmates came just as the modern women's movement was expanding its own critique of American society. It reflected, among other things, the growing discontent that many women felt over media portrayals of feminine sexuality. As Kiss implied, *Playboy*'s political philosophy was in line with progressive, possibly even feminist, ideology, but that mutuality was negated by the magazine's inclusion of the centerfolds. *Playboy*'s response to Kiss reflected Hefner's adamant refusal to acknowledge the feminist challenge to the Playmates. Calling her position on the centerfolds "old and discredited," Hefner totally denied the growing opposition that the women's movement leveled against his magazine. By telling Kiss that she saw only what she wanted to see in the centerfolds, Hefner refused to see that the Playmates were open to interpretation.

Some critics have seen the centerfolds as not just degrading to women, but as obscene or pornographic.[13] Instead, the Playmates should be seen as part of the history of the American pin-up—a sexy image meant to titillate and instigate fantasy, but one that avoids sexual explicitness. World War II made such images pervasive as American GIs looked to pictures of stars like Betty Grable and Rita Hayworth and to *Esquire*'s illustrated Petty and Varga Girls to ease the loneliness of war. Twenty years later, *Playboy* received so many fan letters from troops in Vietnam that Hefner began to send Playmates there on promotional tours.

Renowned film critic Andre Bazin defined the nature of the pin-up in 1946: "The pin-up girl is a specific erotic phenomenon [not to be confused with pornography]." He described the formulaic image,

Let us note the firm opulence of her bosom. . . . [but] an adequate physique, a young and vigorous body . . . still do not define the pin-up girl for us. . . . [A]n infinite variety of suggestive degrees of undress—never exceeding some rigorously defined limits—show off to the advantage the charms of the pin-up girl while pretending to hide them. . . . The veils in which the pin-up girl is draped serve a dual purpose: they comply with the social censorship . . . but at the same time make it possible to experiment with the censoring itself and use it as an additional form of sexual stimulus.[14]

Bazin concluded that this "precise balance . . . clearly distinguishes her from the salaciously erotic or pornographic."[15] Historian Mark Gabor affirmed that the mass-produced pin-up was distinct from pornography, because the latter "accomplishes—and realizes—exactly what a pin-up must not do," it "[acts] out the rituals that are only suggested by the pin-up."[16] Hefner's construction of the Playmates spoke to this tradition. The centerfolds were portrayed as wholesome yet alluring, and meant to inspire fantasy, but they were deliberately constrained within the "rigorously defined limits" both Bazin and Gabor noted.

The famous pin-ups were not the only nude photographs in Playboy. Since its inception, the magazine included various features that justified racy pictures. Stories on cabarets, striptease acts, and sexy foreign films gave Playboy a reason to illustrate articles with images of naked women. "The Girls Of . . ." series highlighted beautiful women from various countries and cultures, such as "The Girls of Scandinavia" or "The Girls of Africa."[17] As the magazine grew into the 1960s, even a few naked men found their way into Playboy through journalistic pieces on countercultural nude-ins and the growth of the adult-film industry. One of the more popular features, "The History of Sex in Cinema," by Arthur Knight and Hollis Alpert, documented in text and image eroticism in avant-garde and mainstream film.

These articles gave Playboy a chance to showcase women other than the Playmates. But it also afforded the magazine an opportunity to present sexuality and nudity more overtly than Hefner allowed in the idealized centerfold. While Hefner insisted that the entire magazine uphold what he considered to be a standard of wholesomeness and taste, the supplementary pictorials provided a space for testing the magazine's own boundaries. For instance, pubic hair was shown in Playboy for the first time not in a centerfold, but in a feature on dancer Paula Kelley in 1969. Likewise, full frontal images of men were included in a feature on campus nudity in 1972. But it was the Playmate centerfolds that made the magazine instantly famous.

Hefner believed that he personalized the centerfolds with stories of the models' families and aspirations, and therefore could not or would not entertain the idea that the Playmates were objectified or dehumanized. Considering the pairing of image and text, Hefner was right. The centerfolds were, in fact, humanized. But to the extent that they still may have been negative portrayals of female sexuality—in their implied availability, eagerness to please, and airbrushed perfection—critics like Marilyn Kiss did not see the difference. But that difference mattered, because the centerfolds' humanization was actually a granting of sexuality. Though the Playmates were undoubtedly a product of the conservative postwar era, compared to the cultural terrain around them they contradicted the notion that the only place for women's desire was in the matrimonial bed. By sexualizing the girl-next-door in his centerfolds, Hefner granted that same sexuality to the women the Playmates represented—the secretaries, neighbors, girlfriends, and colleagues that Hefner told readers could be found all around them.

In 1974 scholars Richard A. Kallan and Robert D. Brooks argued that the primary goal of personalizing the Playmate was to portray her as available and morally upstanding, thus "conferring approval upon her nudity."[18] But personalization did more than that. It challenged the degradation of women's sexuality that was common in that pre-feminist age. Kallan and Brooks pointed out that Playmates were characterized as educated, hardworking, kind, and individualist. Significantly, parents were often mentioned and even included in non-nude secondary pictures, and their approval of their daughters' appearance in Playboy was noted. Kallan and Brooks contend that this merely "added to the Playmate's 'apple pie' character," so that there appeared "really nothing unusual about her at all."[19] More importantly, though, it also made female sexuality a joyous and normal experience, so that there was "nothing unusual" about a woman who celebrated her own sensuality. If a father did not harshly judge a young woman for expressing her sexuality, why should millions of Playboy readers?

This concept of women's sexuality was in contrast to prevailing postwar mores. Historian Elaine Tyler May argues that in the midst of the cold war, conservative America sought to contain the sexuality of those who might have challenged the stability of the family and thus weakened the nation, namely promiscuous women. May says that as the United States worked to contain the spread of communism around the globe, so women were contained within the domestic sphere of home, marriage, and motherhood. Using the contemporary slang for sexualized women, May writes, "Knockouts and bombshells could be tamed... into harmless *chicks, kittens,* and the most famous sexual pet of them all, the Playboy bunny."[20] But did the Playmates represent the containment of women's sexuality? The centerfolds were never portrayed as aggressive, threatening, or controlling—attributes that may or may not be prerequisites for a feminist sexuality. The Playmates were, above all else, constructed as cheery, easygoing girls. That is the important point: in postwar America, "nice" girls lost that vaunted status as soon as they had sex outside of marriage. But the Playmates told the country that women, even the marriageable ones, could have happy, healthy sexuality, regardless of marital status.

The Playmates were constructed as all-American girls who enjoyed sex. Hefner insisted that the women in his magazine were not unlike the women his readers encountered every day. He told his audience that women like the Playmates could be found everywhere, thereby not only popularizing his magazine but also granting sexual autonomy and desire to women. Thus, women who enjoyed their sexuality as a part of their total personality would not be suspect to *Playboy*'s readers, nor would such a lifestyle be attributed only to the most immoral, or conversely the most glamorous, women. It would be offered as a possibility for real women across the country, and ultimately contributed to a changing notion of femininity in an era of sexual revolution.

This was an important part of convincing men that the *Playboy* lifestyle was attainable, but it also it challenged the traditional standards of sexuality that Hefner railed against in his magazine.[21] Portraying Playmates as active sexual beings, *Playboy* insisted that women had desire, indeed a *right to desire,* just as society assumed men did. Importantly, that desire was not problematic for *Playboy.* Hefner did not judge or punish the Playmates for their sexuality. The wholesome centerfolds were not portrayed as wanton whores. To the contrary, *Playboy* celebrated them through photos and accompanying stories, as ideal American women, sexually available, but often educated and employed, and all-around good citizens. Many supposedly dreamed of families and white-picket fences. The accompanying photos to Willy Rey's centerfold, for instance, showed her cooking at home with her mother and then enjoying the "delicious" meal with both her parents.[22]

This celebration of a postwar woman whose sexuality was part of her overall identity, and who treated sexuality as a fun and joyous pursuit—not a deadly serious way of cementing or landing a relationship—was rarely seen in 1950s American popular culture. But for Hefner, the fact that these women took off their clothes for his magazine did not preclude them from participating in the American dream. Other pop culture representations of female sexuality, like those found in many American films of the time, meted out punishment to women who asserted their sexuality too boldly.[23] The Playmates' sexuality, in contrast, was not portrayed as dangerous, and some critics have seen this as proof of the antifeminist, antiwoman nature of the centerfolds. But should one assume that a woman's sexuality must be a threat to men in order to be feminist? Is it any more pro-woman to portray feminine sexuality as something men need to fear?

Some contemporary observers of Playboy noticed something other than female objectification in the centerfolds. In 1971, after almost two decades of Playmates, theologian Herbert W. Richardson wrote an appraisal of Playboy's influence on American sexual mores. Richardson concluded that the magazine's portrayal of women's sexuality was not as simple as mainstream feminists had purported. He argued that the "nonthreatening" Playmates were actually an improvement over traditional notions of femininity. Richardson wrote that with the emergence of Playboy as a significant cultural icon, "several new trends in human sexuality are given expression."[24] He noted,

In [Playboy] we find patriarchalism and the traditional exploitation of sexual anxiety that is found in every "girlie magazine." But to focus on these is to miss the important thing. . . . What is especially unusual about the Playboy-Playmate symbolism is that the sexually attractive woman is here conceived as a friend and equal. . . . The "Playmate" is the girl from whom all the aggressive aspects of human sexuality have been removed. . . . The Playmate is not of interest simply for her sexual functions alone. The photo montage that surrounds the Playmate portrays her in a variety of everyday activities: going to work . . . climbing mountains and sailing . . . figuring out her income tax. She is . . . the Playboy's all-day, all-night pal. . . . The [egalitarian], nonaggressive relation between the Playboy and the Playmate stresses the similarity between the two. He enjoys sex, she enjoys sex. . . .

The implication of this fact is that . . . men and women can be constant companions and the best of friends. It means that their sexual relation will . . . be . . . integrated within . . . their total personal life together.[25]

Richardson showed that at the height of the women's movement, some observers saw the potential in *Playboy* to offer a progressive view of women's sexuality. There is no question that Playmates were meant to appeal to heterosexual men, and they beg questions of power and sexual authority. But the Playmate image was invented at a time in American history when news of women's sexual agency made headlines, as with the publication of Alfred Kinsey's work in 1953. Hugh Hefner challenged those postwar standards when he presented the all-American girl to the world and told us that she liked sex—a subversive proposition in the 1950s.

In the years following World War II, America experienced a stunning about-face in its consideration of women's "proper" place in society. It had turned from an insistence on women's wartime independence and economic contribution outside the home, to a postwar emphasis on domesticity. Men and women were expected to pick up where the country had left off nearly twenty years earlier, when depression and then war had disrupted the traditional processes of domestic settlement. Facing an "antifeminist onslaught,"[26] men were pressured to conform to the standards of the breadwinning dad, and many women were forced out of their wartime jobs and back into traditionally feminine roles. Though a vast majority of women reported they wanted to keep their jobs, "most gave them up without much of a struggle. . . . women's individual desires remained secondary to a shared commitment to families."[27]

The rates of marriage and childbirth after World War II skyrocketed to "mythic proportions,"[28] suggesting that many couples did this happily. On the surface, it seemed that much of middle-class America relished the opportunity to create a peaceful, prosperous suburban existence. With this renewed emphasis on home and hearth came a vigorous sexual double standard. For men, casual dalliances before marriage were usually dismissed as a male prerogative. A woman, on the other hand, was expected to protect her virginity until her sexuality was coaxed to life in the marriage bed. Media scholar Susan Douglas writes, "The message . . . was always the same. Girls . . . didn't have much, if any, sexual desire. . . . If a girl did it before she was married . . . no boy, not even her steady boyfriend, would ever respect her again."[29] So regardless of the independence, sexual or otherwise, that was culturally tolerated during the crisis of war, women were expected to conform to strict standards of propriety in the 1950s.

When women's sexual desire was recognized, it was almost always in the capacity of wife and mother. The years following World War II saw a growing emphasis on Freudianism, which insisted upon sexual expression as part of a healthy development as an individual. Thus middle-class women were no longer thought of as passive sexual creatures, as Victorian standards had assumed. Now they were considered sexual beings that could, indeed *should*, blossom into sexually satisfied women, but only after marriage.

This link between sexuality, family, and nation contributed to what many feminists believed to be "damaging and dangerous times"[30] for women. Prescriptive ideology constrained women's sexuality outside of marriage, and combined with pressures to maintain the wellbeing of the family through the marital bed, led to a culture with very strict notions of proper feminine sexuality. But this view does not tell the whole, varied story of postwar femininity, as reality often revealed a different picture.

Much of 1950s America was fraught with contradiction. It was an era that saw unprecedented prosperity, and yet many Americans found themselves unable to break the cycle of poverty. The United States had just defeated a genocidal dictator, and now led the so-called free world in a global struggle against Soviet Communism, but its own history of racial oppression continued to plague its African American citizens. Such conflicts marked many women's lives. Though social prescription called for limited sexual expression for women, the 1953 publication of Kinsey's study on women's sexuality showed the world that American women had active sex lives both in and out of marriage. It was evident that much more went on behind closed doors than most people were willing to admit. The need to reconcile contradictory expectations extended beyond women's sexual lives as well.

Social and governmental propaganda told women that to be anything less than a happy homemaker was neurotic and damaging. Despite this, women stayed in the workforce in unprecedented numbers, while others entered paid employment for the first time. The rates of married female employment doubled between 1940 and 1960, with an even more dramatic increase in the numbers of working mothers. Historian Alice Kessler-Harris points out, "As in World War II, a vigorous cold war economy demanded a steady and well-educated supply of labor. A combination of expanding educational opportunities for women and heightened expectations for more comfortable . . . living standards tempted middle-income women into the labor force."[31] Moreover, women's social and political activity in the 1950s belied the pressures to domesticate. As Susan Douglas argued, "Just because the feminine mystique had become the official ideology by the late 1950s doesn't mean that all women bought into it."[32]

Those ambiguous and competing postwar tensions—between tradition and progress, domesticity and independence—found their way into the centerfolds of Playboy. Though certain elements of the centerfolds changed over time, including a diversification of race and the eventual unveiling of the pubic area, the basic approach remained the same for decades. As longtime editor Nat Lehrman insists, "The Playboy of 1953 is not that much different from the Playboy of today."[33] Indeed, many of the Playmates of the late 1960s and early 1970s looked remarkably similar to those of a decade earlier.

In contrast to the prevailing ideology that "good" girls remained virgins until marriage, the Playmates were presented with a "freshness and vitality and capacity for having fun, . . . accessible to all girls."[34] In a 1957 interview, Hefner said that he "never thought about any big difference between girls who pose in the nude and girls who don't."[35] Women ended up in Playboy's gatefold in different ways. Potential Playmates could submit pictures to Playboy directly, or, as was often the case, staff or freelance photographers could nominate women they thought were fitting. In other cases, friends and associates of Playboy employees, or Playboy Club waitresses, known as Bunnies, were recommended. If the magazine's picture editor and associate picture editor approved the test shots, they were then submitted to Hefner, who had the ultimate say in who was chosen as Playmate of the Month.[36] Playboy promotional material emphasized Hefner's "personal control of the Playmate cycle—from selection to shooting to publication."[37] Editor Jim Petersen says the Playmates "reflect Hefner's taste in what the ideal American woman looks like."[38] "In order of importance," their "beauty," "figure," and finally their "background" factored into their approval.[39]

For their efforts, Playmates by the late 1960s typically received an initial payment of $1,500; after publication they received an additional $1,000. They were guaranteed another $2,500 if eligible for further promotional work (over 90 percent of the Playmates qualified).[40] Playmates of the Year "[received] a cash bonus and additional merchandise and gifts generally valued at $10,000."[41] This was lucrative work for a young woman in the 1960s. The median annual income for all women in 1967 was approximately $1,600; the vast majority of female workers (88 percent) earned under $5,000 per year.[42] For one or two days of work posing for the centerfold, a Playmate could earn more than most women earned annually; with a year-long promotional contract, she would be in the top 12 percent of female earners in the country. Hefner ushered each new centerfold into the world of *Playboy*, "[L]et me personally welcome you to the illustrious list of young ladies who have graced our celebrated gatefold, been admired by literally millions of young men across the country—and indeed around the world."[43] The women were assured, "To be a Playmate is an experience that appeals to many girls. And whether it be a calculated step toward show-business success, or for the financial rewards, one thing is certain. [You'll] never look better."[44]

Hefner preferred women who were otherwise unknown, and had them photographed in ways that spoke to their ordinariness, granting the centerfolds a perceived availability that he found lacking in traditional pin-ups. Some famous or soon-to-be-famous women like Jayne Mansfield and Betty Paige, posed for *Playboy* during this time, but they were the minority. The most famous of Hefner's centerfolds was his first, Marilyn Monroe, known in the inaugural issue as the Sweetheart of the Month.

Monroe did not actually pose for *Playboy*. Photographer Tom Kelley took the pictures in 1949, before Monroe's fame. The photographs were sold to a Chicago calendar company and continued to circulate into the early 1950s, when it was discovered that the model was the newly famous Marilyn Monroe. Though the calendar had originally been popular in barber shops, garages, and the like, the photographs were presented to the world when Hugh Hefner bought the rights from the Baumgarth Company for $500 and published them in the first issue of *Playboy*.[45] The magazine was a hit.[46]

Included with the rights to the Monroe photos were several other previously photographed nude pin-ups. Those pictures became the magazine's first centerfolds. Models were posed in typical "cheesecake" style, by lying on a bearskin rug, for instance, with no props or particular setting. Miss March 1954, Dolores Del Monte, was one of those original pin-ups. Nineteen-year-old Del Monte hid her work from her parents in 1951, "Because it was the fifties, I did not tell my parents that I was going to model nude that day . . . That just wouldn't float." Actually, since her photo was part of those bought from the Baumgarth Company, Del Monte had no idea her picture had found its way into *Playboy* until her son spotted the photo in a 1979 anniversary issue, making her a celebrity among her family and friends. Looking back, she says, "These are not bad people who pose in the magazine. I am still proud of that centerfold. It was my destiny."[47]

In 1955, Hefner made the decision to change the look of the centerfolds. He noted, "we aren't interested in straight nudes anymore. On the other hand, we aren't looking for straight cheesecake or pin-up pictures either. What we want is a sophisticated semi-nude."[48] Such statements made clear Hefner's desire to not necessarily push the boundaries of nudity, but rather to produce a magazine according to his own standards of taste and propriety. Hefner was adamant that the photos convey a sense of wholesome, sexy sophistication, yet the women were not supposed to look like they had been around the block *too* many times. Hefner explained to a photographer in 1955,

> We want to get our girls into more natural surroundings—preparing for a dinner date, getting ready for bed, rising in the morning, or any of the hundreds of things that a smart, sophisticated career girl might be doing in the semi-dress. . . . We'll be particularly interested in new girls—ones that haven't been seen in either the nude or semi-nude in other magazines. . . . What we're trying to come up with . . . is class-sex. We want to take the Playmates out of the barber shop calendar category and give our readers something fresh and different.[49]

Hefner described Playmates as "[usually] nervous [and] awkward."[50] This was because, for the most part, Hefner preferred women with little or no professional experience, particularly as nudes. He felt this lent an air of innocence and naturalness to the images. The women had to agree to not pose nude again for two years after their appearance in the magazine.[51]

Crude sexuality was never the goal of *Playboy*, and this restraint was evidenced in the photos. One idea for a shoot centered on a model playing Scrabble with an unseen paramour. Her tiles were arranged to spell "Maybe." Hefner loved it. He thought it was a "very clever twist" befitting the tone of the magazine.[52] The suggestion of hesitation reflected situations readers no doubt encountered with three-dimensional women everyday; and it showed that sex in *Playboy*, as in life, was not necessarily a given, but an enticing reason to come back for more.

To further the fantasy, Hefner wanted the photos to appear "real"—posed in recognizable settings, with props that suggested an actual circumstance, and in the early years with himself as part of the image, what Hefner referred to as "nudity with validity."[53] "We want to see fresh, young things . . . dressed as girls really are. We want the surroundings to be logical and the girl real to the reader."[54] Models wore Hefner's unbuttoned shirts, his ties hung in the background of some shots, and his ubiquitous pipe was conspicuously placed in many photos, connoting his supposed association with the women. The camera itself acted as "our guy who is present but unseen," that is, the gazing male reader.[55] Hefner argued, "It is easy for the reader to identify himself with this unseen masculine company and the picture is . . . greatly enhanced by the suggestion of not just a picture but an intimate scene."[56]

In 1955, Hefner took the concept a step further. Miss July was Janet Pilgrim, Hefner's then girlfriend and *Playboy* employee in the subscription department. The picture had Pilgrim (a pseudonym) seated at a vanity wearing an open negligee, with a tuxedoed man in the background. The issue touted her as an average working girl, one who never took her clothes off for a photographer before, but felt that it was acceptable, "just this once,"[57] for *Playboy*. The man in the background was Hefner, and the photo caused a sensation for the magazine.

Letters to the editor poured in praising the photo. The "Boys in River Dorm" at Ohio State University wrote, "Amateur or professional, we think Janet Pilgrim rates with the best." A reader from New York asked, "Is it possible that a girl as beautiful as Miss July actually works in your circulation department?" At least one fan even offered to work in the circulation department for "nothing, or less."[58] With that, Hefner knew he was on to something. Pilgrim graced the centerfold two more times.

One of the more "successful" centerfolds in the early years of *Playboy*, according to Hefner, was Miss September 1955, Anne Fleming.[59] The photo showed a full-length profile of a topless Fleming, wearing only black lace leggings and heels. She was walking up a staircase, presumably to a bedroom. Her left arm trailed behind her, pulling a man's hand up the stairs. The rest of his body was outside the frame, leaving no doubt as to the subject of the photo. Hefner liked it "because it included all of the necessary Playmate elements: a sex situation which also had a touch of humor to it, nice composition in the picture, a soft, sophisticated look, and a girl herself who was both smart and sexy appearing."[60] Apparently readers agreed, because Hefner described it as "one of the most popular we've published. . . . [I]t was strongly confirmed through letters from readers."[61] Ultimately what

figure 4.   Playmate Anne Fleming, September 1955. Reproduced by special permission of *Playboy* magazine. Copyright 1955 by Playboy.

this photo showed was a sexually assertive woman leading a man to bed; she was in control. She was appealing but not whorish; her naked breasts were hardly even visible. The suggestion of a particular romantic interlude was clear enough that readers could likely identify with the situation. These kinds of images flew in the face of traditionally conceived notions of female sexual passivity common in the postwar years.

The sense of wholesome feminine availability was zealously protected and fostered in Hefner's Playmates. In 1956, he was considering Arkansas native Betty Blue as a possible Playmate, but he worried that she might give the wrong impression. "I assume that she isn't a stripper," he commented to photographer Hal Adams, who had submitted her photos for consideration. "The last name is what made me wonder about the stripper possibility. A bit unusual."[62] Apparently, Betty was not a stripper, because she landed herself a spot as Miss November 1956.

Another model was not so lucky, however. Photographer Carlyle Blackwell, Jr., submitted photos for a possible New Year's spread. Hefner liked the "balloon and streamer gimmick," but thought the model was "too nude" and that she had "the hardened look of a stripper . . . the face looks like she's been around a while and we prefer the fresh wholesome look on our Playmates."[63] While it is hard to know exactly how nude the model was, it is significant that a photo could be "too nude." Such a statement speaks to the fantasy that was being constructed in *Playboy*, one that could, given the right circumstances, be within the realm of possibility for the average, red-blooded American man. The new image of the Playmate was born as "a girl with a reputation as unblemished as her body." Russell Miller argues, "The cute, fresh-faced . . . all-American cheerleader Playmate was the greatest imaginable turn-on for Americans accustomed to anonymous pin-ups with knowing eyes and come-hither expressions, threatening broads . . . The attraction of the Playmate was the absence of threat."[64] For postwar Americans, whose traditions were being inundated with threats from the Soviet Union, the civil rights movement, Alfred Kinsey, and others, Hefner's version of female sexuality worked.

Building on the visual appeal of the Playmates, a note on the girl's personality, life, work, or background, as well as her measurements, always accompanied the pictures. Sometimes the women's names were changed in order to sound more appealing or all-American. Betty Blue's description included a play on words, "The etymologist in our Research Department insists the word 'buxom' [originally meant] 'pliable and obedient.' It would be nice to think that Miss November . . . is both, and furthermore that she is 'readily incited; prone; of speech, mild and courteous'—definitions of 'buxom' Noah Webster lists as obsolete. But . . . Betty . . . is far from obsolete."[65] The biography of Miss May 1963 portrayed an unpretentious, down-to-earth gal: "'I want to be a hair stylist . . . because I like styling hair. Good painting has always flipped me. I like classical Spanish music... And dancing the cha-cha. And the sound of rain on windows.' When asked what she wants most from life, she quietly replies, 'Love. Money is nice, of course—but it can't hold hands.' Miss May lives in her mother's home and sleeps in a cozy room full of antique furniture."[66] Hefner noted that Miss May's copy was "some of the best we have ever produced.... [it] does a great deal to make the girl warm and personal and real.... I would say that this copy could serve as a good guide to... our Playmate text for the future."[67]

Ironically, given critics' claims of objectification, Hefner felt that these stories, which were likely a combination of biography and editorial license, helped to challenge the potential that some erotic photography had to de-humanize its subject: "There is relatively little appeal in a nude that has no name... [it] is as interesting as a beautiful chair is, but as a human being, no.... [The story] personalizes the girl, she's not just a rag o' bone and a hank o' hair. She's a living breathing human being."[68] Such details allowed the feature to present "the girl herself as a human being and a personality."[69] Portraying centerfolds as living, breathing women was crucial to the brand of sexuality constructed in the pages of *Playboy*. Erotic photos of women had been available since the early days of photography, but in *Playboy* voyeurs got a story as well, a story that suggested similarly beautiful, sexy girls could be found all across America.

Emphasizing feminine availability, Hefner told his October 1955 readers that the magazine was "still getting some of our models the easy way, using members of the organization. The sweet young thing... on the cover this month is Marilyn McClintock, *Playboy*'s receptionist."[70] The magazine told often-fictitious stories of how the models were innocently discovered in a store or restaurant, and insisted readers could find the same, "We suppose it's natural to think of the pulchritudinous Playmates as existing in a world apart. Actually, potential Playmates are all around you: the new secretary at your office, the doe-eyed beauty who sat opposite you at lunch yesterday, the girl who sells you shirts and ties at your favorite store."[71] The photos were supposed to appear as if the camera happened to catch a nice, average girl on a given day, thus showing readers that the women were possible not just for Hefner, but for them, too. Though this approach was "an illusion," Hefner granted, "it can be a very successful one."[72]

A feature on "Photographing Your Own Playmate" in June 1958 told read-ers that they did not need to hire a professional to strip down for them. They could find willing beauties all around—just as *Playboy* found centerfolds, like the popular Janet Pilgrim, in their own office. The column explained how the magazine got their fourth-floor receptionist Judy Lee Tomerlin to pose in the nude. She had no prior experience, which *Playboy* pointed out was "[p]erfect for our purpose."[73] Aspiring playboys were told that they were not the only ones facing women who played hard to get; "Judy Lee did the proper amount of hemming and hawing for a couple of days; then, finally, she said 'Yes.'" All a man needed to achieve the "naturalness" of "the magazine's famous triple-page, fold-out feature," the reader was told, was a "simple prop like a pillow or towel" and he could have his own Playmate.[74]

Professional or not, photographer Dwight Hooker claimed so many girls wanted to pose for *Playboy* in the 1950s he had to "fight them off with a baseball bat."[75] Even at the height of the women's movement in 1973, twenty-three-year-old associate picture editor Holly Wayne received one hundred amateur nude photos a month from women hoping to appear in the magazine.[76] Anecdotal evidence speaks to the desired ordinariness of many of those girls.

In 1959, photographs were taken of would-be model Bonnie Carroll. Bonnie posed not as a potential Playmate, but rather as a fun-loving attendee of a *Playboy* house party that was featured in the magazine. Having thought better of it, Bonnie later said she had done it because she only had three dollars at the time. She wrote to Hefner asking him to not run the photos,

> I feel terrible about those pictures. . . . It wouldn't be so bad if there wasn't any people sitting around, or if it wasn't Hawaiian. . . . I have a good year-round job now, swimming underwater as a mermaid. My boss, it's a girl, wants girls of only the *very best* reputation. . . . I'd have no worries if I was a blond [sic] in it or a blonde playmate or something . . . [Photographer Bunny Yeager has] got high hopes for me in this business, but I haven't, at least as a brunette I mean. . . . I'm sorry to cause so much trouble Hef, please understand.[77]

Who knows why Bonnie might have felt more comfortable with the photos had the party not been "Hawaiian," or if she was not a brunette, but Hefner graciously agreed to pull them and insisted that Bonnie keep her modeling fee, stating, "What you added to the fun of that house party weekend—just being there—was well worth your fee as a model."[78]

Women who did appear as Playmates in the conservative postwar years had a variety of responses to their experience, but many reflect the all-American personalities preferred by Hefner, as well as the complexity with which the magazine presented femininity. Gale Morin, known as Miss November 1954, Diane Hunter, started modeling when she was seventeen, and today bills herself as an "accomplished swing and ballroom dancer." Reflecting on her centerfold, she says, "It was strictly a better job than the soda fountain I was working at before. I never saw myself as anything less than the girl-next-door. I just did a different job than most girls." Morin stopped modeling when she had children, noting, "I flip-flopped from model to housewife so quickly."[79]

Some women wanted to "flip-flop" the other way—from housewife to model, but instead joined "the legions of 'Playboy Rejects.'" One such woman was Mrs. Carole Waite, by her own description a "tiny . . . red-headed wench." In 1959, Carole submitted photos for consideration a second time, after she was initially told she needed to "lose 10 pounds" and prove she was at least eighteen.[80] Carole wrote a charming letter in the third person campaigning for herself,

> Carole amazes people when she tells them of her three children . . . "I made 'em myself—with a little help that is." Carole has a very happy marriage. She's a good wife and mother a very good cook, and a lousy housekeeper . . . Carole is a feminine female—women don't like her, men can't forget her. . . . I'm thru washing diapers, now I want to do something else, modeling perhaps . . . Carole loves: her Bill, her children, her home, a good time . . . scotch and water (tall glass please) . . . jazz oh yes—jazz, "luscious undies," . . . and spending money.[81]

Carole was rejected once again.[82]

Though she was denied her dream of Playmate fame, it is not hard to understand why women like Carole might have wanted to pose for *Playboy*. Much of postwar American culture emphasized traditionalism and domesticity for women. Many, however, wrestled with the strict double standard. For a wife and mother like Carole, posing in the nude for *Playboy* offered an opportunity to spread her sexual wings and rebel against the norms of suburban conformity and boredom. Half a century later, Carole confirms this view. Looking back, she said that after years of marriage and motherhood, she felt she had "a lot more to offer" the world. She had dreams of being a dentist, or even a scientist—or a *Playboy* Playmate.[83] These disparate ambitions—scientist or Playmate—may seem incompatible, and would certainly have been unattainable, possibly unthinkable, for many American women in the 1950s. But what Carole's story tells us is that both options represented the chance to break the strict boundaries of traditional postwar womanhood. No matter what the Playmates have come to represent to feminist eyes, for a woman like Carole, the pages of *Playboy* signified something "more."

Rebellion against conventional gender norms was the standard for Miss July 1956, Alice Denham. She grew up in a conservative Southern family, saying, "Mother wanted me to be her, and I refused."[84] As a child, she fantasized she was "a boy, . . . an Indian scout . . . always evading the evil white man."[85] An aspiring writer with a master's degree in English, Denham moved to New York in search of a career in 1951.[86] Beautiful and voluptuous, she "fell into modeling" and was able to support her writing on a few modeling jobs per week. She says she would have been unable to write her first novel, *My Darling from the Lions*, if she had had to work a typical full-time job.[87] In early 1956, Denham had an idea—she would pitch her short story, "The Deal," to *Playboy* and offer herself as the accompanying Playmate of the Month. She says, "Hefner loved it."[88]

In her memoir, Denham revealed the ambivalence with which she became a Playmate. Upon meeting Hefner, Denham explained that she was only posing to make "a living," but she chastised the publisher for exploiting women, for "building an empire off women's bodies." She admitted that he quickly reminded her it was *her* idea to pose for *Playboy*.[89] Denham, who had done some nude modeling previously,[90] conceded that she had mixed feelings about the work, "I've always loved it and hated it both."[91] Today, she says she was a "born feminist," and indeed she was active in the movement in the 1960s and '70s. She participated in a sit-in at the *Ladies' Home Journal* to force the magazine to discuss feminist issues, became a member of NOW at its founding, pressured New York Mayor John Lindsay to include an equal rights platform in his administration, and protested for abortion rights.[92]

As a feminist and a Playmate, Denham represented the conflicted relationship that *Playboy* had with femininity. "*Playboy* advanced the sexual revolution," she argued, "by showing Nice Girls, whose centerfold proclaimed their sexual freedom or sexual ease. *Playboy* tainted the sexual revolution by proclaiming to its male audience [women's] sex object status."[93] Denham

figure 5.   Playmate Alice Denham, July 1956. Reproduced by special
permission of *Playboy* magazine. Copyright 1956 by Playboy.

said the magazine was "a two-edged sword: sexism versus freedom," and she acknowledged that while she felt at once "exposed, flattered, and cringing" by the display of her body to the world, she was also "immensely pleased that so many people might read my story."[94] She says she has no regrets about her experience with *Playboy*, because it advanced her career. After her story and centerfold appeared in 1956, Doubleday, Random House, and Houghton Mifflin each contacted her about publishing a novel.[95]

If not all Playmates considered themselves rebels, some understood they were testing the limits of conventional femininity. Joyce Nizzari, Miss December 1958, was introduced to Hefner by famous pin-up photographer Bunny Yeager, and began a romantic relationship with him.[96] Nizzari describes herself, "Although I was never an exhibitionist, I was also not conservative. General standards had little influence on me. What did, however, was my strict Italian father." Nizzari says that she and her mother were eventually able to win her father's approval after she introduced him to Hefner, who "helped to soothe any anxiety."[97] Nizzari and Hefner remain friends, and she currently works at the Playboy Mansion in Los Angeles. She says that her "son feels as if Hef's an uncle, or related somehow, because *Playboy* has been in our lives so long."[98]

Other glimpses into the motivations of would-be Playmates can be seen in questionnaires that women were asked to fill out when they submitted photos for consideration. They inquired about physical measurements, family, interests, ambitions, and the like. [99] The answers illustrated that many of the women who wanted to take their clothes off for *Playboy* were indeed average, all-American girls.

Linda Allison of Weehawken, New Jersey, was only seventeen in 1968, but with the signed consent of her mother she tried for the centerfold. Allison had modeled for retail advertisements, and acted in a Gilbert and Sullivan production at her high school. Her favorite book, other than those by "Papa Hemingway," was *The Power of Positive Thinking*; indeed, when asked what she was "particularly wild about," she answered, "Life in general. It's great!" Allison hoped to become a social worker, and planned to use her modeling fee "for the purpose of furthering my career and education."[100]

Lynda Jean Veverka, known to *Playboy* readers as Miss October 1966, Linda Moon, had Cherokee blood and wanted to be a beautician. She enjoyed sewing and horseback riding, and loved Mexican food and 7-Up cola. Veverka hoped to be a Playmate "because it would be a new experience."[101]

Attesting to Hefner's claim that he found many of his Playmates in his own office, nineteen-year-old *Playboy* receptionist Mimi Chesterton posed for the magazine and became Claudia Jennings, Miss November 1969. Chesterton loved "sour green apples," mentioning them twice on her data sheet, and she described herself as "a person deeply troubled [by] the world situation and given to moments of thought, especially with the racial problems." She wanted to be a stage actress, "If I eventually get up my courage and hit New York I feel it could only be beneficial having been slightly exposed to the public already. (I didn't mean that literally!)"[102]

Regardless of the sociopsychological reasons that may have motivated women like Mimi to pose, in the end there were cash and prizes, in fact, a "Queen's Ransom" offered to the lucky few, the Playmates of the Year. By the mid-sixties winners of the title were awarded automobiles and a treasure trove of kitsch, including a ten-speed Schwinn bike, a bumper pool table, and lamé stretch pants "all in Playmate Pink," as well as suntan lotion, a platinum-blonde wig, and a gallon of Kahlua.[103] With the wealth of consumer goods available to postwar Americans, apparently Playmates of the Year reaped the benefits.

As Hefner deliberately constructed centerfolds to portray an image of safe feminine availability, he did not make the photos as explicit as legally possible. No matter, there were still occasional debates among readers as to the appropriateness of certain pictures: for obvious reasons, bust size was a hot topic. One reader found Miss March 1962's thirty-nine-inch bust "simply disgusting," while another denounced her as an "udder disaster."[104] Writer Max Eastman took the time to offer his thoughts on the voluptuousness of the Playmates. "[Y]ou are running nudes that are *too* full-bosomed. . . . I get a feeling from some of your recent Playmates that I have to cultivate my mother complex rather than my sense of beauty and adventure."[105]

American popular culture was fixated on breasts in the 1950s. Film scholar Marjorie Rosen argues that the period was marked by "mammary madness."[106] The obsession centered on "enormous white breasts"[107] that would not only connote earthy sensuality, but also the overflowing abundance of postwar prosperity. Given the popularity of Freudian psychoanalytic theory at the time, the breast fetish suggested as well the implicit association of motherhood—another obsession of the era. Celebrity biographer Donald Spoto notes, "In postwar America, psychoanalysis and psychiatric sessions were very much the vogue . . . for those who felt drastic action was needed to resolve life's ordinary demands."[108] Scholar Marilyn Yalom writes, "In the psychoanalytic scheme of things, breasts are the source of a person's deep emotions. Freud posited that sucking at the breast was . . . 'the starting point of the whole sexual life.'"[109] She argued, "[W]e must give [Freudian breast theories] credit for uniting the two major strands of breast history into a powerful psychological paradigm: the maternal breast and the erotic breast have become one."[110]

Yalom argues that popular postwar conceptions of womanhood were defined by notions of "sweetness, wholesomeness, and health" associated with ample bosoms[111]—and by extension, with the Playmates. Clinging to the portrait of womanhood that he articulated in the 1950s, Hefner continued to promote the Playmate as he always had, even as the country struggled through the 1960s. More than a decade after the first centerfold appeared on newsstands, Playmate Tish Howard, Miss July 1966, looked as if her picture could have appeared ten years earlier. She posed in front of a set of lockers that held a letterman's sweater, and she wore only one ankle sock. Her back to the camera, she smiled over her right shoulder. With a tennis racket and a pair of Keds at her feet, she was the epitome the sexy coed. Upon evaluation for a *Playboy* promotional contract, Howard was described as "an excellent representative for *Playboy*—she is intelligent and well-bred."[112] Another evaluator called her "The perfect Playmate. Genuine, natural, lovely, sweet, etc."[113] As *Playboy* and the rest of the country moved into a new era, the Playmate continued to represent the same vision of wholesome sexuality that she had for years.

As the social and sexual changes of the 1960s drastically transformed American culture, *Playboy* cheered the move toward a more libertine society. Hefner had always supported a philosophy of individual liberty and civil justice, and as the decade wore on, the country was catching up to his vision. Even some Playmates found themselves caught in the spirit of the times. Gloria Root, Miss December 1969, apparently saw no contradiction between posing for *Playboy* and working for the revolution. She described her "ideal man" on the data sheet she filled out when she tested for the magazine. He had "dark, long hair," and she hoped he would not "work to perpetuate the 'system.'" Root explained herself as "young, sexy, somewhat intellectual." She liked "money, clothes, cars, demonstrations, riots and anything for the revolution."[114] Her eventual *Playboy* layout declared her a "Revolutionary discovery," and the accompanying photographs showed her at an antiwar rally.[115] Miss December, the "sometime scholar and full-time radical,"[116] did not comment on the feminist movement, nor indicate if she felt herself a part of it. But in her own eyes at least, Gloria Root saw her life and politics as cutting edge and progressive. To her, appearing in *Playboy* did not contradict those beliefs.

It was different for Miss September 1963, Victoria Valentino. Valentino had just discovered she was pregnant when her centerfold was shot, and gave birth the day after her issue hit the stands.[117] She says that as her political views changed in the late 1960s, her view of *Playboy* changed as well. She was "going to love-ins and marching in the streets against Vietnam. *Playboy* was something I tried to avoid . . . my ever-evolving socio-political and spiritual consciousness was always causing me extreme grief [because of my experience as a Playmate]. I didn't know how to make it fun . . . I didn't understand how to integrate it all." Today, she has embraced her connection to *Playboy*, but like Alice Denham, still sees a contradiction: "[The magazine] raised consciousness and gave women permission to experience themselves as sexual beings . . . a good thing. It gave men the opportunity to have sex with less responsibility . . . not a good thing . . . I think it was good for both genders, but in different ways."[118]

Despite the evolving social landscape that had such an influence on Valentino's perspective, most of the Playmates remained sexy girls-next-door—even if that sometimes meant the politically conscious girls-next-door. The centerfolds hardly changed, even as Americans themselves began reevaluating their own sexual standards. Beauty standards shifted along with political consciousness, but *Playboy* steadfastly resisted the fashionable androgyny of the time, noting that popular model Twiggy was more appropriate for the magazine *Boys' Life* than for *Playboy*.[119] Only certain hairdos or contemporary articles of clothing revealed the passage of time among most Playmates.

For Martha Smith, Miss July 1973, posing for *Playboy* at the height of the women's movement did not compromise her politically informed liberal views. In fact, she found it the "perfect time" to appear in the magazine, because of the freeing of sexual constraints and growing acceptance of nudity that marked the era. Smith saw the money earned from nude modeling as a route to independence and freedom from the traditional gender norms with which she had grown up. Her family lived in Detroit, and her older sister, herself a model, had already appeared in secondary nude features in *Playboy*.

But in general Smith reflects that her "upbringing . . . was entrenched in . . . stereotypes, being raised in middle-class America, with a kind of 'Ozzie and Harriet' hierarchal prototype . . . I had strong desires to pursue a career." She goes on to say, "It wasn't the traditional program in my family for the girls to chase careers . . . [but I] couldn't bear the idea of marrying and being a housewife. It seemed compromising."[120]

Posing nude for *Playboy* was not "compromising" for the headstrong Smith, but marriage and motherhood was. Smith was very politically engaged at the time, noting that Vietnam, the Munich Olympic massacre, the era's assassinations, and other traumas greatly affected her and informed her view of the women's movement. While she is opposed to "labels" such as "feminist," Smith insists she "couldn't be a stronger advocate for equal rights, equal pay and opportunities." But she was opposed to the way in which some feminists challenged femininity and beauty culture—a position *Playboy* vociferously articulated. Smith says that compared to the "horrors" that played out in America's streets and abroad in the late 1960s and early 1970s, the "stop-shaving and wearing makeup contingent" of the women's movement did not appeal to her.[121]

As a Playmate in a feminist era, Smith was often asked if she felt that she was exploited by *Playboy*. She unequivocally answered,

> No, I never had that feeling or even the notion. I looked upon that entire episode of my life as one of a professional career choice that was right for me at the time, that I was very nicely compensated for, [as a] good job opportunity. . . . I didn't feel a need to compromise any of my own views or morals in order to do my job, as might have been the case had I been working for, let's say the Nixon administration . . . It was in general a heady and exciting time for me . . . I felt happy, modern, independent and free . . . I felt neither oppressed nor in need of being liberated from anything or anyone.[122]

Smith says that posing for *Playboy* changed her. It gave a shy, awkward young woman a "welcome" sense of sophistication, savvy, and confidence.

If Playmates like Smith had to confront their own personal politics in a changing time, the magazine had to do the same and the issue of race became an obvious question for Hefner. When *Playboy* began what would become one of its most noted features, the celebrity interview, the magazine approached celebrated jazz musician Miles Davis. Davis was initially wary of giving an interview to *Playboy*: "It's a magazine for whites. . . . another reason that I didn't want to do it was because *Playboy* didn't have black or brown or Asian women in there. All they have are blond women with big tits and flat asses or no asses."[123] Ultimately, Davis agreed to be interviewed by Alex Haley for *Playboy* in 1962. But he was right. No woman of color appeared as Playmate until August 1964 when the magazine included its first Asian centerfold, China Lee.[124]

It should come as no surprise that a magazine like *Playboy* would first break with its tradition of Caucasian centerfolds with an Asian American woman. The United States, and the West in general, had a long tradition of cultural fascination with Asia and its women. Scholar Sheridan Prasso says that the region has held a seductive air of mystery and sensuality for Westerners. The charm of Japan and the Polynesian islands especially grew in the postwar years. After the conflicts of World War II, Korea, and eventually Vietnam, soldiers brought home with them not just enthralling stories— or lurid secrets—of adventures in Asia, but also tens of thousands of war brides, as well as a new appreciation for Asian and Polynesian culture, if only as kitsch. As historian Bill Osgerby points out, the 1950s and early '60s saw the rise of Eastern-inspired fads like tiki bars, luaus, tropical shirts, bamboo furniture, and surf music. Additionally, scholar Christina Klein writes that thousands of students, tourists, and the like, as well as the cold war's diplomatic expansion into the region, fed into Americans' focus on all things Asian. Osgerby argues that in an era of expanding consumption, "the mythology of the island paradise [stood for] consumerism's beguiling promise of indulgence and unabashed pleasure seeking in a land of plenty. . . . where [postwar Americans] could throw off the work ethic and the inhibitions of prudish sobriety to luxuriate in an Eden of sensuality."[125]

By the time *Playboy* ventured to include an Asian American centerfold in 1964, the conflation of Asian women with sexual availability was firmly established in many readers' minds. Sheridan Prasso calls this the myth of the "Asian Mystique—the fantasy of the exotic, indulging, decadent, sexual Orient."[126] As Prasso and others have demonstrated, many Westerners have additionally perceived women of Asian heritage as docile and subservient. Centerfold China Lee explicitly acknowledged this stereotype in *Playboy* when she declared, "the popular image of the shy and retiring Oriental female is long overdue for a change."[127] Although *Playboy* emphasized the American-born Lee's ethnic heritage, referring to her as the "China Doll" and the

"Oriental Charmer," it also challenged the stereotypes associated with Asian women. Lee's biographical sketch described her traditional upbringing and her family's line of "Oriental restaurants." Lee said, "In this sort of environment; the men dominate and females are forced into the background. I rebelled, and I'm glad I did." *Playboy* slyly noted, "So, we might add, are we."[128] For a Playmate like China Lee, rebellion meant taking her clothes off for a national men's magazine. But for a woman from a conservative background, Asian or otherwise, such a move could have symbolized a true rejection of the traditional expectations of restrained womanhood.

If *Playboy* highlighted Lee's ethnicity to make her more appealing, its next foray into racial diversity played out differently. In March 1965, the magazine finally published its first African American Playmate, Jennifer Jackson.[129] A waitress in the Chicago Playboy Club, Jennifer Jackson enjoyed "exotic cuisine, outdoor sports, avant-garde drama, progressive jazz and 'the joys of trying something new.'"[130] Though the postwar modeling and advertising industry had opened up to African American women, their images were excluded from white publications. The rise of popular black magazines like *Ebony*, however, offered their models an opportunity to claim a space in America's beauty culture. Historian Laila Haidarali argues that the celebration of black pin-ups "became a signifier of democratic promise by representing economic and social triumph in a period when these goals remained unfulfilled for many African-Americans."[131] She adds that the black pin-up possessed a power that "simultaneously objectified, and then restored, respectable middle-class status to African American women's bodies. Successful and sexual, these images redressed the denigrating and pervasive stereotypes of African American women."[132] That power shifted the first time an African American Playmate appeared in the otherwise white *Playboy*. Hefner tread into dangerous territory by including Jennifer Jackson. He was raising the specter of white exploitation of the black body, and he knew it.

Unlike editorial commentary on China Lee, this time the editors made no mention of Jackson's race. Personally and publicly, Hefner fully supported civil rights and equality, and in fact quit a job with the Chicago Carton Company in 1949 due in part to his employer's anti-Semitic and racist hiring practices.[133] Hefner biographer Thomas Weyr writes, "Hefner . . . had always been blind to color bars,"[134] but he "[agonized] over black sex. He understood the ambivalence in black communities about depicting their women for white delectation."[135] Hefner said, "Black women were always viewed as sex objects

figure 6.   *Playboy*'s First African American Playmate, Jennifer Jackson, March 1965. Reproduced by special permission of *Playboy* magazine. Copyright 1965 by Playboy.

and made welcome in the white man's bedroom, and not much good would be done for civil rights with that."[136]

Nonetheless, changing social standards, as well as Hefner's support for civil rights, dictated that women of diverse ethnic backgrounds needed to be included in the gatefold, although models like Lee and Jackson would still represent only a rare departure from the standard Playmate in these years.[137] Young, white blondes continued to be the focus of *Playboy*'s gatefold celebration, reflecting both Hefner's personal taste in women and larger cultural ideals.[138] But in the 1960s, many Americans considered *Playboy* a standard-bearer of feminine attractiveness, and Hefner's inclusion of Jackson struck a blow to the country's longstanding racist beauty standards.

When asked many years later why he took so long to include black Playmates, Hefner said, "we [publishers] all took too long, only I was there ahead of most everybody else."[139] Hefner is aware that his magazine was slow to include women of color in its gatefold. But given the context of the time, Hefner believes that *Playboy* took an important initial step in the direction of integration in a mainstream magazine. He defends his position,

> Even though it is absolutely clear that the majority of Playmates have been white, we had black bunnies in the very first [Playboy] club in 1960 . . . when I did [the television program] *Playboy's Penthouse* in 1959, the very premise of which was that it was a party in my penthouse apartment, there were black performers and black guests, socializing in that environment, and because of that . . . I knew that we would not be distributed in the South, and I took that as a small price to pay [for integration]. When we opened the first club, we hired [a] black . . . stand-up comic to work in a non-black nightclub, Dick Gregory. . . . I supplied the seed money that made possible *Essence* magazine, and took no money out of it at all.[140]

Biographer Steven Watts adds to this list: "significant" financial support to civil rights charities; a controversial policy of racial integration not just among Playboy Club Bunnies, but also among patrons; a $25,000 reward for information on missing civil rights workers in Mississippi in 1964; and all profits from the highly successful Playboy Jazz Festival in 1959 were donated to the Chicago Urban League. Because of this activism, some African Americans saw Hefner as an ally.[141]

Regardless, Jennifer Jackson, like other Playmates, has had conflicted feelings about her appearance in *Playboy*. She went on to become a wife, mother, and social worker, but acknowledges that her centerfold is "part of history."[142] While working at the Chicago Club, Jackson was approached by *Playboy* photographer Pompeo Posar. She initially resisted, fearing her parents' reaction. Ultimately, though, she agreed to pose not to challenge

America's vicious stereotypes of black womanhood, but to get back at a boy-friend with whom she had just separated. By the time her centerfold was published, Jackson had moved to New York City and gotten married.[143]

To her surprise, Jackson says her husband and family were happy when they found out about her appearance in Playboy. Although her father was too embarrassed to mention it to her, she "heard through the grapevine that [he] was very proud." Initially she felt ashamed, and did not fully appreciate the trailblazing nature of her photos until she began to receive mail from Afri-can American soldiers in Vietnam. She says that she then realized she had done something to make them "happier," to feel like they could "be men of the world, too . . . having my picture in Playboy, for African-American males, meant they could be a part of that elite manhood." She did not get much mail from black women, although a few "older" women expressed disapproval of her pictures.[144]

Regarding Hefner, Jackson likewise has mixed feelings. She says he is a "glorified pimp, clearly. I like him, but he was a pimp." Reacting to the level of outrage from some readers over her centerfold, Hefner told Jackson he could not offer her a standard Playmate promotional contract, which would have had her traveling the country to make public appearances, because he could not adequately "protect [her]," particularly in the South. But Jackson argues that Playboy was one of the "more liberal magazines you could think of" in the 1960s. She also acknowledges the important role that Hefner and the Playboy Clubs played in advancing the careers of black entertainers and in challenging segregation and racism when the original Chicago Club and others employed black Bunnies like her. Jackson insists, "He was a pio-neer . . . [I] had only appeared in Ebony otherwise." She argues, "[Madison Avenue] changed in the seventies," and that Hefner helped to bring about that change.[145]

If Jackson and Hefner received letters from both supporters and detrac-tors, such sentiments were reflected in the published letters to the editor. Readers had plenty to say about Miss March. P. Justin Mullen of Hartford, Connecticut, praised Playboy, "In your leadership of the avant-garde in mod-ern America, you have taken another giant step forward. . . . I am looking forward to more Jenny Jacksons and China Lees, to show that beauty has no racial barriers."[146] G. Donald Lovett of Alabama appreciated the way in which the editors did not call attention to Jackson's race: "she was merely treated . . . as another American young lady with the physical endowments necessary to qualify her for the pull-out page. It was a blessing to see her treated as just another citizen and human being."[147] Mrs. Phyllis G. Rosalli of New York City wrote to say that she and her husband found the centerfold "an absolute delight," while Captain Pat Stiles, Jr., of Walker Air Force Base in New Mexico cheered, "Kudos to my favorite icon smashers."[148]

Of course, there were critics. "Interested Readers" from the University of Maryland returned their copy of the centerfold to *Playboy*: "At the risk of being labeled bigots, racists, reactionaries and sundry other things . . . we entreat you to return to your time-tested format of Playmate selection."[149] A letter signed "A University of Mississippi Student" said, "I do not need the foldout in the March issue and I am returning it to you. There are two too many Negroes at this university now,"[150] referring to the integration of the school by African American James Meredith in 1962.[151]

Ultimately, race was not the only controversy that the Playmates, or Hefner, would weather. In its early years, *Playboy* faced several challenges from antiobscenity crusaders in the American government, law enforcement, and religious groups. Charges of obscenity leveled at works of popular and high culture were not uncommon in the postwar years; William Burroughs's *Naked Lunch*, the comedy of Lenny Bruce, comic books, and D. H. Lawrence's *Lady Chatterley's Lover* were all targets.[152] In this atmosphere, Hefner deliberately conceived *Playboy* as the "classy" men's magazine, based on its literary emphasis, its upscale consumer celebration, as well as the glossy, high production value of its pages. The sophistication of the magazine came from packaging sexuality in the accessories of an upwardly mobile lifestyle, mixing the risqué, some said obscene, with the mainstream world of commodity and class, thus allowing *Playboy* to be offered to a broad audience. These elements helped to buffer the sexual content of the magazine at a time when hysteria over explicit material gripped much of the nation. But *Playboy* was far from immune to allegations of obscenity. Some Americans saw *Playboy* as a bastion of pornography, even if it lacked the violent "meat grinder" orientation that would come to define its more explicit imitators.[153] The uproar over smut in the 1950s was another manifestation of cold war fears that dictated sexual conformity and family stability, but it was not the first time that the question of obscenity focused the nation's attention.

The proliferation of pornography in the second half of the nineteenth century brought with it a host of antivice movements and crusaders.[154] Most notable among them was Anthony Comstock, a zealot dedicated to eradicating the obscene from American culture. Beginning in the 1870s and lasting through the early twentieth century, Comstock and his legacy dictated public discussion of sexuality, obscenity, and reproductive health. The tide began to turn in the 1930s, however, as public opinion slowly shifted in support of expanded conversations about sex and birth control, and as the courts began to rule against the censorship of books such as James Joyce's *Ulysses*.[155]

By the time Hugh Hefner began publishing *Playboy* in 1953, the conservative political and social mood of the era once again brought the question of obscenity into the national spotlight. Activists across the country, many of them religiously minded, protested against and successfully banned thousands of books, films, magazines, comic books, and the like, claiming harm to society and especially children.[156] Nonetheless, times were changing. In the 1940s, the U.S. Postal Service, acting as national censor, had failed in its attempt to restrict the bulk-mailing privileges of *Esquire* magazine, the top "girlie magazine" of its day. But the postal service continued to target explicit men's magazines, and focused its attention on *Playboy* in 1955, and again in 1958. Each time, the courts ruled against the postal service's claims of obscenity.[157] At least as early as 1955, the FBI kept a file on Hefner and tracked his personal and professional life for evidence of obscenity.[158] Then in 1957 the Supreme Court handed down the *Roth* decision, an important, if vague, precedent defining obscenity as "appealing to the prurient interest" and "devoid of 'the slightest redeeming social importance'" according to community standards. Similarly in 1958 two nudist magazines won mailing privileges when the court "suggested that nudity, per se, was not pornographic."[159] So a supportive legal stage was set for *Playboy*'s major run-in with censors. This time Hefner was put on trial when the city of Chicago prosecuted him over a nude pictorial of actress Jayne Mansfield.

In June 1963, Hefner was arrested in his home for "publishing and distributing an obscene publication."[160] Describing the experience to his readers in *Playboy*, Hefner wondered if "the whole thing [was] just a bad dream caused by the frankfurters and Pepsi [I'd] consumed just before retiring."[161] The arrest was real, but some Chicagoans were not convinced. One *Chicago Sun-Times* reporter asked an obvious question, "Why now? *Playboy* has been publishing nudes of voluptuous dishes for years."[162] Prosecutor John Melaniphy argued that the pictures in the June 1963 issue were different because a (fully clothed) man was shown on a bed with Mansfield, and the captions, which read "'she writhes about seductively'" and said that she was "'gyrating,'" made these particular photographs obscene.[163] At least one Chicagoan agreed and wrote to *Playboy* to express his support for the charges, "You rotten moron, the law is finally catching up with you . . . You are lower than the Madison Avenue scum. Hang your head in shame—you and your crackpot Bunnies."[164]

On the stand, Hefner defended himself by arguing that his magazine upheld community standards,

> [T]here is a continuing attempt [on my part to maintain those standards], since we are not interested in simply a small circulation magazine that would appeal to a very limited number of people, or one that pushes to the outer limits of legal acceptability . . . we are interested in reaching a goodly part of society. . . . I think I am able to . . . keep in touch with what the community standards are and how they are changing. . . . [Those standards] very much played a part in the making of my decisions as editor and publisher of *Playboy*.[165]

In a private memo to his staff, Hefner made his case less diplomatically. He assured his employees that "*Playboy* has never been judged obscene by any court in the land." He argued against the city of Chicago's claim that the Mansfield pictures "were not art" but instead were "suggestive," by admitting that they were not meant to be artistic, but no matter, that fact did not make them obscene.[166] To his staff and readers alike, Hefner insisted that the arrest was not really about the pictures, but rather served "to emphasize . . . the importance of the separation of church and state."[167] Suspecting conspiracy he asked, "Were these photographs the real reason for the action taken against us? Or is it possible that The *Playboy* Philosophy itself, critical of the church-state implications in the Chicago justice [system] . . . , and emphasizing that true religious freedom means freedom from as well as freedom of religion, supplied the motive?"[168]

Indeed, Hefner had long been railing against undue religious influence on American government and law, particularly in the form of censorship. He cited the Catholic National Office of Decent Literature (NODL) as a particularly egregious enemy of free speech.[169] The NODL published monthly lists of books and magazines that were not recommended for Catholic youth. But Hefner noted that their lists included Hemingway, Faulkner, Orwell, and other important works of literature. By threatening boycotts, Hefner argued that the NODL was able to put pressure on book dealers across the country to conform to their standards.[170]

In the Philosophy, Hefner argued, "Chicago remains one of the few major cities in America that is dominated by a single religious denomination—that is, where a majority of the officials in power belong to one church and where their administrative decisions sometimes appear to be predicated more on religious dogma than civil law."[171] Hefner felt that it was the NODL that pressured the city of Chicago to prosecute him, and Illinois assistant state attorney James R. Thompson seemed to confirm it when he publicly noted, "Citizens report to the State Attorney's office books and magazines suspected of being obscene."[172] Prosecutor Melaniphy admitted that he would have a difficult time convicting Hefner on obscenity charges. Indeed he was right, as Hefner was eventually cleared of all charges by a hung jury.

By the time Hefner faced obscenity charges in 1963, the country was in the midst of massive social and sexual upheaval. By the end of the decade, American attitudes regarding sex and obscenity would be drastically different than those Playboy confronted in the 1950s. In fact, Playboy's insistence on good, clean, all-American sex met its biggest challenge in the midst of the sexual revolution it had encouraged. The taunt came from a more explicit magazine, Penthouse, in the form of the "pubic war."[173] After publishing in Europe since the mid-1960s, Bob Guccione brought Penthouse to the United States in 1969. He immediately targeted Playboy's audience with full-page ads in major newspapers declaring, "We're going rabbit hunting."[174] Penthouse imitated Playboy in its journalistic features, fiction, advice columns, and in its style of pictures, except Guccione's concept was to inject more explicit sexuality throughout, including more female anatomy than Playboy had ever dared. The challenge forced Hefner to rethink a photographic policy that was, by the late 1960s, seemingly rather prudish. Biographer Russell Miller argues that the Playboy centerfolds "denied that the world was changing. The 'permissive society' had arrived and the Playmate had not noticed."[175] Guccione put it this way: "[Playboy was] still fighting the sexual revolution . . . Our starting point was that the revolution had already been won."[176]

Guccione began pushing the limits of sexual explicitness when he published photos of women with clearly visible pubic hair in 1970 and a "full-frontal centerfold" in August 1971.[177] He, and editors at Playboy, initially expected the stunt to be met with obscenity charges, but none came, and his magazine shot up in circulation.[178] Hefner thought the move to "go pubic" was "cheap, pornographic crap."[179] *Playboy* had recently published two secondary features that included photos with vaguely hinted at pubic hair, but no Playmate had been so exposed. Feeling the pressure of rising *Penthouse* circulation though, Hefner grudgingly made the decision to shoot a Playmate with visible pubic hair in January 1971 and a full-frontal Playmate in January 1972.[180] Even then, most Playmates would not regularly show pubic hair until 1973–74.

What this contested evolution spoke to was the conservatism with which Hefner approached the Playmates. He "agonized"[181] over the decision to go pubic; picture editor Vincent Tajiri "was very, very unhappy about it."[182] Hefner wanted to continue his formulaic conjuring of the sexy, wholesome girl-next-door, while Guccione's centerfolds expanded the boundaries of mainstream eroticism.[183] The move to more explicit photos "obsessed everybody" at *Playboy*, editor Nat Lehrman says, "many people . . . thought it disgusting" to go further with the photos.[184] In fact, Lehrman says the hesitation was appropriate because *Playboy*'s circulation, which began to sag in 1973, did not improve with greater explicitness.[185] Longtime editor Jim Petersen says there was a "great tension, a great internal war was fought" over the issue.[186] Petersen explains that as *Playboy* inched in the direction of *Penthouse* in the mid-1970s, "Hefner said, 'No, you don't copy second-place. You don't follow them out the window.' He reeled us back in. And it was one of his major spiritual and business decisions . . . Hefner woke up and said, 'No.' He defined what *Playboy* was, and would continue to be, and he said we'll live within these limits, and *Playboy* survived and *Penthouse* barely survived."[187]

This points to an audience that had come to expect certain standards from Hefner's magazine. Competing publications, such as *Penthouse* and *Hustler*, which was founded by Larry Flynt in 1974, continually upped the ante on raunch in the industry. But raunch was not part of *Playboy*'s style. Looking back, *Playboy* editor Nat Lehrman says, "*Playboy* . . . fought all the battles" for sexual freedom and against censorship, allowing newcomers (like Guccione) to then go further than even Hefner thought appropriate.

To many observers, the Playmates and other nude pictorials symbolized all that was wrong with *Playboy*. But from the early days of the magazine, Hefner's stated intention—to portray the sexy girl-next-door—was not lost on readers. As late as 1972, in the midst of the feminist revolution, Mrs. L. Rosen of New York City echoed the position of theologian Herbert W. Richardson when she disagreed with the accusation that *Playboy* objectified women: "many of those who attack *Playboy* are unwilling to acknowledge . . . that the man-woman relationship . . . typified by the Playmate is an enormous improvement on former American roles for the sexes." Mrs. Rosen continued her analysis, "In the old, unliberated days, sex was . . . seen as something the man did to the woman . . . The Playmate symbolizes a new relationship . . . one that reflects the progress of egalitarian and libertarian trends in our society."[188]

In sexualizing the girl-next-door, and thereby granting sexual desire and autonomy to American women, Hefner's fantasy version of sexuality became real and livable, something that could, theoretically, be attained by both men and women.

For men, it meant seeing the women around them as desirous, sexual beings, and thus potential sex partners. For women, it meant claiming an autonomous sexuality for themselves. Hefner not only acknowledged but insisted that women were as sexual as men. Hefner sees the Playmates, whom Steven Watts calls "icon[s] of sexual liberation in the 1950s," as part of the political statement of *Playboy*.[189] It was part of a strong desire "to break down traditional roles" for men and for women, and to change what Hefner saw as outmoded laws and attitudes regarding sex.[190] But while the Playmates were the most noted element of the *Playboy* world, Hefner spent at least as much editorial energy on constructing a new vision of masculinity, one that relied heavily on the all-American pursuit of consumption.

3

Selling the Dream:
Playboy and the Masculine Consumer

If girls were the only motivation for buying our magazines, they wouldn't sell. People would buy sheer smut. We, on the other hand, are Taste City.[1]

HUGH HEFNER, 1961

In 1953, *Hugh Hefner was an unknown cartoonist taking a* gamble on a sexy new magazine. Shy and awkward, he reinvented himself in *Playboy*. Hefner told the world he was a dapper Casanova, and he invited American men to a grand cultural party hosted within *Playboy*'s pages. Surprisingly, maybe even to Hefner, people accepted his invitation. More than half a century later, the party continues with a new cohort of American men and women arriving in droves, wearing rabbit-logo t-shirts and necklaces, popularizing a reality television show about Hefner's girlfriends, and gallivanting at a new generation of Playboy Clubs in Las Vegas and other major cities.

Playboy has undoubtedly made its mark on the world with its voluptuous centerfolds and the hedonism of its founder. But there is much more behind the recognizable rabbit logo than just sex and parties. From the start of the magazine in 1953, Hefner promoted a complete lifestyle of which women were just one part. Clothing, stereos, high-end appliances, and hobbies like yachting were pervasive throughout the magazine, and usually took up more pages than talk or images of sex. Certainly, these pursuits were sold to men as the tools that would help them attract women. Each one of these components of the *Playboy* lifestyle, however, was equally important in constructing the magazine's particular brand of manhood. According to long-time editor Jim Petersen, the "attitude" of the gentleman bachelor "trumps everything," even sex.[2]

Consumerism played a central role in that experience. Hefner compares *Playboy* to the Sears Roebuck catalog of the early twentieth century, a "wish book" that offered a seemingly infinite number of enticing consumer items to Americans. According to him the catalog "brought to rural America . . . a more sophisticated potential in terms of fashion and furnishings." Likewise, Hefner argues, "*Playboy* has always been a wish book, or a dream book. A book of aspiration and fantasy."[3] Readers like Karl D. Brown, Jr., of Florida, confirmed this notion, "where else could a small-town yokel like me learn a little about wine and food selection as well as accepted methods of dealing with the fairer sex? If mine is a *Playboy* inspired dream world, it suits the hell out of me."[4] Much of the fantasy lifestyle was just that, an unattainable vision of luxury in which many American men could never indulge. Nonetheless, chasing the American dream through rampant spending was as much a priority in *Playboy* as was the ability to seduce women.

The "attitude," as Petersen calls it, consisted of a sense of style, urbanity, and a general joie de vie. The magazine prominently expressed that attitude through regular features on the traditionally feminine pastimes of fashion, cooking, and decorating. Hefner considered these articles a "glamorous reflection of the romantic, good life."[5] In turn, readers responded to the columns with questions and comments. Through these conversations, *Playboy* offered its readers a unique vision of masculinity. Hefner's bachelor was a far cry from the "inner-directed" traditional American man.[6] The rugged, self-sacrificing family man of previous generations had given way to a man who lived for the moment; a man whose notion of domestic responsibility meant keeping his wet bar stocked and ready for an impromptu midnight gathering. The midcentury consuming male was, depending on one's perspective, considered a predictable product of the affluent times, or a result of the era's supposed "crisis" of masculinity. As columnist J. Robert Moskin lamented at the time, "The American male has begun to dress for women; the men's toiletries industry now does a $480 million business each year. . . . men are now told how they, if they wear the right hat, may be the chosen one, the loved one—a role that used to be reserved for women."[7]

In contrast, *Playboy* was part of the cohort that saw consumption as a desirable pastime for American men. While Hefner critiqued the traditional expectations of men, he did not offer a radically different view of American masculinity. His magazine promoted male-centered heterosexuality and celebrated capitalism through rampant spending. As scholar Bill Osgerby points out, *Playboy* "undoubtedly challenged both the traditional 'breadwinner' archetype and the Cold War ideologies of 'domestic containment.' But this was a challenge that took place from *within* the parameters of dominant ideological discourse."[8] So *Playboy* pushed the boundaries of acceptable heterosexual male behavior, but did so without presenting a drastic challenge to the status quo. Men were offered a version of liberation, but not encouraged to overthrow the system. Contemporary analysis of *Playboy* by popular theologian and *Playboy* critic (and eventual ally) Harvey Cox argued that the magazine "fills a special need for the insecure young man with newly acquired time and money on his hands . . . *Playboy* speaks to those who desperately want to know what it means to be a man . . . in today's world."[9]

During the 1950s, while much of America trumpeted the proud cold warrior, *Playboy* celebrated the fun-loving bachelor who knew how to match his belt to his shoes. The result was an objectified postwar man, a male reader whose appearance, home, and lifestyle were newly scrutinized according to the particular standards of the urban playboy. Not just the Playmate, but the bachelor himself—albeit fully clothed—was put on display and offered up for critical evaluation in *Playboy*. Many observers have noted a sexual objectification in its centerfolds. But men were also commercially objectified in the pages of *Playboy* through its relentless consumer drive.[10]

Men's wardrobe, manners, taste in music, and bedroom décor were placed under a microscope and evaluated with a self-consciousness traditionally reserved for women. Simon Marquis points out that traditionally, self-scrutiny "is permissible, even attractive in women; it is perceived as weak and unmanly in a man."[11] *Playboy* challenged this dynamic. After a reader perused the nude centerfold, his attention was often turned onto himself. Was his casual wear up-to-date? Was his record collection hip enough to impress his girlfriend? Scholars James K. Beggan and Scott T. Allison argue, "[*Playboy*] encouraged men to adopt attributes and learn skills that women would find desirable so that women would find them more attractive. . . . the implication . . . was that men should surrender sovereignty to women over how men should choose to define themselves."[12] Beggan and Allison, in other words, see the guidance in

WHAT SORT OF MAN READS PLAYBOY?

A young man who knows his way around—uptown or downtown—the PLAYBOY reader's arrival signals the start of an eventful evening. And with good taste—from wine to women—he's a man who dines and drinks out often. Facts: 89% of PLAYBOY readers enjoy at least one drink, 43% at least three, in a restaurant or bar each week. For 30%, it's just natural to end an evening with a cordial note. Sure lift for your beverage sales: a campaign in PLAYBOY. It will do wonders for your spirit. (Source: *Playboy Male Reader Survey* by Benn Management Corp.)

Advertising Offices: New York • Chicago • Detroit • Los Angeles • San Francisco • Atlanta

figure 7.   "What Sort of Man Reads *Playboy?*" ad, April 1964. Reproduced by special permission of *Playboy* magazine. Copyright 1964 by Playboy.

Playboy's lifestyle columns as leading the reader to the ultimate goal of sex. The association is apt, and one that Hefner has acknowledged.

Today, Hefner agrees that there is a connection between masculine consumerism and objectification: "men . . . want to be sex objects, too." He cites himself as an example, "Why did I smoke the pipe? Why did I wear the smoking jacket? Why do I wear cologne? Why did I purchase the rotating round bed? All because of wanting to be a sex object in the best sense of the word."[13] Many feminist critics would doubt that there exists a "best sense" of objectification, but Hefner acknowledges that constructing manhood in such a way was a goal for himself and for his magazine.

But as historian Becky Conekin correctly observes, the lifestyle features functioned as more than mere guides to ultimate sexual attractiveness or conquest. They were at least as important as the centerfolds in creating a sense of "fantasy, desire and aspiration" in the magazine. Consumption was a goal in and of itself.[14] In the process of creating a self-conscious, consuming male, Playboy brought modern constructions of masculinity and femininity into closer alignment. Beggan and Allison argue that "the central gender theme in Playboy magazine was the integration, rather than polarization, of masculine and feminine representations." They add that Playboy "reduced gender role strain by legitimizing a broader definition of masculinity."[15] Apparently, given the wild success of the magazine, Hefner's readers bought into this image of modern manhood. Many men seemed to want the freedom to experience life outside the confines of traditional domesticity, at least in fantasy. Moreover, they wanted the freedom to spend their fattening wallets on the array of new consumer goods flooding not only the pages of Playboy, but American society as well.

By the time Hugh Hefner took up his campaign to get bachelors spending in the 1950s, the American century had already emerged as one defined by consumption.[16] But the economy boomed like never before after World War II. The early years of the cold war fueled massive military production and government spending, creating jobs and financial growth. With the help of the GI Bill, millions of families rose into the middle class, got an education, and bought homes in the newly thriving suburbs. Postwar prosperity allowed Americans to buy more consumer and luxury goods than previous generations could have imagined.

The period saw a "historic reign of prosperity," according to Lizabeth Cohen, "longer lasting and more universally enjoyed than ever before."[17] With the emergence of shopping malls, a vast highway system, and other innovations, Americans had a wealth of new buying opportunities. The cold war provided a jingoistic context for this shopping boom as consumer spending became equated with capitalist freedom and democracy. Purchasing consumer items came to represent patriotism in the face of drab communism. As Cohen notes, politicians emphasized "the potential power of American consumer goods to win the hearts and minds of people in the so-called developing world. . . . Faith in a mass consumption postwar economy hence came to mean . . . an elaborate, integrated ideal of economic abundance and democratic political freedom . . . that became almost a national civil religion."[18]

In the 1950s, not just women and men, but teens and even children became important markets for products like hula hoops, records, and other luxury-oriented consumer goods and spaces. Despite "poverty, periodic recessions, a slow growth rate, and other economic problems," historian J. Ronald Oakley argues that there was a "general public belief that the nation never had it so good."[19] The middle class saw an unprecedented economic and consumer expansion, resulting in great national confidence. Per capita income rose by 48 percent during the fifties, as the expanding economy created a record number of jobs. Luxury spending reached an all-time high, as wartime saving gave way to advertising-age consumption. Credit was more readily available than ever before. Americans bought homes, automobiles, televisions, and swimming pools, as well as convenience products like TV dinners and McDonald's french fries. Clothing fads, for men as well as women, caught on because of the growing class of Americans with disposable income.[20]

In spite of all this, shopping was still considered a traditionally feminine pastime. Oakley writes, "much of the advertising was based on the assumption that women did most of the buying, not just for themselves but for their children and husbands."[21] Even so, the fifties saw a new emphasis on the male consumer, who "played an ever greater role" in the economy.[22] Lizabeth Cohen observes that Americans witnessed the "growing importance of men's authority over the family purse," and that the media portrayed middle-class husbands and wives as a "family team" shopping for groceries together.[23] In the 1950s, the conventional stereotype that associated women with spending began to break down as all Americans, regardless of gender, were called to serve their country in the name of domestic stability and capitalism.

Reflecting the enormous growth that marked so much of American commercial and popular culture of the time, the magazine industry experienced a phase of expansion in the postwar years. Mass-circulation journals had been popularized in the late nineteenth and early twentieth centuries, but the modern market was drastically different than the one general-interest magazines, such as *Life* and *Look*, enjoyed in the first half of the century.[24] Although generalist magazines remained prevalent in the consensus-driven 1950s, postwar economic and social changes made the cultural landscape increasingly amenable to special-interest magazines, and particularly to *Playboy*.

Prosperity and competition from television set the stage for what media scholar David Abrahamson calls a revolution in the magazine industry. More Americans than ever before had the means and leisure time to not only pursue magazine reading but also a host of consumer-driven recreational activities like boating, cooking, or amateur science. With the "triumph of self" in the sixties, according to Abrahamson and others, specialized periodicals—those that cultivated unique personal interests—helped Americans to "reinvent themselves."[25] It also meant that the popularity of new, finely targeted periodicals overwhelmed the traditional, generalist magazines, which tended to promote a "benign sense of contentment . . . faith in the status quo."[26] The pursuit of individual fulfillment through niche consumption became the order of the day.

The case was especially true for men. Various magazines had long appealed to male or female audiences, but along with the family-oriented generalists, women's publications like *Ladies' Home Journal* dominated the market before World War II. But in the new middle-class economy of the postwar years, men's leisure pursuits helped drive the rise of special-interest magazines.[27] Abrahamson argues that with more time and money to spare, and a diminishing sense of traditional manhood, growing numbers of men looked to magazines to confer on them identity and status and to guide them through the expansive horizon of consumer abundance.[28]

Playboy was at the forefront of these industry transformations in a number of ways. Its rise in the mid-fifties foreshadowed the growth of special-interest periodicals that followed a decade later. And without a doubt, Hefner took the lead in articulating the self-centered, consuming heterosexual male for American magazine readers. Further, Abrahamson points out that editorial voice became increasingly important to the success of special-interest journals. Editorial persona helped establish rapport with readers and gave them a sense that their conversation with expert editors made them in-the-know, too.[29] With Hefner's self-conscious public personality as the randy, urban sophisticate, and then with the writing of the *Playboy* Philosophy, *Playboy* quickly developed an unmistakable identity.

That identity was buttressed by *Playboy*'s stylish design and production value. Hefner's empire started out small, in fact he laid out the first issue of *Playboy* on his kitchen table in south Chicago in 1953, but from the beginning he had a clear vision of the grand lifestyle magazine he hoped to create. Previous jobs in the industry had given him an understanding of the business and contacts among distributors, and friends and family invested $8,000 in the fledgling HMH Publishing Company.[30]

Hefner auspiciously chose as his art director local graphic artist Art Paul, who designed the "cool, sophisticated, slightly irreverent" look for which Steven Watts says *Playboy* became known. Vince Tajiri, who was soon brought on as photo editor, formulated a photographic approach that was "slick but candid, a cross between advertising photography and photo journalism." Likewise, artist LeRoy Neiman joined the staff and brought with him a style of illustration that was "impressionistic with elegant, elongated figures and bold slashing colors."[31] Hefner said, "I wanted a magazine that was as innovative in its illustration and design as it was in its concept. . . . The notion of breaking down the walls between what hung in museums and what appeared in the pages of a magazine was unique at the time."[32] This combination of "commercial and noncommercial art gave *Playboy* a uniquely progressive edge over most publications at the time," argues art critic Steven Heller.[33]

Mindful of the glossy, chic quality he hoped to achieve, Hefner shunned the low-end advertisers initially willing to associate with his magazine. Journalist Gay Talese, in his summation of *Playboy*'s impact on the sexual revolution, said that Hefner "was an optimist and positive thinker." Talese noted that in creating an image of sexy, urban elegance, "Hefner would not print any advertising that focused on male problems or worries. . . . [He] did not intend to desecrate this dream with advertisements reminding male readers of their acne, halitosis, athlete's foot, or hernias."[34] However, by 1955, *Playboy* had grown in popularity and reputation, and the magazine landed its first major advertiser, Springmaid sheets. Soon ads for upscale clothing, liquor, automobiles, perfume, and electronics began to fill the magazine, placing *Playboy* at the "center of a consumer bonanza in 1950s America."[35] Thus, Hefner and his team created a product that emerged as one of the most sophisticated consumer magazines of the postwar years. Moreover the modern, hip look and high quality of the magazine helped to legitimize its risqué nature.

With his own magazine on the market, Hefner joined in the new celebration of the masculine consumer. *Playboy* promoted men's fashion, travel, decorating, gift giving, cooking, and other activities that demanded spending. In the process, he expanded the reach of the consuming man by telling him that it was all right to frivolously spend money on himself.[36] David Halberstam writes, "For men whose parents had not gone to college, *Playboy* served a valuable function: It provided an early and elementary tutorial on the new American lifestyle. . . . It midwifed the reader into a world of increasing plenty."[37] In contrast to the family purchases that Lizabeth Cohen notes, *Playboy* did not expect men to focus on the traditional domestic acquisition of lawn mowers, barbeques, station wagons, and dinettes. They could follow fashion trends. They could stock their bars. They could buy sporty two-seaters just big enough for the bachelor and his date. Undoubtedly, many readers could not live up to such high standards, but they could look to *Playboy* as a guide to their fantasies and aspirations.

Not just an emphasis on consumerism, the overall lifestyle that Hefner prescribed was a unique view of American manhood. Instead of domestic obligation, the bachelor's primary responsibility was to himself and his party guests. He did not fret over the looming threat of the cold war, but rather focused on updating his wardrobe. When he was unsure of himself, sexy centerfolds told him that the good life was within his grasp.

The culture of male acquisition was not new to the 1950s, and the emergence of *Playboy* was not the first time American men ventured into the world of consumerism, although it would signal an expansion of self-centered male spending.[38] Bill Osgerby points out, "since the beginning of the century there had existed articulations of masculinity grounded in an engagement with consumer culture and hedonistic desire—and during the postwar era they were newly invigorated."[39] *Playboy*'s prominent articulation of masculine consumerism took its cue from the leading men's magazine of the prewar years, *Esquire*.

Established in 1933, *Esquire* carved out a unique place for itself in the American cultural landscape. Historian Tom Pendergast calls it the first "single coherent embodiment of modern masculinity," while Kenon Breazeale adds that it co-opted feminine consumer indulgence for the purpose of restoring a vibrant masculinity that had been supposedly lost amidst the misery of the Depression.[40] Founders David Smart and William Weintraub, whose backgrounds were in marketing, saw their new magazine primarily as a moneymaking "vehicle for men's apparel ads."[41] Scholar Hugh Merrill notes that *Esquire*'s unique contribution was "in exploiting the market for advertising directed toward male consumers, a field that no magazine had tried before."[42] Additionally, under the editorial leadership of Arnold Gingrich, the magazine drew on a larger cultural critique that associated the feminine consumer with a "gullible vulnerability to consumerism's trashy faddishness," and decried women's growing consumer power.[43]

Esquire capitalized on this criticism by reestablishing the ideal consumer not as a frivolous woman, but as a savvy man, and the consuming male would remain a significant focus for *Esquire* in the years to come. Pendergast argues that the magazine "completed the project of casting men as consumers that advertisers had been perfecting for years."[44] Regular columns on fashion, cooking, and decorating opened the domestic space to masculine consumption. *Esquire* served as a guide to navigating the urbanizing landscape of 1930s America.[45] The magazine avoided charges of effeminacy or homosexuality by including risqué illustrations of beautiful women and constant commentary on the pitfalls of modern femininity.[46] *Esquire*'s "absorption in heterosexual sexuality, especially via the illustration and the cartoon," according to Pendergast, "rescued consumerism for a male audience."[47]

Hefner's association with *Esquire* began with his brief employment in their subscription department in 1951. He left the company when they relocated to New York from Chicago.[48] Hefner admired the magazine, but was disappointed in its eventual rejection of the bawdiness that had marked it in the 1930s and '40s.[49] When Hefner conceived *Playboy*, he had the popular men's magazine in mind, and he imitated and expanded upon everything in *Esquire*, from its fashion columns to its centerfolds. As Breazeale points out, by the time *Playboy* emerged, *Esquire* had set the precedent for eroticized masculine consumption.[50]

Hefner says that it was *Playboy*'s implicit (and later in the Philosophy, explicit) support of capitalism that shielded him from broader critiques that might likely have otherwise surfaced in the climate of the 1950s.[51] Hefner acknowledges that his brand of masculinity "absolutely" embraced traditionally feminine characteristics and hobbies, such as conspicuous consumption, as well as "cooking, caring about your own apartment . . . caring about something more than sitting in front of the television or bowling,"[52] pastimes Hefner associates with traditional manhood. He says that *Playboy* was generally not criticized for these associations because "Consumerism has always been all-American. . . . The intimate interconnection between capitalism and consumerism and sexuality is obvious . . . People who attack capitalism are perceived as being radical and un-American."[53] For the most part then, the consumerist *Playboy* was free to reinvent American masculinity in any form it chose.

What made *Playboy*'s consumerism unique was the context of its time. Unlike the lean, desperate years in which *Esquire* thrived, postwar America was wealthier than ever. There was vastly more opportunity to cultivate consumers of either gender. Additionally, it witnessed a revived domestic ideal in which men were required to be devoted, and consuming, husbands and fathers. So in the pages of *Playboy*, the consuming male was in lockstep with his times as the magazine celebrated spending as a central experience of the middle-class American lifestyle. Yet simultaneously, the playboy challenged his era's dominant gender expectations by recasting his spending spree not in the interest of the family, but in his interest alone.

Like its predecessor *Esquire*, *Playboy* included columns promoting an urbane lifestyle for modern men. While *Playboy* emulated its competitor on many levels, there was a difference in attitude in the newer publication, not the least of which was its sexual explicitness. Upon comparison of the publications, Hefner argued that his magazine "far more accurately reflects the tempo and thinking of the times."[54] *Esquire* catered to mature, professional, urban men and by the 1950s had become a staid, established publication. According to biographer Hugh Merrill, the average *Esquire* reader in the late 1940s was almost forty years old.[55] The magazine's overall tone had grown serious and dignified. By the 1950s, its sexual nature had been toned down because editor Arnold Gingrich believed that the popular Varga pin-ups for which *Esquire* was known had tarnished the magazine.[56] *Playboy* catered to a similar, albeit younger, demographic and placed a greater emphasis on playful irreverence.

Many *Playboy* readers were either current or former *Esquire* fans, and they responded positively to the unique elements of the new magazine. A reader from Philadelphia wrote, "Congratulations on the first real man's magazine to hit the market in 15 years."[57] The readers that Hefner and his staff were editing for were a select group of American men. Stated repeatedly in editorial comment, as well as reinforced through articles and advertisements, the magazine catered to the "indoor, city-bred male."[58] Readers approved, "I whole-heartedly back your idea of staying at home. I'm getting tired of reading about 'Joe Jones' Jaguar Jaunts for Jerks,' . . . other 'men's magazines' have one idea in mind—EVERYBODY OUTSIDE!"[59]

These men were the targeted demographic from the magazine's inception, and a reader's survey conducted in September 1955 revealed *Playboy*'s audience to be well conceived. Aiming at the "sophisticated, intelligent, urban . . . man-about-town, who enjoys good, gracious living," the results of the survey showed the average reader to be twenty-nine years old, which was ten years younger than the average reader of "the other class men's magazine" (*Esquire*); over 70 percent of *Playboy*'s readers were college educated ("a greater percentage of college-men than any other national magazine"); half were unmarried; nearly 75 percent of readers were either students, businessmen, or in the professional fields; they paid "considerably more than the national average" for clothes and automobiles; and over half took vacations abroad. *Playboy* readers also read *Life*, *Esquire*, *Time*, and the *Saturday Evening Post*.[60]

The reader's survey painted a picture of a demographic that was well educated, gainfully employed, and presumably regarded as upstanding citizens. Of course, there were many men outside of the major metropolitan areas that were not part of the targeted demographic but liked *Playboy* nonetheless. A man from New Matamoras, Ohio, told Hefner, "I enjoy every page of your wonderful magazine . . . life here on the farm gets a little dull and your magazine adds just the spice necessary."[61] Other men apparently felt the same way. With its inaugural issue in December 1953, *Playboy* printed 70,000 copies. By the end of the first year, the print run increased to 175,000. With the thirteenth and fourteenth issues (January and February 1954), circulation jumped to 250,000 copies, and was at 350,000 by April 1955.[62] Apparently, the combination of "humor, sophistication, and spice" had struck a chord with many American men.

Regardless of its insistence on elegance and sophistication, *Playboy*'s editors understood that they were promoting a lifestyle that was often out of reach for its readers. In one example, an executive from a Pittsburgh advertising firm privately wrote to Hefner on behalf of his client, Swift Homes, Inc. Swift was promoting precut homes that could be assembled as vacation cottages by "a calculating bachelor armed only with unskilled, but enthusiastic friends, and as much beer as necessary."[63] Editorial director A. C. Spectorsky responded that second homes were certainly in line with the *Playboy* lifestyle, but that readymade homes easily assembled by a bunch of drunk bachelors was not. He admitted, "Realistically, we believe there are a great many more of our readers who would find it possible to avail themselves of a cottage like yours, than would have the money to erect the rather elaborate [places] we [portray]. However, we feel that by stimulating our reader's dreams and aspirations, we move him to action in a [higher] financial bracket . . . than if we lowered our price range for the houses, cars and boats which we occasionally feature."[64]

Part of a man's "dreams and aspirations," at least according to *Playboy*, was to develop a refined taste in dining. *Playboy*'s regular food and drink columns, written by chef Thomas Mario, showed them how. The food column began as a simple recipe page featuring a particular dish or alcoholic drink each month. Soon it became a long column devoted to the history of the dish, appropriate settings in which to serve it, and ways of preparing the featured food. Hefner said of the column, "One of the single, most important motivations for publishing articles on food and drink . . . in a men's magazine is the opportunity it affords us to include lush, elegant, romantic illustrations . . . depicting the urban male wining and dining alone with a beautiful girl, or in a happy party atmosphere with friends."[65]

Like the clothing column, the food column often skirted the boundaries of traditional masculinity. Even the manly art of grilling steak was reworked for the playboy lifestyle. Mario noted "a man-about-town going on an outdoor picnic is not the old-fashioned type whose idea of fun is to build a primitive trench fire in the Andes or to construct a mud reflector for a rough stone barbecue on a mountain side." Of course, steaks were a mainstay of the suburban backyard barbeque, but *Playboy* removed the taint of domesticity from the meal. The playboy preferred "to invite his lady fair out to the terrace to impress her with his own idea of grilled *filet mignon marchand de vin*."[66] Later, on the topic of salad preparation, Mario insisted that "a good salad maker must have many of the traits and skills that we sometimes think of as feminine," adding, "but for some reason it takes a man to master the really fine art of the salad bowl."[67] Whether it was oysters, Beluga caviar, or hamburgers, Mario turned around the old adage and pointed out that the way to a woman's bed was through her stomach.

While the kitchen was being co-opted from the ladies in the pages of *Playboy*, aspiring chefs could retain their masculinity with the knowledge that they were tossing around a salad to seduce a woman as well as to maintain a modern, youthful lifestyle. The kitchen space itself was transformed from women's domain into tool of the playboy. Scholar Joanne Hollows maintains, "*Playboy* tried to construct the private sphere as a heterosexual masculine space that was based on a rejection of . . . the feminized domestic that was perceived to be dominant in the era."⁶⁸ She notes that in the early years of the magazine, there was "a sense of unease about how to make cooking masculine," so writer Thomas Mario made "very explicit connections between food, cooking and sex," and likewise emphasized the role of food in entertaining, rather than in the family.⁶⁹

Playboy argued that in the ideal bachelor pad, the kitchen was no place for old boxes of TV dinners to pile up and for dishes to go unwashed. A dining room was necessary for a "full-production gala dinner, as no 'dining alcove' is." And of course no self-respecting bachelor would think of having "all night poker games, stag or strip," without "pull-down globe lighting." Avoiding the isolation that so many women faced while slaving in the kitchen during holidays and dinner parties, "the urban male [who] prides himself on his culinary artistry" could pull back sliding screens to open the kitchen "onto the dining room, so [he] can perform for an admiring audience while sharing in the conversation."⁷⁰ Thus, the playboy was displayed for his guests, but avoided the pitfalls of domesticity.

In addition to monthly columns on food, *Playboy* included semiregular features on interior design and architecture. Though these pieces did not appear as often as the other columns, they were quite popular. In fact, in April 1959, Hefner deemed the September 1956 penthouse feature "the most popular single feature ever to appear in these pages," noting that readers were still writing letters about it.⁷¹ Fine furniture, hi-fi stereos, and wet bars were always part of the lifestyle, but in the 1956 feature, *Playboy* designed an elaborate plan for the ultimate bachelor pad. The effect was "a man's world which fits your moods and desires, which is a tasteful, gracious setting for an urbane personality." Primavera panels, dustproof closets, and a terrace overlooking the "winking towers of the city beyond" created a sophisticated backdrop for entertaining.⁷²

Great attention was given to the detail of his surroundings. A guided tour of the penthouse revealed,

The floor beneath us is cork tile. The smooth plaster wall is in dramatic contrast to the stone hearth, which has a painting on its right and a raised planter with climbing vine on its left. The apartment's sense of masculine

richness and excitement stems in part from such juxtapositions of tex-
tures . . . and for visual impact the unadorned brick wall which closes off
the bath and the kitchen area. Turn to the window wall. Here's drama and
contrast again, a view of the city through casements richly hung with white
dacron and slate gray silk shantung overdrapes.[73]

The ultimate penthouse was decked out with the most cutting-edge, fashionable furniture and technology. An ultrasonic dishwasher, a touch-cool
induction heating stove, as well as "weatherproof, metal, terrace furniture,
all by Salterini," adorned the apartment. But the traditionally unmasculine
preoccupation with decorating his bachelor pad would be tempered with
a bedroom equipped with buttons that would gradually lower the lights,
draw the curtains, turn on romantic music, and even start breakfast in the
morning—leaving time for the playboy to start the day off right with early
lovemaking.

The state-of-the-art technology allowed the man to never leave the side
of his romantic interest for the evening, thus there was "no chance of missing the proper psychological moment—no chance to leaving her cozily
curled up . . . with her shoes off and returning to find her mind changed."[74]
Throughout the magazine, sexuality was injected into most topics, thus
foregrounding virile heterosexuality amidst the more effeminate pastimes
of fashion, cooking, and decorating. Historian Elizabeth Fraterrigo argues
that the *Playboy* penthouse answered the postwar "need for masculine
space," amidst "the backdrop of new postwar suburban housing forms,"[75]
while architectural specialist Beatriz Preciado notes that the cultivation of a
domestic space for the urban bachelor was "at once heterosexual and gender
segregated." Preciado sees sexual conquest as the primary goal of the *Playboy* penthouse, going so far as to call the apartment the "first mass media
brothel."[76]

In fact, Preciado argues that in publicly displaying the sexy bachelor
penthouse in the pages of *Playboy*, it became the magazine's "pornographic
object *par excellence*."[77] In other words, the reader was a voyeur, leering at a
place wherein sex, above all else, was intended to occur. While she acknowledges the important role of consumption in the *Playboy* pad, Preciado pri-
oritizes the pursuit of sexual conquest in the apartment. But consumption
was key to the *Playboy* universe. Preciado's view understates what we might,
in her conception, call the orgy of spending that was an equal goal to sex in

Playboy. As much as affirming the masculine libido, the seduction meant to take place in the pad legitimized the virility of the bachelor's shopping spree.

The magazine celebrated rampant spending on home design and personal entertainment and encouraged men to purchase a variety of luxurious domestic accoutrements. In March 1959 *Playboy* ran a feature on the latest in stereo equipment. In a memo to Spectorsky, Hefner emphasized, "the important thing . . . is to remember that this article isn't going to sell any stereo equipment directly—it is only calculated to stir up the interest of readers in stereo[s] . . . to get them into the stores looking around . . . and buying. In other words, everyone in the stereo industry will benefit tremendously from the article. . . . The important thing is, we are plugging a stereo as a concept, and that should move *everyone's* merchandise."[78] It was in the interest of Hefner and *Playboy* to bolster sales of stereos and other popular consumer items. If Hefner made stereo connoisseurs of his readers, then they would be compelled to come back each month to learn the latest on such products, ensuring both the popularity of his magazine as well as advertising dollars. As the centerfolds cultivated the taste of American men in the sexy girl-next-door, the product features refined men's growing aptitude as postwar shoppers.

Probably the most iconic element of the bachelor pad was the *Playboy* bed. Originally illustrated in the May 1962 rendering of *The Playboy Town House*, it was made real for Hefner in his Chicago mansion and promoted in print again in April 1965. Eight and a half feet in diameter, the round, vibrating, fully rotating bed included a control panel for television screens and stereos. The amorous couple need not ever leave the comfort of the bed for additional entertainment. Anything one might hope to do in a bed, including "slumber [or] late-night TV viewing" or enjoying the "romantic glow softly emanating from an Italian marble fireplace," was possible with the touch of a button. Anticipating a party, the bed could turn away from the fireplace toward a "conversation area on the other side of the room." The headboard "superstructure" housed a small refrigerator and filing cabinets, and functioned as "a desk, table or snack bar."[79] Not everyone found such a versatile bed appealing, though. One disgruntled woman from Minneapolis wrote the Advisor to complain that her pending marriage was threatened by her fiancé's insistence on having a round marriage bed.[80]

More than the interior design features, though, it was the monthly fashion features that attempted to cultivate reader aspirations to "a [higher] financial bracket," as Spectorsky had described. *Playboy*'s fashion features typically promoted classic, sophisticated looks. Since its inception, *Playboy* included a monthly feature on the latest trends. Readers responded, particularly in the fifties, with questions and comments in the letters to the editor column. Later, such questions were dealt with in the *Playboy* Advisor. Seasonal fashions were covered in detail, and annual features on college trends were included.

In the early years of the magazine, features consisted of descriptions of clothes and were accompanied by illustrations (and later photos) of men wearing the items. By the late fifties, photos began to include women in order to make the columns sexier and likely to reinforce the heterosexuality of the magazine and its readers. Soon lists of retail stores were included to guide readers to the purchase of items they saw in *Playboy*.

Fashion was a major element of the prescribed playboy lifestyle, and one to which the readership responded. Imitating the fashion features of *Esquire* throughout the fifties and early 1960s, *Playboy* typically promoted the Brooks Brothers tailored suit and the preppy style of the Ivy Leaguers. The official *Playboy* look of the season was outlined by fashion editor Jack J. Kessie in the January 1955 issue.[81] Tedious details of the appropriate attire for a man-about-town were given: "Our man would choose suits with the natural look ... with flap pockets and a deep hook vent in the back. ... For ... relaxation without a jacket he chooses shepherd check gingham ... His hosiery follows the solid-color line, tending toward the darker shades."[82] The exalted cold warrior of the day might not have been caught dead in gingham, but the *Playboy* man had his own priorities.

Readers took the advice seriously. Following this article, a tailor from Houston started a dispute over the merits of Northeast fashion versus Texas style. His letter reflected the potential challenge *Playboy*'s version of masculinity posed to traditional heterosexual manhood. The Houstonite explained, "That stuff may go in the East, but down here anyone dressed the way Mr. Jack J. Kessie says ... [would be called an] 'Ivy League Fruit.'"[83] Not everyone agreed, however, as the tailor's comments spurred letters from all over the country. Some Southerners agreed; others were ashamed of the styles he attributed to Texas. Northerners made fun of the "lime colored shirts" and "pleated pink ties" he endorsed. Still others ignored the Texas fashion controversy, and maintained that the Kessie look was outmoded.[84] This conversation suggests the seriousness with which many readers treated fashion, and, by implication, the rapidly expanding consumer culture in which many *Playboy* fans participated. They embraced the expanding role of the playboy as a postwar fashion connoisseur. In spite of the pressures of early cold war living, many men welcomed the fun and lightheartedness of the *Playboy* lifestyle, which in the fifties meant pondering summer wear over *Sputnik*, at least while perusing the magazine.

The fashion columns of *Playboy* spoke not only to the consumerist drive of the 1950s, but also to the image of masculinity that Hefner and his editors prescribed. A column by Kessie on appropriate Christmas gifts for the playboy shunned "real western cowhide handkerchiefs [and] he-man aftershave scents distilled from male goat glands and put up in hairy bottles" in favor of an imported Scotch Shetland herringbone jacket that was "about as handsome as any we've seen."[85] *Playboy*'s clothing articles provided explicit detail for all manner of playboy dress—casual weekends in the country, college football games, formal evenings out. Fabric, texture, cut, and color were all described in exhausting detail.

The magazine's preoccupation with fashion avoided any hint of effeminacy, however, as the articles were always tempered with the manly interests of the bachelor. For example, in October 1955, the fashion editor explained the waistcoat color combinations that "we like" for the college playboy, which included "red, wine, navy, and black check on a yellow background, or a black, light blue, brown and yellow check on a white background." He elaborated, "All wool vests of imported miniature tartans, including Black Watch (green-black); MacDuff (red-green) or Dress MacLeod (yellow-black), provide a wonderful dash of color for any occasion," tacking on at the end, ". . . including a panty raid." Or with the recommendation of "a [crew neck] long sleeve pullover made of pure llama," for "serious beer drinking."[86] Such descriptions reassured young men about their tenuous masculinity and undercut potential suspicion of one so interested in the traditionally feminine pastime of fashion. Postwar American culture dictated that one appeared to be nothing less than virulently heterosexual. But the pages of *Playboy* operated safely within the path laid by the prewar *Esquire*, which had begun to push the bounds of acceptable masculine consumerism. Hefner reiterated that a man could feel comfortable questioning whether his blues really matched, or if his three-button blazer was so last season, because everyone knew he was a playboy.

The fashion columns, like other aspects of the magazine, enthusiastically promoted not just style, but *spending*. In a profile on shoes in the March 1961 issue, A. C. Spectorsky wanted the magazine to promote an extensive collection of shoes and shoe care products. His editorial memo revealed not just a haughty sense of fashion, but the sense of class he hoped *Playboy* would have: "We will want to put down the idea (in a positive way, of course) that a couple of pairs of shoes are all a guy really needs. We . . . want to indicate . . . that the shoe wardrobe should be as extensive and varied as the clothing." A wide variety of shoes was not enough: "In the matter of care we want to show shoe trees, shoehorns, shoe shine kits, electric shoe polishers, etc." Keeping in mind the class status of the magazine's ideal reader, Spectorsky was careful to point out, "We certainly don't want to imply that our reader is going to shine his own shoes—though, of course, he may. We should directly state . . . that this is done for him. . . . We can say that . . . the domestic's job should include—high on the list of things to do—seeing that your shoes are shined." Spectorsky quipped, "There's nothing that so betrays the plebian who is trying to look well dressed, as run-down heels or unpolished shoes."[87]

The resulting article compared the "gentleman's shoe wardrobe" to "the multifarious milieus in which he earns his bread and lives his good life." Calling a good collection of shoes "socially and esthetically important," men were advised that the "newest news" in footwear was "olive . . . so prominent in spring suitings." Indeed, shoes should be changed "twice a day." The article closed with the hetero-confirming note that women prefer "a man who can keep both feet on the ground, put his best foot forward, stay on his toes, and kick up his heels—all at the same time. We can't tell you exactly how to go about it, but we do know it's a lot easier in the right pair of shoes."[88] So *Playboy*'s version of manhood was constructed as the sum of its fashionable parts. It was not enough to have stylish shoes. A man was required to have many stylish shoes and a vast array of shoe care products. Only then could he get the girl, be a true playboy, and live the high-spending postwar American dream.

Other examples of this push toward abundant self-improving consumerism were offered. Regarding grooming accessories, men were told they needed much more than a simple razor and deodorant. One feature showed grooming products in spaces along a board game, with a nightgown-clad woman at the end—presumably the prize for winning the game of hygiene and personal appearance. The products included a "Tensolator [to provide] bodybuilding isotonic tension," a portable steam bath, "Persian Leather soap

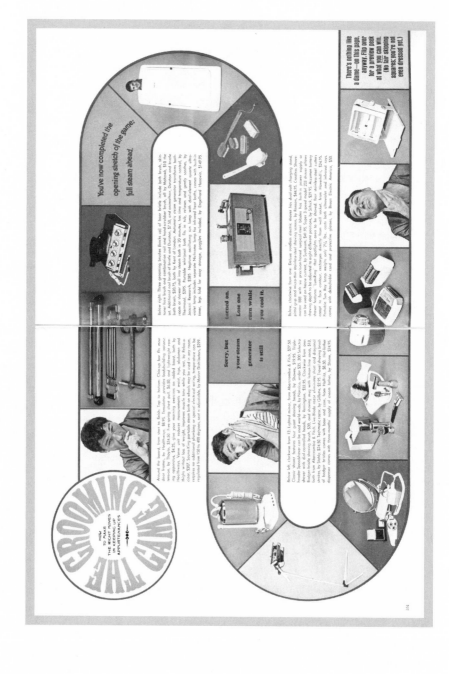

THE GAME THE GROOMING

HOW TO MAKE THE RIGHT MOVES IN KEEPING UP APPEARANCES

You've now completed the opening stretch of the game; full steam ahead.

Turned on. Lose one turn while your cool it.

Sorry, but your steam generator is still.

There's nothing like a game—on this page, anyway. Flip over for a preview peek at what you can win. (No fair skipping squares; you're not even dressed yet.)

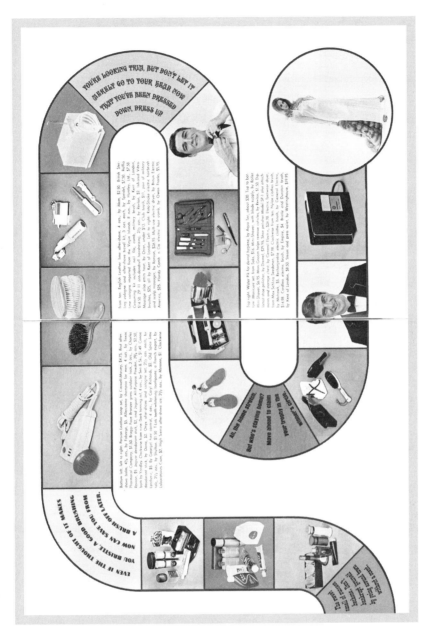

figure 8.   *Playboy* guided postwar men through an expanding consumer culture in part by emphasizing male attractiveness and sex appeal (March 1967). Reproduced by special permission of *Playboy* magazine. Copyright 1967 by Playboy.

set," "Raffia lime cologne imported from the Virgin Islands," face bronzer, tooth-whitening paste, a variety of hair and clothes brushes, manicure sets, scalp massager, and the like.[89]

Playboy saw itself as a "fashion leader" for men. Nearly as much thought and consideration went into conceiving the fashion pieces as went into choosing the monthly Playmate. In this, the magazine demonstrated an awareness of its readership's economic standing, no matter its idealized well-to-do man. The shoe feature was just one example of the ways in which *Playboy* offered fashion as an aspirational experience to its fans. As Hefner explained in the Philosophy, "Our editorial emphasis is on entertainment and leisure-time activity rather than on the ways in which man earns his daily bread and yet the articles, on the creature comforts and the infinite variety of man's more elegant, leisure-time possessions, clearly stress that these are the prizes available in our society in return for honest endeavor and hard work."[90]

A yearly feature on holiday gift giving provided an opportunity for *Playboy* to sum up its grand vision of spending for the American bachelor. In December 1960, Robert L. Green offered men tips on subtle ways to hint at the consumer items they hoped to receive from their lovers at Christmas. Without such guidance, Green warned, "the results can be . . . disastrous . . . as when a well-intentioned girl presents a guy who digs Swedish modern with an early American cut-glass decanter."[91] Who knows how many readers would have recognized the differences between Swedish and American design, but according to *Playboy*, they *should*.

Like the lifestyle columns featured throughout the year, "Gifting the Guys" reinforced the strict standards of the playboy bachelor. Men were instructed to look around themselves—at their wardrobe, their apartment, their "sports car or . . . boat"—and consider what was missing. "How many times," Green asked, "have you visited friends and admired their taste and the way they have done their apartments? . . . Look around your own pad . . . and check off the things you would like to replace. By doing all this, you'll be amazed at the list of possible gifts you'll amass."[92] Traditional economic roles—men as earners and women as consumers—was turned upside down in *Playboy* as women were expected to provide men with the missing pieces of their domestic design dream.

In *Playboy*, it became acceptable for the bachelor to coyly suggest that his girlfriend might buy for him "a well-constructed, compartmentalized, hand-tooled, plush-lined box" for his assortment of cuff links, tie tacks, and the like.[93] Similarly, any hip fellow, Green suggested, should have "a liqueur chest from Hong Kong that has chiseled brass fittings and drawers lined with Chinese silk brocade."[94] For *Playboy*, luxurious fabrics were not to be left to the ladies; sensuality in one's living space as well as in sex was of primary importance to the refined urban man. Part of being a true playboy, readers were told, was not just getting a women into bed, but getting a woman to pamper and spoil you with gourmet kitchen items, "If the lightness of your soufflé or the bouquet of your Boeuf Bourguignon is of real meaning to you, there is an almost endless display of fascinating utensils . . . cooking aids and cook books that will help you . . . [including] omelet pans . . . copper molds . . . chafing dishes . . . pastry tubes."[95]

Green subtly acknowledged that such an attitude might appear less than traditionally masculine to some readers. But he countered by explaining that women mistakenly assume that "if a gift is a gadget it has masculine appeal, ipso facto. . . . It has some strange Freudian connotations about virility: the more virile the guy . . . the more complex must be the gadget."[96] Challenging this notion, he pointed out, "One especially masculine item for the gourmet is a stainless steal chafing dish, with a teak handle, from Maison Gourmet, Ltd. . . . Or . . . a set of prosciutto ham holders made of stainless steel . . . and have an ivory-handled slicing knife, extra long."[97] Phallic imagery aside, these consumer goods more traditionally filled a bride's hope chest, not a bachelor's kitchen. But the reader was continually reminded of his heterosexuality, because the gift giver was, in fact, a "smiling [girl] in expectation of [his] rapture."[98]

These articles served to objectify masculinity and define it based on the consumer items with which a man surrounded himself. One of the most blatant examples of male objectification was in the October 1964 issue. The "Fall and Winter Fashion Forecast" featured male models imitating mannequins. They were positioned in stiff, contrived poses. They wore vacant looks on their faces and had black lines drawn around their necks and hands to mimic the different parts of a mannequin fitting together. Fashion director Robert L. Green opined that *Playboy* got the "best of both worlds" by "utilizing live models to play the parts of mute mannequins, which "better . . . show off the style, stitch and weave of every garment."[99] Green informed his readers, "well-dressed men will be wearing clothing that is shaped to the contours of their bodies."[100] A detailed account of the trends was provided, "Our man's the very model of a modern fashion plate in his water-repellent wool topcoat with fly front, bal collar, raglan sleeves, black zip-in wool lining."[101]

The live mannequins used in the feature were a simple gag, but nonetheless demonstrated the fact that for *Playboy* masculinity was a deliberate, malleable construction. It was not just women who were scrutinized by the bachelor's discerning gaze; men themselves were presented for appraisal and comparison by readers. Another example was a three-page centerfold in the September 1965 issue. But it was not Miss September, Patti Reynolds; it was the "Pin-up Man on Campus," a fully dressed man promoted by the Dickies clothing company. The foldout ad accompanied a page that showed coeds examining photos of Dickie-clad men. The ad read, "New Trend in Pin-Ups: College girls pin down the male look they like: tall and trim (the Dickies Look)." A short article was included: "*Playboy*'s Playmate may not be the only well-pinned item in this issue. If campus coeds continue a new fad, the man in the Dickies Slacks . . . may join the fold and decorate dorms at Vassar, Smith, Stanford, and other girl-populated places of learning."[102]

While this advertisement was likely conceived outside of *Playboy*, it played on the pin-up phenomenon that Hefner had helped to popularize, and obviously had the approval of the magazine's editors, given its inclusion. It turned the traditional notion of woman-as-object on its head, making men the object of women's gaze in the ad itself, and making masculinity the object of reader scrutiny. Bill Osgerby said of this approach, "the male form was . . . constructed as the object of a voyeuristic gaze that threatened to rupture the heterosexual assumptions central to dominant articulations of masculinity."[103] Men and women alike were forced to consider the Pin-up Man of the Month as a sex object, one that depended on the right clothes and attitude. In much the same way that women had been for years, men were encouraged to dress according to the standards of *Playboy* (and, in this case, Dickies) in order to appeal to the opposite sex and to live up to the standards of the media.

Occasionally, *Playboy* addressed other issues of male appearance. In April 1965, "the noted men's hair stylist" Jay Sebring offered men a "comprehensive guide to individualized haircuts and correct hair care." He scolded readers, "The condition of most American men's hair is deplorable." Sebring detailed the ways in which readers could improve upon their much-neglected heads, noting, "The type of shampoo that should be used is critical," while proper conditioning can "build body in fine hair." Periodic hot-oil treatments were recommended, and he emphasized the importance of regular haircuts. According to Sebring, "no hair should be left on the head that isn't absolutely necessary for fullness and outline." Moreover, men were obliged to consider the shape of their face, "protruding ears," and "problem" noses when choosing a style.[104] Such physical scrutiny was typically associated with femininity. Nonetheless, a man had to consider more than a modest crewcut, because the playboy understood that "*any* hair style looks better on a man than a crewcut."[105] Features such as these fostered, or exploited, in men an insecurity that turned their attention away from the monthly centerfold and toward their own mirrors.

Other examples included a man who wrote to the Advisor column for guidance on how to lose weight. It seems he indulged too heavily in the good life promoted by *Playboy*, "good liquor, gourmet food and beautiful women." He apparently found himself with an "'in-fat-uating new look.'"[106] Another reader worried that he was too scrawny and wanted advice on building his biceps.[107] Despite the occasional concern of such readers, brawn was never a priority in *Playboy*. Placing a premium on muscle would have contradicted the urbane, leisurely life the bachelor was supposed to lead. Scholar Richard Dyer writes, "developed muscles indicate a physical strength that women do not generally match . . . [and are] the means of dominating both women and other men. . . . The 'naturalness' of muscles legitimizes male power and domination."[108] So the absence of brawn in the magazine, like much of the *Playboy* lifestyle, ironically blurred the gender lines by neglecting that avenue of male exceptionalism and authority.

Hefner took these columns seriously. In a memo regarding a planned spread on facial hair in the September 1968 issue, Hefner informed Spectorsky that he was "rather disturbed" by the piece's emphasis on "sideburns and beards when the really big news in face hair at the moment is mustaches."[109] Ultimately, Spectorsky concurred, and the article "Hair Today, Gone Tomorrow" showcased mustaches on the feature's opening page. The piece highlighted a trend in removable "false" facial hair—mustaches as well as sideburns, beards, and goatees. Accompanying photos showed a dashing male model posing with a variety of women—a different girl for each falsie he wore. The faux pieces ran from $25 for the "Zapata mustache" to $100 for the "Mariner's beard."[110] The feature demonstrated the malleability of a man based on his appearance. Whether he needed to appear sophisticated, strong, youthful, or whimsical,[111] he could easily change his persona with "instant" facial hair the way women changed theirs with cosmetics. However, the article failed to advise the reader on how to deal with his date's disappointment at the culmination of a romantic evening when she discovered his sideburns were fake.

By the early 1970s, men were increasingly eroticized—and objectified—in *Playboy*. In February 1972, for instance, a fashion feature on "Super Skivvies" profiled the "wild new styles" in men's underwear, a rare feature in the magazine. The piece showed several pictures of men in trendy undergarments. The models' faces were not shown in the photos, a tactic unheard of among Playmate photos. Rather, the pictures were of parts of the men, from chest to groin. Almost every photo had a nude woman out of focus in the background. The women were likely included to temper the homoerotic gaze that was required of male readers as they perused the lineup of scantily clad men. The feature described one of the garments, "something for well-built guys to crow about is this rooster-appliquéd superslim stretch nylon knit bikini." Such articles and accompanying photos indicated that it was not just women that needed to purchase accoutrements of seduction, like sexy underwear. According to *Playboy*, men were also expected to present themselves as desirably as possible to their partners. In order to do so, men needed to reevaluate all aspects of themselves, right down to their skivvies.[112]

The notion of male display was heightened with the increased use of celebrities in the fashion features. In March 1972, Clint Eastwood showed off the stylish sweaters of the season.[113] A subsequent issue's feature used both James Caan and Burt Reynolds to showcase flashy male jewelry. The piece noted, "if you think all that glitters belongs only on girls, tell it to these guys." Caan and Reynolds demonstrated that manly men could appreciate gold by Gucci as well as the Playmate hanging on their arms, Connie Kreski.[114] Burt Reynolds appeared in *Playboy* again the next month, but he was not sporting the latest fashion trends. He was nude. Reynolds had recently posed for a centerfold in the women's magazine *Cosmopolitan*.[115] The photo found its way into *Playboy* in the magazine's own gatefold. Miss August 1972, Linda Summers, was photographed on the beach with a pair of glasses in her hand and the Reynolds centerfold laid out before her. The clear implication was that *Playboy*'s centerfold, herself an iconic object of male visual consumption, was turning the process of gazing on its head. She was offered for appraisal as Playmates had always been; but the picture also indicated that the woman had her own desire and her own appreciation for men as sex objects.[116]

figure 9.   Playmate Linda Summers, August 1972. Reproduced by special permission of *Playboy* magazine. Copyright 1972 by Playboy.

Playboy included other nude men in various pieces in the early 1970s. A September 1972 pictorial on campus nudity portrayed full-frontal male nudity.[117] An annual article on sexy film stars celebrated men as well as women. In one such feature, Burt Reynolds proved a favorite of *Playboy* when he was profiled once again. He was spotlighted in the piece's opening photo. In fact, it was the only full-page photo of a sexy star, male or female. The picture showed Reynolds reclined on a bearskin rug—a traditional prop for the female pin-up. Reynolds wore no pants, and his naked rear was clearly visible.[118]

Though *Playboy*'s reputation was built upon the objects of straight male desire—women like centerfold Linda Summers, not men like Burt Reynolds—masculine consumption was central to the lifestyle Hefner promoted. His authority extended to the style features as well as the selection of the Playmates, though no one found him to be a fashion plate, infamous as he was for wearing white tube socks with everything, including formal wear.

Hefner's magazine increasingly incorporated images of eroticized men by the early 1970s, particularly to promote fashion. While this transition was apparently smooth, Hefner seemed to be anxious about the larger question of *Playboy* as a consumer leader in a society whose politics, fashion, and tastes were rapidly changing.

For instance, Hefner chastised his editors in a two-and-a-half-page memo in 1967. In it he outlined why he felt the recent fashion columns were "remarkably uninspired." Hefner was disappointed that *Playboy* had not featured an article on the "single really hot piece of news on the subject of the 'informally formal'"—the "turtleneck shirt in conjunction with formal attire." Moreover, he wondered why the recent piece on the trendy "Edwardian . . . jacket is frustrated by neglecting to button the top of the jacket" in the accompanying photo. To make matters worse, the "velvet . . . formal suit with ruffled shirt" had been paired with a "foppish tie." Hefner admitted he had "nothing personally against ruffled shirts," but thought they were more appropriate with a traditionally cut suit, as shown in a "smashing photo" recently in *Esquire* that presented the style with a "masculine appeal that most readers would like to have in their dress."[119] In the late 1960s, *Esquire*'s fashion pages typically promoted trends more appropriate to older, professional men, such as features on cuff links and "other old elegances."[120] Although *Playboy* targeted a younger demographic, Hefner apparently still considered his predecessor a stylish model on which to base his own sense of fashion.

In addition to *Esquire*, Hefner went on to cite *Vogue* as a standard on which *Playboy* should be basing its fashion coverage. He concluded, "our fashion layout . . . has got to show off the fashions in a way that makes them desirable to our readers, so that [they] really do want to purchase and wear [the clothes] after seeing them pictured in *Playboy*."[121] If the magazine could accomplish this, it would be a necessary asset to its readers as they traversed the expansive consumer landscape. In addition, Hefner and his editors were undoubtedly aware that manufacturers and retailers who spent their dollars on *Playboy* ads would have a reason to continue to do so.

Given Hefner's clear, unwavering vision of the lifestyle he hoped his magazine would promote, he took "serious exception" to the publication of the February 1968 food feature.[122] The piece profiled "gooey" desserts like pineapple baked Alaska and brandied date pudding. Hefner thought the accompanying photo spread of two dashing couples erupting into a food fight was "more suitable for *Mad* magazine than *Playboy*."[123] He was also displeased with the title, "Let Yourself Goo."[124] Hefner was concerned that the magazine had "more success in projecting the humorous side of its personality than the truly elegant side."[125]

Several of his editors, however, found the piece "lighthearted, surprising, young and delightful."[126] Photo editor Vince Tajiri defended his work: "I think that occasional departures towards some of the zaniness of our times is important." Speaking to *Playboy*'s shifting place in the contemporary cultural scene, Tajiri said, "I fear the disaster of the dinosaurs. I believe that our audience is growing increasingly younger (especially as we age), and the youth are coming up more aware, more hip, more irreverent and it is essential for us to reflect some of these moods and attitudes."[127] Spectorsky concurred, "We are . . . pretty close to taking ourselves terribly, squarely seriously. Our preoccupation with elegance can approach that of the insecure man who will never be a true sophisticate and knows it. . . . And we risk having the world pass us by."[128]

In spite of Spectorsky's fear of irrelevance, Hefner continued to be inspired by the icons that he idolized when he started *Playboy*. Biographer Thomas Weyr notes, "Hefner . . . remained hooked, for all the styles that came and went, on 'the kind of thing men like Fred Astaire and Carry Grant and some other extremely well-dressed men have continued to wear no matter what else was in fashion."[129] For example, one late sixties fashion feature profiled suits in "The New Edwardian: The Pierre Cardin Look in an Elegant Ensemble for Well-Dressed Occasions." At the moment when hippie culture was being co-opted by the mainstream, *Playboy* continued to celebrate the classic, tasteful "tradition of Savile Row." In an utter rejection of the times, the piece described the look, "What is the Cardin look? First of all, it is not Mod."[130]

Thomas Weyr pointed out that by 1968, *Playboy* was begrudgingly forced to update its look for the changing era.[131] However, even as the magazine paid lip service to the changes in fashion that accompanied the upheaval of the late 1960s, the monthly fashion feature continued to celebrate a more stylized, refined look. In April 1969, fashion director Robert L. Green lauded "revolutionary new trends in men's attire." He did not promote love beads, raggedy denim, fringed vests, or other styles associated with the young, "revolutionary" generation. Instead the profile highlighted the "elegant apparel" of the season, which included "sport jackets" and "no-button suit[s]."

figure 10. After establishing itself as an icon of sophisticated masculine style, *Playboy* struggled to find its place in the increasingly irreverent, casual culture of the late 1960s ("Let Yourself Goo," February 1968). Reproduced by special permission of *Playboy* magazine. Copyright 1968 by Playboy.

Likewise, a feature in August 1969 called "Avant-Garb" showed a "silk brocade double-breasted evening suit."[132] Fashion features such as this did not ignore the styles of the day, but rather incorporated new details, such as wide collars and loud prints, into the magazine's preferred polished looks.

As the 1970s began, *Playboy*'s sense of itself was challenged not just by the rise of feminism, but by the triumph of the new antifashion. In February 1970, Spectorsky sent a memo to fashion director Robert L. Green about what he and Hefner considered "a continuing problem." Spectorsky felt that the magazine was "over-stressing casualness. It almost looks as if we are in

a campaign to abolish the necktie and to ignore the fact that the vast majority of our readers go to work approximately 50 weeks of the year." Casualness in dress, Spectorsky seemed to believe, was out of step with how many
professional men, the type *Playboy* traditionally courted, dressed on most
days. Yet he was aware of the growing discrepancy between the style *Playboy*
had cultivated and the ways in which that style was increasingly irrelevant
to a younger generation: "I am requesting that we hew a good deal closer
to proper urban-executive garb, while recognizing the fact that the casual
look—which our young readers dig—is making inroads against conservative appearance as never before."[133] So while times were changing, there remained among the old guard at *Playboy* a desire to uphold the standards it
had set for itself and its readers a generation earlier.

Playboy understood that its audience was composed of more average,
middle-class men than wealthy fashion elites. In 1970 Spectorsky reiterated
the "ground rules" on style features to fashion director Robert L. Green. "Our
top priority is the interest and guidance of our readers—all of them, not just
those who lead [country]-weekend lives and dwell close to high-fashion bou-
tiques." Apparently referring to a question of whether ready-to-wear clothing
should have been separated in the pages from couture fashion, Spectorsky
was insistent, "The notion of practicing segregation in our pages, whether
in matters of race or fashion, is simply unacceptable. . . . The best of it can
and must be integrated—and in sufficient abundance to show we . . . aren't
really a restricted-clientele journal of fashion snobs." Reflecting *Playboy's*
overall philosophy, Spectorsky noted, "Our role in demonstrating fashion
leadership is to work within the establishment . . . not to overthrow it."[134]

Readers like Gary Reed from California challenged this attitude, calling
Playboy's "encouragement of luxury consumption" its "fatal flaw." In the face
of diminishing world resources, Reed thought that the magazine's promotion of consumption was an "obscene contradiction" to its professed political beliefs. Editors responded that only further technological advances
would protect the world and its populations, not returning to a "simpler"
preindustrial society. Rather, *Playboy* insisted, continual progress would actually elevate more people to a healthier, more efficient "simplicity of abundance."[135] To a similar criticism from another reader, *Playboy* responded, "we
feature many products that *Playboy's* readers find interesting and attractive,
but that doesn't imply advocacy of elitist luxury living or wasteful exhaus-
tion of the earth's resources."

By the end of the decade, more and more young Americans were taking to the streets in military-surplus jackets. *Playboy* itself had become highly political in the preceding decade. But in its fashion features, the magazine continued to promote the style of the upwardly mobile, consuming middle-class man. The standard *Playboy* look was geared toward a night of cocktails at a posh club, not a protest march. *Playboy* had to keep its politics out of its fashion features. While Hefner and most of his editors sat left of center politically, they could not publicly embrace the radical critiques of capitalism that dominated much of the contemporary dialogue. If *Playboy* had taken the "revolutionary" trends too literally, it would have challenged its own status as a consumer magazine.

The *Playboy* consumer lifestyle was a product of the 1950s, from its girls-next-door to its insistence on dapper, Cary Grant–like sophistication. *Playboy*'s original vision may have been innovative and ahead of its time, but by the late sixties, it seemed that time had caught up to *Playboy*, and most of its editors—with the possible exception of Hefner—knew it. The editorial anxieties over some of the late sixties consumer articles suggested the precariousness of *Playboy*'s position as a sociocultural arbiter in an era of revolution. They also demonstrate that every aspect of the magazine, from girls to "goo," was meticulously conceived to further the magazine's notion of masculinity. No matter how young editor Vince Tajiri felt *Playboy*'s audience might have been, Hefner insisted on maintaining a level of manly elegance. By the 1970s, many American men were growing fuzzy beards and long hair, and trading in their neckties for tie-dye, but *Playboy* clung to a notion of bygone taste and refinement. Though the magazine had long touted hedonism and pleasure, gooey food fights and overly casual fashions signaled the boundaries of Hefner's inhibitions.

Playboy, like much of postwar American culture, presented consumption as the most direct path to happiness, but the magazine had it limits. Occasionally a reader surpassed even *Playboy* in his obsession with stuff. A wealthy young man from Atlanta detailed how he usually "snowed" women with high-end liquor and expensive things and then easily took them to bed. His usual seduction failed to win over one "sweet, beautiful goddess" who refused to date the "spoiled aristocrat." The Advisor admonished that he should adjust his "'principles, morals and standards'" if he ever hoped to find a good woman.[136] Similarly a young man said he had fine clothes, a sports car, and the like, yet could not find a date. The Advisor asked, "Are you interested in a girl who wants to go dating or shopping? A catalog that might interest young women would say something about your personality."[137]

Hefner affirms that his magazine was intended not just as a girlie magazine, but as a lifestyle guide for postwar men.[138] *Playboy* celebrated the pursuit of American women and the American dream through rampant male spending. But men were warned against taking the pursuit too far. They were told that they should evaluate themselves based on the ideals portrayed in the magazine, but apparently not to the detriment of good manners. Traditional criticism of *Playboy* has focused on its objectification of women through its centerfold. But clearly, men's desirability and refinement was scrutinized in the magazine's monthly features on fashion, cooking, and design. Moreover, as the mainstream culture became more sexualized, *Playboy* responded with subtle nods to male sexual objectification. Though rampant materialism was a consistent focus for Hefner, by the mid-1960s the magazine began to take itself more seriously and expanded its focus to more meaningful political and social issues. What developed was a surprisingly compassionate and fair treatment of male/female relations, a view that was documented in the growth of readers' letter columns in the magazine.

4

Lack of Love Is a Tragedy:
Playboy and Romantic Values

I'm willing to bet that your "personal god" is a cool cat with a
crazy beard, twisting around in bunny heaven with a host of
cotton-tailed angels. . . . Perhaps you . . . should try marriage.[1]

AN IRATE READER TO HEFNER, DECEMBER 1963

*W*hen Alfred Kinsey published his groundbreaking study of
male sexuality in 1948, America took notice. Kinsey showed the country that
its rigorous standards of heterosexual monogamy were for many people just
talk. In reality, American men participated in a variety of sexual practices
both in and outside of marriage. Hugh Hefner was a twenty-two-year-old
veteran and student at the University of Illinois in 1948, and says he was "very
much influenced" by the report.[2] When he read Kinsey's study, he found
an articulation of his own unease with the American sexual system. Hefner wrote a rave review of the book for the university's humor magazine in
which he criticized "our society's very hurtful hypocrisy related to sex, and
the gap that exists between our behavior and our supposed beliefs."[3] With
the publication of Kinsey's parallel study of American women, just months
before the first issue of *Playboy* hit the stands in 1953, Hefner had the fuel he
needed for his crusading fire. As biographer Thomas Weyr argued, "Hefner
recognized Kinsey as the incontrovertible word of the new God. . . . Kinsey
would add a dash of scientific truth to the *Playboy* mix."[4]

Although Hefner saw himself as carrying the banner of sexual liberation hoisted by Kinsey, some contemporary observers perceived the opposite. Pop psychoanalyst Rollo May declared *Playboy* among the "new puritans," and argued that in its "vacuous" representation of women the magazine was "not 'sexy' at all but . . . has shifted the figleaf from the genitals to the face."[5] Ultimately, the most accurate interpretation of *Playboy*'s version of sexuality probably resides somewhere between total liberation and utter dehumanization. But in order to decipher the magazine's portrait of sex, one must look at more than the centerfolds.

Much of the contemporary and historical debate over the meaning of *Playboy* has tended to focus on its most obvious site of sexual representation, the Playmates. But sex was found not just in the center of the magazine. As *Playboy* evolved into the 1960s, sex became increasingly prominent in the various readers' letter columns, particularly in the Advisor, begun in 1960, and the Forum, which first appeared in 1963. The Advisor was an advice column that covered everything from sex to stereos; the Forum was devoted to debate on contemporary social and political issues. In these columns *Playboy*'s editors had the opportunity to speak directly to their readers. Editors like Nat Lehrman, who oversaw the Advisor and Forum for much of the sixties, were inundated with letters from readers asking for advice on personal issues.[6] This is not to say that commentary, sexual or otherwise, was not found in other parts of the magazine. Certainly articles, cartoons, fiction, and interviews provided spaces for *Playboy*'s editors to remark on sex and relationships. But it was in the readers' letter columns that *Playboy* most fully articulated a thoughtful, coherent sexual ideology.

Playboy's take on sexuality included more than a hedonistic fixation on wholesome-yet-available naked women, as portrayed in the ubiquitous centerfolds. In the early sixties, the magazine shifted away from the antimarriage/antiwoman vitriol of its previous years and instead presented a more compassionate view that emphasized personal responsibility in romantic relationships. The shift may have been jarring to readers who remembered early articles like "Don't Hate Yourself in the Morning." But in its second decade, *Playboy* began to take itself more seriously, and the ideological move reflected the magazine's newfound sense of importance. One of the results of that change—or maybe what caused it—was Hefner's strong rapport with his readership.

That relationship between publisher and reader translated into practical advice that condemned deception and infidelity, and insisted on respect for others. In addition, the columns supported sexual liberation for men and for women, as long as that expression did not violate the terms of romantic responsibility. That meant that *Playboy* denounced the double standard, and it promoted tolerance for difference, including homosexuality. Together, this balance of responsibility and free expression added up to a sexual value system that honored commitment and sociopolitical equality. In short, *Playboy* updated traditional romantic values with modern views of sexuality.[7]

This morality found its way onto the pages of *Playboy* from the personal worldview of Hefner and his obsession with the notion of romance, a fixation he held since his youth.[8] His politics and fantasies became the magazine's, and his crusade for sexual liberation was based in part on his perception of America's religious past. He called the country's Puritan roots a "stifling [insidious] influence in America . . . that has pervaded our culture since the nation's beginnings."[9] Hefner's own religious life included strict Methodist parents and, according to him, a childhood marked by emotional and sexual repression.[10] Hefner carried throughout his life a sense that the codes, regulations, and biases of organized religion were at the heart of America's failure to live up to its ideals.[11] He argued, "a man's religion should make him a better person—more tolerant, sympathetic and understanding. . . . Too often organized religion has had the opposite effect, placing its emphasis on orthodoxy instead of understanding and emphasizing ritual and dogma rather than the spiritual founding principles of faith and love."[12] So while *Playboy*'s advice columns promoted traditional values like commitment and monogamy, they rejected the Judeo-Christian ideology from where those values often came.

The magazine used its letter columns to express these views each month, particularly through the Advisor. Editors usually responded to questions with the compassionate, intimate—and, when necessary, scolding—voice of a big brother.[13] Demonstrating the magazine's delicate hand with reader letters, Hefner answered many questions himself in the early years of the Advisor. Editors sent Hefner drafts of the column, and according to senior editor Nat Lehrman, Hefner "would . . . rewrite them extensively. . . . He always tried to answer the question in as deep and sensitive way as he could."[14] Many readers looked to *Playboy* as a reliable source of advice, and they used the Advisor to express their desires, dilemmas, and insecurities.

Nat Lehrman edited the Advisor from 1965 to 1973, and insists that the vast majority of letters *Playboy* published were real. Lehrman said that before he took over the Advisor in mid-1965, letters were sometimes forged, but that he changed this practice.[15] Likewise, Jim Petersen, who followed after Lehrman and remained editor of the column for over twenty years, maintains that the published letters were representative of those submitted by readers overall. He says that letters to the Advisor peaked in the early 1970s, averaging over one thousand submissions per month, and that typically between one-quarter and one-third of all letters were from women. Petersen admits that he occasionally created composite letters to address issues he thought would be important to readers, but by and large the majority of published letters were real.[16]

While there is no comprehensive collection of letters in the *Playboy* company archive, monthly office reports counted and summarized submissions, and they back up Petersen's claims.[17] The reports were distributed among Hefner, all top editors, and staff, further illustrating the seriousness with which the magazine treated reader correspondence. Nonetheless, in choosing which letters to publish, the magazine molded the kinds of topics that it wanted to address, as well as the types of readers the magazine wanted to portray. Historian Joanne Meyerowitz and sociologists James Beggan et. al have relied upon the reader letters in *Playboy* to understand the cultural context in which the magazine operated. Meyerowitz analyzed women's letters to the editor in *Playboy* and argued that the letters pointed to postwar women's complex views of gender and sexuality and revealed their unpredictable responses to nude centerfolds, which ran the gamut from condemnation to celebration.[18] Beggan's statistical analysis of the Advisor found that the column consistently promoted compassion, tolerance, equality among men and women, and challenged stereotypes and the double standard.[19] More significant than many of the letters, though, was the editorial response offered. Those replies demonstrated *Playboy*'s position on a variety of issues regarding sex and relationships and the ways in which Hefner perceived his audience.

Although Barbara Ehrenreich points to *Playboy* as a major contributor to the postwar male "flight from commitment,"[20] *Playboy*'s advice column actually put forth a set of values that included a surprising degree of old-fashioned monogamy, commitment, and respect for marriage. In *The Hearts of Men*, Ehrenreich writes that *Playboy* celebrated the man unencumbered by familial commitment and domestic obligation. This position was certainly an element within the magazine, particularly in its early years. But this characterization neglects the magazine's many comments on the sanctity of marriage and the obligation that romantic partners owed to one another. For regular readers, of which there were millions throughout the 1960s, editorial comment in the letter columns presented a consistently supportive approach to committed relationships, often declaring "sex with love is . . . superior to sex without."[21] *Playboy*'s advice columns insisted that relationships between men and women required fidelity and mutual respect. In fact, *Playboy* repeatedly stated, even monogamy could be exciting and fulfilling if approached with "honesty, imagination, and love."[22] Regardless of the magazine's reputation for hedonism, the Advisor insisted, "The lack of sex is an inconvenience; the lack of love is a tragedy."[23]

In spite of *Playboy*'s libertine reputation, this approach to romance represented a break with the tradition of male privilege. In the history of American sexuality, masculine hedonism in matters of sex was often tolerated, or even encouraged, according to class and status.[24] Though religious, moral, and reform leaders officially condemned sensual indulgence, men of previous generations typically exploited lower-class women and prostitutes for sexual pleasure. Historian E. Anthony Rotundo, for instance, writes of the "exploitative, impersonal nature of these liaisons," in which men believed that "sex and nice girls should have nothing to do with each other."[25] Although Hefner was considered one of the twentieth century's most celebrated hedonists, his magazine's advice to readers denounced the traditional, class-based sexual hierarchy. Sex with prostitutes, while not condemned in *Playboy* for ethical reasons, was not promoted as a masculine right. Purchasing sex ran counter to the idea that the playboy should be suave enough to get it for free. In the advice columns, the magazine insisted that a playboy need not exploit women for sex, for he was man enough—and moral enough—to romance his equal.

In addition to the Advisor, the magazine's sexual morality was further defined in Hefner's rambling editorial "The *Playboy* Philosophy." The Philosophy ran from December 1962 to May 1965 (with a few random columns later as Hefner became reinspired). In the Philosophy, Hefner explained to "friends and critics alike—our guiding principles," and offered "a few personal observations on our present-day society and *Playboy*'s part in it."[26] He laid out his worldview on sex, censorship, religion, capitalism, race, and countless other issues of the day. Perhaps more important than the Philosophy's editorials was the Forum, a readers' letter column that addressed issues Hefner raised in his editorials and various other contemporary topics. Biographer Steven Watts calls the Forum a "journalistic seismograph."[27] Likewise, Thomas Weyr argues that the Forum was "the most vibrant channel of communication between editor and reader" and reflected "a huge response [to the 'Philosophy'], so diverse in content and opinion as to make the 'Forum' the most uninhibited 'town meeting' in the nation."[28] In the Forum, editors articulated a progressive view of sexual politics. That perspective included a celebration of heterosexual liberation for men and women. But it also included a distinct tolerance for, if not outright embrace of homosexuality, which was necessary to Hefner's overall vision of sexual freedom.

Hefner admitted "a strong personal prejudice in favor of the boy-girl variety of sex."[29] But *Playboy* was an important and compassionate vehicle for the discussion of gay and lesbian issues years before the Stonewall riots of 1969. The magazine's official position on the issue supported free expression and legal protection regardless of sexual orientation. By the start of the gay liberation movement at the end of the sixties, *Playboy* claimed it "consistently defended the civil rights and civil liberties of homosexuals,"[30] and for the most part it did. Indeed, editors reported on legal and political developments relevant to gays and lesbians in the Forum, as it did for various other causes supported by *Playboy*, such as abortion rights, free speech, and drug law reform.

Nonetheless, Hefner's primary allegiance was to heterosexual masculinity. As the nation confronted the changes of the 1960s, America, and Hefner himself, continued to wrestle with shifting standards of gender. As evidenced by postwar cultural conversations around the crisis of masculinity, as well as occasional commentary in *Playboy*, homosexuality was often associated with the decline of traditional manhood, or even perversion. For example, in 1955, Hefner expressed an aversion toward homosexuality similar to the dominant psychiatric and cultural beliefs of the period, which classified it as a psychological disorder.[31] In a letter, Hefner called homosexuality a "mental sickness . . . indicative of a maladjusted sex life," and went on to point out that "*Playboy* is dedicated to the healthy and the heterosexual."[32] This animosity, though, was atypical and surprising given his record of support for sexual liberation for all, and particularly his celebration of the work of Alfred Kinsey, who noted relatively high rates of homosexual experience among men and theorized a sexual continuum on which most individuals fell somewhere between exclusive hetero- and homosexuality.[33]

The explanation of Hefner's ambivalence was likely as historian Jonathan Ned Katz describes: "In the twentieth century the threat of homosexuality was often used by sex liberals as argument for sex education and greater heterosexual freedom. . . . [S]ex-liberal reform actually helped to secure the dominance of the heterosexual idea."[34] For instance, scholar David Allyn points out that noted sexologist Albert Ellis used such a tactic to challenge the heterosexual double standard, as did Hefner's female double, Helen Gurley Brown.[35] Similarly, sex-ed champion Mary Calderone of the Sex Information and Education Council of the United States (SIECUS), "a close friend and ally"[36] of Hefner, "encouraged sex education on the grounds that it would prevent children from growing up to become homosexual adults."[37] Allyn notes that in spite of its heterocentrism, SIECUS "represent[ed] the liberal wing of the medical profession,"[38] even in the late 1960s. So while Hefner was a lifelong champion of sexual libertarianism, his priority would never be gay men and women.

Closer to his official position, though, Hefner publicly expressed a defense of homosexuality in the same year. In August 1955, *Playboy* ran a science-fiction piece by Charles Beaumont called "The Crooked Man." The essay told the futuristic story of a world in which heterosexuality was considered abnormal and deviant, and homosexuality was the standard. Thus heterosexuals were persecuted and subject to surgery to correct their "problem." Apparently *Esquire* originally bought the article but decided against running it. *Playboy* then "snatched it up," Hefner told Ray Bradbury, because "a good story is a good story."[39]

One reader criticized the piece, calling it, "an absurd hypothetical topsy-turvydom . . . a paper-tiger enemy." The editors replied to this letter, "We saw it as a kind of plea for tolerance—shoe-on-the-other-foot sort of thing. At any rate, it's a story that prompts thought and discussion, and that's why it is important."[40] Mainstream American society would slowly begin to reevaluate its entrenched homophobia by the 1970s. But in the 1950s, that painful process would have seemed a long way off. The country was suffering the political and psychological traumas of McCarthyism, when homosexuals were considered easy prey for communists and purged from government jobs. Urban gay and lesbian communities became more visible after the Second World War, but the dominant culture viewed homosexuality with suspicion and outright hostility. Yet in 1955, a whisper of sympathy and tolerance found is way into the pages of *Playboy* magazine.

By the 1960s, homosexuality was gaining increasing attention in the popular media. From Hollywood to popular literature to investigative journalism, gay men and lesbians became a hot topic. Historian John D'Emilio writes that a "noticeable shift took place in . . . the sheer quantity of discourse about homosexuality," but he noted, "much of it was exploitive and derogatory."[41] *Time* magazine called homosexuality a "pathetic little second-rate substitute for reality . . . a pernicious sickness." But others, like *Life*, "acknowledged a range of opinions, including those of homophile leaders."[42]

Paralleling the larger cultural discussion, *Playboy*'s role in the conversation about homosexuality increased by the mid-1960s with the inclusion of the Advisor, Philosophy, and Forum. The topics relevant to gays and lesbians ran the gamut, but the Advisor always treated the subject with respect. In one 1964 Advisor response, *Playboy* reassured M. M. from California that he need not fret over his girlfriend's lesbian sexual experimentation in college.[43] Later that year, the Advisor encouraged a woman who worried about her family's objection to her friendship with a gay man.[44] In April 1964, Hefner expressed support for homosexuality in the Philosophy: "our belief in a free, rational and humane society demands a tolerance of those whose sexual inclinations are different from our own—so long as their activity is limited to consenting adults in private and does not involve either minors or . . . coercion."[45] Hefner argued that pervasive homophobia existed in the United States because "The American male's concern over his masculinity amounts to an obsession."[46] Even though his magazine was in the business of privileging straight men, Hefner seemed to recognize that gender was not a natural state of being, but rather a self-conscious construction intimately tied to American notions of sexuality. His statement suggested there was room to expand accepted definitions of manhood to include homosexuals, too.

Hefner's perception of sexuality's crucial role vis-à-vis American manhood was astute. Historians have documented the degree to which twentieth-century masculinity came to depend on rigid distinctions of sexual orientation in order to validate the gender order. Such notions stood in contrast to the previous century, wherein ideals of middle-class masculinity were determined by a man's character. Historian Kevin White shows that men were expected to exhibit "[s]elf-control, discipline, delayed gratification, and self-sacrifice."[47] Sex was a component of manhood, as the Victorians believed that men embodied lust, but men were expected to keep their desires in check. For the middle class, and thus the dominant culture, manhood was achieved by living a life of propriety and hard work, not merely by having sex with women.

By the turn of the twentieth century, men's traditional seats of power were challenged in a number of ways, most especially by women's rising economic and political power and changes in the labor force. As middle-class men slowly ceded authority in public life, George Chauncey argues, they embraced a new ideal of manhood that rested on heterosexuality, thereby establishing sex as the basis of a stable masculinity. Jonathan Ned Katz has shown that these renegotiations of sexuality were bolstered by contemporary sexology, which offered new, rigid definitions of "heterosexual" and "homosexual," or normal and deviant sexual orientation. American understandings of sexuality shifted as sex became seen as a core component of identity, and no longer a set of behaviors taken up or abandoned at will. By midcentury, manhood was proven primarily by one's sexual attraction to women. The dichotomous view of exclusive orientation had taken hold.

Building on the challenge that his hero, Alfred Kinsey, mounted against this prevailing dichotomy, Hefner complicated middle-class notions of heterosexuality. As a product of a conflicted time, Hefner's relatively enlightened perspective on homosexuality, like *Playboy* itself, bridged two eras and was likely derived from his own personal experience. As a young man in Chicago, a pre-*Playboy* Hefner sought sexual excitement, which at one point included an encounter with another man.[48] A casual experience such as the one Hefner had was not unheard of in the first half of the twentieth century. George Chauncey argues that for earlier generations of men, particularly within the urban working class, male sexuality was sometimes experienced rather fluidly. Men had the opportunity to find sexual relief with effeminate gay men, much like they could with female prostitutes, without their manhood being called into question.[49] Though Hefner's own background was middle class, his need for sexual adventure upheld a receding standard that allowed for such fluid definitions of masculinity. At the same time, given Hefner's forward-looking commitment to sexual liberation, his gay experience was also likely an expression of a sexually experimental nature that many Americans would take up in the sixties.

Apparently Hefner's early sexual experience with men did not necessarily challenge his heterosexuality; nor, however, did it guarantee unconditional support for gay men in the pages of *Playboy*. While Hefner publicly promoted sympathy for the homosexual community, he likewise believed that there was the possibility that a gay man could "find his way back to a predominantly heterosexual life" if society's repressions did not force him "into a nether world inhabited almost exclusively by homosexuals."[50] Hefner challenged discrimination against, and persecution of, homosexuals. But he, like many midcentury Americans, believed that gay men could be, and possibly should be, rehabilitated into active heterosexuality. Given homosexuality's status as a mental illness at midcentury, clinical treatment was commonly offered as a cure.

Actually, some psychologists thought that *Playboy* itself could help accomplish this. In April 1967, Gerald C. Davison, Ph.D., assistant professor of psychology at the State University of New York, Stony Brook, explained his novel approach to curing a young man of sadistic sexual fantasies. He used behavioral therapy, "counter-conditioning" the man's erotic response using *Playboy* centerfolds. Apparently, the patient was "cured" and able to lead a "'normal' . . . healthy heterosexual" life.[51] Likewise, psychologist David H. Barlow of the University of Vermont reported a similar therapeutic approach to treating gay men by "reinforcing proper responses to the appropriate heterosexual objects (in this case, the *Playboy* pictures)."[52] *Playboy* noted that this type of work was "clinical substantiation of the point often made by Hefner . . . that the best way of reducing sexual deviation in society is to place significantly greater emphasis on healthy heterosexuality."[53]

One reader claimed he had been cured of homosexuality and was now engaged to "a very wonderful and understanding girl." He noted, however, that "In a sane society, homosexual and heterosexual individuals should be able to live and work harmoniously, without fear or hatred," and he "commended [*Playboy*] for discussing homosexuality as frankly as it discusses heterosexuality."[54] The letter paralleled the position of Hefner—that rehabilitating homosexuals who wanted to lead straight lives was a worthy goal. But in the meantime, according to *Playboy*, they should be treated with dignity, tolerance, and the protection of law. In July 1968, *Playboy* elaborated its position: "[We deplore] senseless prejudice against homosexuals. . . . [A]ny society . . . liberal enough to drop its 'legal of social proscriptions' against homosexuality would also be permissive about sex in general. That society would automatically contain fewer of the irrational taboos and restrictions that are known to cause distortions (such as inversion) of normal sexual behavior."[55]

In other words, Hefner did not support discrimination or hostility toward homosexuals. But he—like most Americans—did not believe that gays and lesbians were necessarily "normal," rather that a repressive society forced some men and women into supposedly deviant practice. He proposed that a freer society, one liberal enough to accept homosexuality, would be a society free of sexual "distortions" and, most importantly, would embrace heterosexual expression. Hefner's support for gays and lesbians was necessary to his overall vision of a society liberated from sexual repression.

The question of whether behavioral therapy, with centerfolds or not, should be used to turn gay men straight ignited a controversy in the Forum. In March 1969, Franklin E. Kameny, Ph.D., founder and president of the Mattachine Society and chair of the Eastern Regional Homophile Conference wrote to the Forum to defend homosexuality as "a preferred orientation or propensity, not different in kind from heterosexuality." He went on to say, "Homosexuality is not intrinsically inferior to heterosexuality; it is not a second-best condition." *Playboy* offered a lengthy response:

> We share your distaste for emotionally charged words such as "sickness" to describe what is more aptly called a "deviance" (the neutral term used . . . to denote a departure from behavioral norms) . . . [T]he exclusive homosexual is not following a preference at all but, rather, a compulsion based on phobic reactions to heterosexual stimuli. . . . [H]omosexuality, when compulsive and phobic, is in itself a problem that exists *in addition* to the problems caused by society's attitude. For this reason, homosexuals should not be discouraged from seeking therapy when they want it. . . . In spite of our disagreement on these issues, we share your belief that the situation of the homosexual in America today would be vastly improved were it not for an intolerant and hostile society that subjects him to enormous stresses. To do away with that kind of social intolerance has been a constant and fundamental purpose of "The *Playboy* Forum."[56]

Rita Laporte, president of lesbian organization Daughters of Bilitis, Inc., asked, "You assume, without proof or argument, that homosexuals are under a compulsion to engage in sexual acts with their own kind. Haven't you also noticed that so-called normal people are in the grip of phobic reactions to homosexuals? . . . I am surprised at your advocacy of sexual conformity."[57] William Edward Glover of Los Angeles wrote, "Liberal, tolerant and well-intentioned as your answer was, it still amounts to a put-down of homosexuals, based on sheer prejudice."⁵⁸

Playboy's editors responded that they only found problematic "the exclusive homosexual," that is, an individual who was capable of sexual response only with members of their own sex, rather than at least occasional arousal with someone of the opposite sex. To the question of the "exclusive heterosexual," *Playboy* acknowledged, somewhat subversively, "heterosexuals often respond positively, occasionally even erotically, to the attractiveness of members of their own sex." In the case of a man who worried about a homosexual experience he had as a teenager the Advisor responded, "Your experience is trivial and important only to the extent of your own concern about it. Psychiatrists point out that such experiences are commonplace and harmless."⁵⁹ Similarly, a confused college student wrote that he had never had sex with a girl he "really liked," but had "come close to falling in love with a few of [his] male friends," and had one homosexual experience. The Advisor thought that he was too young to commit himself to either hetero- or homosexuality: "At your age, it's not unusual to be fond of your male friends. . . . you're a young man who responds to a variety of stimuli."⁶⁰

This view of sexuality as a continuum, with most people at some point responding to either sex, was in keeping with the conclusions that Kinsey had promoted a generation earlier. *Playboy* argued that a range of sexual feelings for and experiences with both sexes—"nonexclusive" sexuality—was healthy and natural. Sexuality, Hefner told his readers, was a fluid, personal experience, an understanding that his own life had affirmed. As sociologist James Beggan et al. wrote, "By facilitating candor, the Advisor created a relatively open forum for the discussion of liberated sexuality and the redefinition of the appropriateness of a wide range of sexual behaviors."⁶¹ Though the magazine celebrated the virtues of heterosexual desire each month, Hefner and his editors did not react to the possibility of gay "stimuli" with macho insecurity, fear, or hysteria. Rather, they told their readers that it was all right to desire other men, at least occasionally, and as long as they left themselves open to women at some point as well.

Even with Kinsey's continuum though, the magazine's critical eye focused on homosexuals because Hefner believed that the biology of heterosexuality—not reproduction per se, but the anatomical fit of heterosexual intercourse—was "one of the fundamental satisfactions of a full human life. The exclusive homosexual . . . is practicing self-deception," or, according to

Playboy, was compulsive and phobic. The editors went on to clarify, "let us be absolutely clear . . . we raise these points only to defend those homosexuals who seek psychotherapy and were condemned as 'immoral' by Dr. Kameny. . . . We are not pressing therapy on anybody . . . if they are happy."[62]

Hefner's views on homosexuality were conflicted. On the one hand, his ardent belief in sexual freedom demanded that he support the rights of gays and lesbians; but his public devotion to heterosexuality left him wavering on a total intellectual embrace of homosexuality. *Playboy*'s approach to the issue was sympathetic, not celebratory. But many gays and lesbians found public sympathy hard to come by in the 1960s. For instance, a CBS-TV poll in 1969, the year of Stonewall, showed that a majority of Americans "look on homosexuals with disgust, discomfort or fear."[63] So in spite of the magazine's conditional support, many gay men saw an ally in Hefner.

In 1964, Charles Philips, president of the Janus Society, a Philadelphia gay-rights organization, called Hefner's early editorials on homosexuality "the most profound and realistic appraisal of sexuality found in the American press to date. . . . *Playboy* and Hefner stand almost alone in advancing a sane concept of sexuality."[64] An anonymous reader wrote, "As a homosexual, I have learned not to expect a great deal of tolerance from members of the heterosexual world. . . . I was very surprised . . . to read your statements. . . . Your attitude is intelligent and open-minded and I only wish it was more common."[65] Another said, "As a practicing homosexual myself, I know all too well that many otherwise liberal persons will not speak out for *our* civil liberties, out of sheer fear that somebody might think that *they* are 'faggots' themselves. Your courage is truly admirable."[66]

One man who had recently come out asked the Advisor which states were "safe," that is, those without laws forbidding homosexuality.[67] Some gay men used the pages of *Playboy* to speak to each other. One affirmed a previously published letter that decried "the popular stereotype of the 'promiscuous faggot,'" and described his engagement to another man. "Unable to have a sanctified marriage contract, we feel that we will be married in the eyes of God, for we love each other as much as any heterosexual couple. Our only regrets will be the lack of a formal ceremony."[68] Lew Norton of Los Angeles responded to a letter from a gay man who had criticized effeminacy: "At the heart of all our problems is the ingrained belief that, being homosexual, we are not men. . . . Open effeminacy, as you may not realize, is a form of defiance that takes great courage. . . . To me, a man is someone who knows what he is, accepts it and spends his life fighting to make the most of it. By that definition, real men are perhaps the smallest minority group, but there is nothing in your or my homosexuality that necessarily excludes us from it."[69] *Playboy* was known then, as it is now, as a paean to male heterosexuality. Nonetheless, some homosexuals found Hefner's philosophy progressive and supportive, and therefore considered his magazine an appropriate place to discuss their roles as men and their position in society.

In particular, police harassment of gay men was a common topic in the Forum.[70] By the late 1960s, numerous letters had been printed by men who claimed to have been arrested or physically attacked by members of vice squads. In the December 1967 issue alone, just under one-third[71] of the letters published were about homosexuality, with five discussing police and governmental harassment and entrapment of gay men. James Wittenberg of San Jose pleaded, "although I do not rob or kill or defraud, I am a criminal, because I am a homosexual."[72] Another man who witnessed a police assault in a gay bar asked, "Who or what am I harming merely by my existence?"[73] Alternately, a straight man wondered, "If the laws and mores in America are changed to accept homosexual behavior, who is going to protect me, the average American male, from homosexuals and perverts?" *Playboy* responded, "Legalization of homosexual acts in private . . . and public acceptance of such behavior does not automatically mean that sexual assault . . . will also be accepted. . . . But we believe you exaggerate the threat to the average American male."[74]

Though *Playboy* was unapologetically heterosexual, some gay men and lesbians found comfort in Hefner's campaign for sexual freedom. Today, Hefner is blunt: "The only thing that defines homosexuality as perversion is our fucked up set of values. And all of that is related to the notion that the only purpose for sex is procreation."[75] His current view reflects the increased cultural acceptance of homosexuality as a legitimate lifestyle. But once again, there is an implied benefit to heterosexuals in Hefner's theory—if society truly celebrated sex for pleasure and personal expression, and thus embraced homosexuals, then Hefner's crusade for straight liberation would be complete. No matter *Playboy*'s position on homosexuality, though, it was first and foremost devoted to straight masculinity. But the air of unabashed hedonism promoted in the centerfolds and lifestyle columns was not to be found in the readers' letter columns. Instead, editors exhibited a surprising sensitivity to the complexities of sexual and romantic relationships.

By the end of the sixties, many Americans were questioning the traditional assumptions of marriage, as they did so many other institutions in those years of upheaval. Couples experimented with living together before marriage or decided to not get married at all. Some chose "open" relationships without sexual exclusivity, or even "wife swapping" as an expression of modern love. Throughout the decade, *Playboy*'s popularity continued to rise on the promise of the freewheeling bachelor lifestyle Hefner first articulated in 1953. But the magazine did not roundly encourage immature sexual self-interest, no matter the message the centerfolds or racy cartoons might have sent. Rather, through the Advisor, *Playboy* articulated an old-fashioned respect for monogamy and the sanctity of marriage.

Many readers went to *Playboy* for guidance not on bedding their dates, but for more domestic pursuits. Some men actually looked to the magazine for matrimonial guidance. The Advisor counseled on shopping for engagement rings,[76] and on the appropriate color for the gown of a pregnant bride (it could be white if she so desired).[77] A man from New York who wanted to know how he could attend the birth of his first child sought advice from *Playboy*.[78] The Advisor admonished readers to "consciously and willingly accept the changes in freedom" that accompanied parenthood.[79] In 1964 *Playboy* spelled out its official position on marriage. The Advisor explained that the magazine was not against marriage, but rather "We're opposed to early marriage for either sex, because we believe that each person should have the opportunity to live on his own, away from parents, for a number of years before considering marriage. Living first as an independent, single adult is the best way to develop the maturity needed to make marriage work."[80] Almost a decade later, *Playboy* responded to a reader who criticized open marriages. The magazine updated its position for the changing times: "people should feel free to follow whatever moral code they prefer, as long as they don't harm others and don't try to force their views on the unwilling. . . . [W]e don't think the conditions of [marriage] need to be inflexible . . . [as long as] the terms be freely accepted by both parties."[81]

Longtime editor of the Advisor, Jim Petersen, confirms this as an editorial ideology for Hefner. Petersen argues that *Playboy* was less concerned with challenging the institution of marriage than with reevaluating the traditional approach to matrimony. He says that Hefner believed that men in their twenties were "entitled to a decade of adventure." After this period, Hefner believed, individuals would make better marriage partners.[82] This idea was promoted, for example, to a young woman racked with guilt about having sex with her fiancé: "We think the better a couple know each other in every way, the greater the likelihood of success in marriage."[83]

So *Playboy* viewed nonmarital sex not just as a pleasurable pursuit, but also as a means of building a foundation for a satisfying, long-term relationship after marriage. Moreover, for those men not involved with one particular woman, but rather enjoying a number of partners—the man supposedly celebrated by the magazine—the Advisor often advised greater discretion. To one such man exhausting himself with a variety of partners, the Advisor said, "We suggest you . . . concentrate on fewer girls, with whom you can share a high degree of affection, understanding and relaxation. Sex, after all, is more than the joining of genital parts; it's a process of giving and receiving and—like any gift—it's enjoyed most when shared with a friend or a loved one."[84]

Even for those men in their "decade of adventure," though, the Advisor served as an experienced, yet sensible, confidante. To an insecure, twenty-year-old reader fretting over his virginity, *Playboy* cautioned that he should not compare himself to anyone else, "Each person progresses at his own rate, and further sexual adventures will come your way when you're ready for them."[85] For a man from New Jersey who wanted to abstain from sex until marriage, the Advisor told him to "stick to his guns" in the face of peer pressure.[86] Similarly, *Playboy* chastised men for trying to bully women into having sex before they were ready.[87]

Further evidence of *Playboy*'s respect for commitment can be seen in the Advisor's constant warnings against infidelity. An available reader from Seattle was told to steer clear of his attractive, and married, upstairs neighbor.[88] W. L. H. of Illinois described the "joys" he had discovered since his wife agreed to his extramarital dalliances. The man wanted advice on how to get her to set out on her own as well. The Advisor responded, "We suggest . . . trying to achieve greater sexual compatibility within your marriage, which seems to us a lot more constructive than playing around outside it."[89] Likewise, the Advisor affirmed the desire of a woman to resist her husband's pressure to "participate with him in a wife-swapping group." Wondering if she was "selfish and old-fashioned," *Playboy*'s simple response to her was "No."[90]

Although the magazine's reputation was for portraying women's sexuality as best when it was easy and undemanding, the Advisor warned against putting a marriage on the line for casual sex. A wife from Illinois admitted that she felt she could not be satisfied by one man, and was thinking of taking up "purely physical activities with other men." Was this the makings of the ideal playmate? No. The Advisor flatly stated, "Seek your satisfactions with your husband. It's a lot easier to build on a relationship that already has many established strengths than to try to develop a stable of strangers."[91] One man was on the verge of an affair with his secretary, despite having a "wonderful home life." The Advisor told him that his domestic bliss was "more important" and "more difficult to come by" than an exciting affair.[92] As traditional monogamy was challenged throughout the culture, *Playboy* clarified its position on extramarital sex in 1971: "We don't flatly oppose extramarital sex, although we are strongly opposed to the deception that usually accompanies it. We simply don't think a marriage that is valued . . . is bolstered by lying and sneaking."[93] These Advisor comments demonstrated that *Playboy*, far from promoting selfish male hedonism, insisted upon respect and honesty for men and for women in committed relationships. *Playboy* did not necessarily condemn multiple sexual partners, or even sex outside of marriage. But the magazine stood by the notion that the priority for any spouse was not instant gratification; it was sexual and emotional responsibility.

In contrast to its reputation for merely promoting callous, male sexual privilege, the Advisor challenged the double standard, which was declared "anti-feminine," and "an immature and outdated attitude."[94] For example, to a soldier overseas who insisted that he should be free to cheat, but that his wife at home should not, the Advisor responded, "since your wife is the same distance from you as you are from her, the same standard of behavior—whatever it is—should apply to both of you."[95] In an era when unwed mothers were often demonized, *Playboy* addressed the hypocrisy that judged women yet let men off the hook for premarital sex. For instance, a woman from Washington, D.C., worried that her premarital pregnancy (resulting in adoption) would ruin her future marriage prospects. The Advisor responded, "Only an up-tight character would hold this against you—the kind of man who, most likely, would insist that his bride be a virgin. . . . Often women seem to bear the entire blame for an illegitimate birth; but, to our way of thinking, any man of integrity is aware that for every unwed mother, there is also a father."[96]

A "20-year-old maid" wrote to the Advisor because she was torn between society's expectations and her own expectations of women: "Sometimes I think I might just prefer to be a bachelorette and have fun the rest of my life, but then the nagging fear of becoming an old maid hits me." The Advisor counseled, "'Old maid' is a state of mind. . . . It's a put down of the female sex. . . . If you'd rather [remain unmarried], then you should try to rid yourself of the outdated characterization of your life style. By all means don't fall into the trap of an early marriage while you're trying to make up your mind."[97]

Regardless of the magazine's status as "entertainment for men," *Playboy* was a place where women readers could find helpful, reliable advice particularly relevant to them. Women's voices were regularly heard in the Advisor, and their inclusion made sense, because by 1970 *Playboy*'s female readership reached 25 percent.[98] Scholars James Beggan et al. argue, "By printing [women's] letters, the Advisor encouraged the abstract 'presence' of women in what had begun as a homosocial environment. The participation of women in what many have alleged is a sexist, exploitative, and misogynist setting, together with the respect given them by the Advisor and his advice to readers that they treat the women in their lives in a similar manner, would have been influential in subverting . . . stereotypes. . . . and allowed women to establish a strong and independent presence in the magazine."[99]

Women's presence in the column was felt in a variety of ways. One woman from Tucson asked the Advisor how to reduce pain when she lost her virginity.[100] Various women and men found the magazine an appropriate source of information on women's health, especially regarding contemporary controversies over the birth control pill. The pill was initially seen as the liberation of women's sexuality—or, depending on one's viewpoint, its downfall—when the drug was introduced in 1960. By the end of the decade over eight million women were taking the pill,[101] but questions had arisen as to the side effects and safety of the contraceptive, and many people began to view it with suspicion. A man from Dayton, Ohio, told the Advisor that he and his wife were confused, "Just how dangerous *is* the pill?" *Playboy* explained the competing views of the pill and its risks and benefits, and advised all women to speak to their doctors.[102] One young woman asked about the proper use of a diaphragm,[103] while the Advisor repeatedly reported on attempts to develop a male birth control pill.[104] Miss R. Hansen of Cleveland wrote to the Advisor to publicize a report on rampant errors in gynecologic textbooks.[105]

As some women and men found *Playboy* an appropriate source of information on contraception and health, readers raised questions about women's sexuality that were clearly informed by feminism. One of the issues feminists tackled in the late 1960s was women's sexual satisfaction, particularly the politics of orgasm. Anne Koedt started the conversation in 1968 with her widely read essay "The Myth of the Vaginal Orgasm," which reasserted the primacy of the clitoris in female sexuality.[106] Soon feminist consciousness-raising groups took up the issue, and women all over the country reevaluated their most intimate experiences. But such groups did not have a monopoly on the conversations about shifting notions of women's sexuality. One woman from Philadelphia wondered aloud in *Playboy* if she should fake orgasm to avoid hurting her partner's feelings. The Advisor responded, "Fact number one is that most women do not achieve orgasm every time they have intercourse. Your boyfriend ought to learn to be able to accept that information without suffering from a bruised ego."[107]

Likewise, the Advisor assured a man, and thus millions of readers, that it was normal for women to experience more intense orgasms solo than through intercourse.[108] A woman reader described the "problem" she had reaching orgasm in the missionary position. *Playboy* responded, "First . . . there's nothing peculiar about a woman's reaching orgasm more easily in the female-superior position. . . . Once you accept the fact that there is nothing wrong with you, the next step is to communicate with your husband. Tell him what pleases you and what turns you off. . . . don't stop communicating."[109] This was not old-fashioned, male-centric advice. Rather it reflected contemporary views informed by the growing political consciousness of women. This response not only comforted the inquiring reader, but educated men on being sensitive to the perspective and experience of their partners. A man from San Francisco wondered how to evaluate his sexual performance. The Advisor assured him, "a man is a good lover when he is willing to please his partner, tries to get her to communicate her wants and needs to him and has a relaxed, happy, unself-conscious attitude toward the sex act, seeing it as an experience to be enjoyed rather than as a feat to be performed."[110] Portraying sex as much more than a game of conquest, *Playboy*'s advice column promoted healthy, mutually satisfying relationships.

That is not to say that the Advisor, or any part of the magazine, condemned casual sex. *Playboy* celebrated the joys of sex just for the fun of it. However, advice insisted upon personal responsibility, and often acknowledged the potential for harm that could accompany thoughtless promiscuity. To a concerned father of a sexually precocious fourteen-year-old daughter, the Advisor counseled, "what your daughter clearly needs . . . is a set of moral values. . . . You should devote several of those heart-to-heart discussions to her confusion of indiscriminate and irresponsible sex with sexual freedom, making clear that freedom of any kind entails responsibility. . . . [Otherwise] she'll achieve neither love nor freedom, but only empty, pointless promiscuity."[111]

In another case, a Georgia reader impregnated two women behind his girlfriend's back. The Advisor counseled that he should approach each girls' parents about how best to proceed, "Once you have arrived at an honest settlement of the girls' problems, get yourself some help in understanding how to live with a person as irresponsible, deceitful and self-centered as yourself."[112] In a total reversal of 1955's "Don't Hate Yourself in the Morning," *Playboy* insisted that men had a "moral obligation" to pregnant partners.[113] In the Advisor, men and women alike got reliable advice on maintaining fair relationships and living up to romantic responsibility. Rather than a flight from commitment, editorial commentary, at least in the letter columns demonstrated the opposite. In the vast majority of cases, individuals who fled from such obligation did not find sympathy in *Playboy*.

Playboy's commitment to responsible heterosexuality was further evidenced by its celebration of the work of noted sexologists William Masters and Virginia Johnson. In 1966, Masters and Johnson released *Human Sexual Response*, considered by many at the time a groundbreaking scientific study of the physiology of sex.[114] Intravaginal cameras and other equipment were used to document the physical changes of sexual arousal and response as never before. Significantly, Masters and Johnson challenged the Freudian insistence on the vaginal orgasm, acknowledged sexuality in the elderly, and "[served] as a direct attack on the double standard."[115] Press coverage of the study and its follow-up, *Human Sexual Inadequacy* in 1970, made the books bestsellers and Masters and Johnson celebrities.[116] Like Kinsey's studies years before, Masters and Johnson were eventually criticized for their statistical methodology, despite the contribution they made to the scientific understanding of sexual physiology.

Also like Kinsey, they had a devoted fan in Hugh Hefner. The exploration of sex, whether in a laboratory or in his magazine, was a priority for Hefner. He called Masters and Johnson's work "the most significant and important of its kind being accomplished anywhere in the world."[117] A reciprocal relationship developed between Masters and Johnson and *Playboy*, with "each willing to help advance the cause of the other."[118] The Playboy Foundation gave multiple grants of $25,000 to $75,000 to Masters and Johnson, the most generous it had awarded.[119] Longtime Advisor editor Nat Lehrman cultivated a close professional friendship with the pair and profiled their work in a 1968 *Playboy* interview.

For their part, the researchers called *Playboy* "the best available medium for sex education in America."[120] They asked Lehrman to edit a version of their highly technical studies for the general public, which was published by Playboy Press.[121] Lehrman's introduction to the book demonstrated the editorial priority of *Playboy* as reflected in its readers' letter columns. Lehrman argued that one of Masters and Johnson's most important contributions was to "see sex from the point of view of *both* the male and female. They don't . . . regard the woman as a supplement to the man, whose sexual needs derive from his. . . . No, Masters and Johnson argue that male and female sexual response are very much alike . . . In the Masters and Johnson system neither sex uses the other."[122] The influence of the researchers on *Playboy* was further articulated when Masters and Johnson became "chief consultants" to the Advisor and Forum.[123]

The mutual support between *Playboy* and Masters and Johnson demonstrated the commitment of each to expanding understanding of human sexuality, and, in particular, heterosexuality. The subjects of Masters and Johnson's research were straight, married couples.[124] The scientists themselves believed monogamous marriage to be the appropriate locale for sexuality, as David Allyn writes, "in their eyes, heterosexuality and monogamy were sacrosanct."[125] Even if their priority was heterosexuality, Masters and Johnson, like Hefner, did not believe that homosexuals were worthy of social ostracism. However, they too saw some benefit to exploring the possibility of turning them straight. In their interview with *Playboy*, the duo said that they were conducting physiological research into homosexuality, and were particularly interested in lesbians. Masters summed up their research goals, "We hope eventually to move into some concept of sexual reversal for those who wish it." Significantly, however, he added, "From what we know now . . . we can't conceive of homosexuality of itself as an inversion or abnormality. It seems to be a basic form of sexual expression."[126] So while William Masters and Virginia Johnson were vocal champions of the sexuality Hefner described as "the romantic boy-girl" kind, they were sex liberals and believed in freedom of expression. Masters, Johnson, and Hefner found straight sex the best sex, but were far from critical of the rights of gays and lesbians. The views of all three found direct expression in *Playboy*'s letter columns.

Journalist Morton Hunt further articulated these views for *Playboy*'s readers in August 1971. Hunt was a regular contributor to the magazine and had previously written a piece on psychoanalysis in October 1969 and had published several books on modern women and relationships, including *The Affair: A Portrait of Extra-Marital Love in Contemporary America*.[127] He also wrote for *Playboy* a controversial article on the feminist movement called "Up Against the Wall, Male Chauvinist Pigs" in May 1970.[128] In August 1971, *Playboy* published another Hunt piece entitled "The Future of Marriage." Disregarding the antimonogamy rants of *Playboy*'s early years, Hunt concluded that marriage was not in decline, as some contemporary observers either feared or hoped, but rather that the institution was evolving. He argued that marriage was changing with the times, and for the better. It was shifting away from "patriarchal monogamy," he wrote, "into new forms better suited to present-day human needs."[129] He said that the new models—which were variously informed by feminism, commune movements, gay liberation, and the like—incorporated modern ideals of equity, companionship, and sexual adventure.

To those who were alarmed by rising divorce rates, Hunt proposed that divorce was actually good for marriage: "Far from being a wasting illness, [divorce] is a healthful adaptation, enabling monogamy to survive in a time when patriarchal powers, privileges and marital systems have become unworkable."[130] Hunt prophesized, "in the future, we are going to have an even greater need that we now do for the love relationships," he continued, "Such relationships need not, of course, be heterosexual. With our increasing tolerance of sexual diversity, it seems likely that many homosexual men and women will find it publicly acceptable to live together in quasi-marital alliances."[131] Hunt's piece was an important article that affirmed the values promoted in the Advisor and Forum. He insisted that monogamy was a worthwhile, even necessary, state for most people, and therefore valuable to society.

By the 1960s, Hugh Hefner had earned a reputation as the ultimate playboy. His magazine became the nation's go-to guide for male privilege and hedonism. That image was based partly on the centerfolds but also on the personal lifestyle that Hefner exhibited to the world. But there was much more to *Playboy* magazine than just welcoming women and lavish parties. As evidenced by the vibrant debate that took place in the Forum and the myriad questions submitted to the Advisor, many people did, in fact, read *Playboy* for the articles—and for the letter columns. What they found in the text was a clear statement on romantic responsibility. Men and women alike—and equally—were advised against deception and infidelity. They were told to treat one another with respect, regardless of differences. In the process of dispensing this advice, *Playboy* articulated values of social equity and individual freedom.

It was through the readers' letter columns that the magazine presented a unique sexual ideology. That ideology did not seek to radically alter traditional romance; it did not put down marriage or monogamy, nor advocate male "flight from commitment." Rather it offered an updated version of commitment that honored women's sexual autonomy, promoted delayed marriage as a means of ensuring personal development, and respected sexual difference. The Advisor guided readers through intensely personal, and even painful, matters like sexual insecurity or police harassment. Like the many other issues addressed the Forum, the growing women's movement elicited a spectrum of opinion by *Playboy*'s readers. Only this topic, however, challenged the magazine's very existence in a tumultuous and changing time.

5

The Battle in Every Man's Bed: *Playboy* and the Fiery Feminists

I was a feminist before there was such a thing as feminism.
That's a part of the history very few people know.[1]

HUGH HEFNER

*It may seem obvious that Playboy and the women's move-*ment would come to blows by the early 1970s. Indeed they did throughout the previous decade. In 1962, journalist and future feminist leader Gloria Steinem famously went undercover to work as a Playboy Club Bunny waitress. Writing for *Show* magazine, she claimed poor working conditions and sexual harassment of women.[2] Six years later in Atlantic City, radical feminists denounced the "Unbeatable Madonna-Whore Combination" promoted by *Playboy* and the Miss America pageant.[3] Many feminists decried *Playboy*'s use of centerfold Playmates and Bunny waitresses as objectifying and degrading.[4]

Despite these oft-cited critiques, *Playboy* took a progressive stance on women's rights and was particularly vocal in support of abortion, as evidenced by the magazine's articles, editorials, and the charitable donations of the Playboy Foundation, the philanthropic arm of the magazine, which contributed thousands of dollars to abortion rights organizations before *Roe v. Wade.* In addition, the Foundation provided the American Civil Liberties Union (ACLU) with money for their work on women's rights, and it helped fund daycare centers for working mothers—all indications that *Playboy*'s gender politics, while complex and contradictory, were surprisingly sympathetic to women's interests. Biographer Steven Watts argues, "Hefner upheld certain long-standing attitudes about males and females, but he disrupted others. Partly by design, but largely by accident, he helped set the stage for a revolution in attitudes about women."[5] Indeed, by the early 1970s the magazine served as a progressive forum for discussions of women's expanding roles in society.

The magazine had to actively support liberated womanhood for several reasons. Ideologically, the hedonism central to the *Playboy* lifestyle would not have been possible without women free to live and love with abandon. For *Playboy*, the bachelor lifestyle depended upon the man's sexual desirability to sexy and savvy women. If women were constrained by the Victorian double standard, then the playboy would lack the ultimate validation of willing and able sexual partners.

Professionally, Hefner and his editors needed to address the movement because they saw their magazine as a serious journalistic vehicle. If *Playboy* had not dealt with feminism, it would have been ignoring an important cultural and political trend. As a publication that was considered "a standard-bearer for liberal causes"[6] like civil rights, the war in Vietnam, and the emerging drug culture, if it had failed to discuss women's liberation critics would likely have used the opportunity to accuse the magazine of not taking the needs and concerns of women seriously. This would have bolstered feminist criticism of *Playboy* and further demonized Hefner in the eyes of many American liberals. Lastly, many *Playboy* readers demanded that the magazine deal with the question of feminism. Men and women alike wrote letters to *Playboy* airing their diverse views on the subject, and they challenged the magazine to do the same.

Critics have argued that *Playboy*'s progressive gender politics merely served the needs of the randy playboy, for liberated womanhood meant greater sexual satisfaction for men, and legalized abortion freed men from the constraints of fatherhood. Today, Hefner simply calls the accusation "pathetic" and insists, "*Playboy* was there from the beginning, before feminists even had their voice, fighting for birth control and abortion rights . . . they couldn't be more wrong."[7] Longtime senior editor Nat Lehrman, in a self-congratulatory echo of these sentiments, claims that *Playboy* "came out on [these] important feminist issue[s] before the feminists had figured out what their issues were."[8]

Hefner and Lehrman's comments are an obvious exaggeration, particularly regarding the history of feminist activism. Their defensiveness suggests that they were still unable to comprehend the feminist criticism of their magazine, forty years after the fact, but nonetheless saw themselves as women's political ally.

Playboy employees from the sixties have their own take on the issue and insist that the dominant political philosophy of the editors, writers, and staff was liberal and in some cases radical.[9] Hefner's personal political views, spelled out in the editorial series the *Playboy* Philosophy, showed a man committed to liberalism. Hefner supported civil rights, the separation of church and state, and was against the war in Vietnam. From his perspective, and the perspective of most of his editors, support for women's liberation was natural and even necessary. By 1970, however, Hefner perceived two versions of feminism. One was a supposedly rational and mainstream faction that promoted liberal goals like antidiscrimination laws, and the other was an extreme and militant version that allegedly wanted to overturn heterosexuality. It was a simple dichotomy that failed to comprehend the diversity of the feminist movement, which included not only these two poles but also a wide range of activism that combined varying goals, agendas, and priorities.[10]

Playboy supported the brand of liberated womanhood as embodied by Helen Gurley Brown in her 1962 bestseller, *Sex and the Single Girl*, which celebrated the traditional dance of heterosexual seduction, but also called for women's economic independence and sexual and reproductive freedom. Reflecting the competing visions of feminism that emerged by the late 1960s, however, *Playboy* reacted with equal hostility to radical feminists who critiqued traditional norms of feminine beauty and heterosexuality—the things on which the *Playboy* universe was built. Hefner saw the feminist critique of his magazine not as a valid grievance, but as reflecting an "antisexual element within the women's movement," and says he "felt that [antisexuality] was the thing that was unique, that deserved attention."[11] Hefner insists that the militant view of him is "lost, is confused, is really truly not thought out," but this is "for understandable reasons"—not because he thinks there may have been a real power imbalance symbolized by the Playmates, but, he says, because the feminists shared in the repressive, Puritan heritage of America.[12] Claiming the moral high ground, Hefner saw himself as a champion of sexual liberation for all and not as a purveyor of patriarchalism. He interprets the feminist critique of his magazine as a critique of sexuality itself.

Thus *Playboy* balanced precariously between legitimate support for liberal feminism and hysteria over the challenge posed by militants.

Hefner and many of his editors saw no tension between their personal stance on feminism and *Playboy*'s nude centerfolds. Senior editor Murray Fisher bluntly stated, "The magazine . . . is an intelligent magazine. It is also interested in tits and ass. So are men. . . . *Playboy* didn't think one more important than the other, nor see any contradiction between them."[13] Hefner says, "The suggestion that somehow you can have a society that celebrates sexuality and then feels demeaned by images of sexuality is bizarre."[14] Hefner rejects the feminist premise—that such images of women are not a celebration of sexuality, but rather a privileging of heterosexual male power and desire.

Longtime editor Barbara Nellis, a self-identified feminist and civil rights activist, now takes a different and decidedly more lighthearted view of the centerfolds than Hefner or, for that matter, many of his critics. To the extent that the pictures may have been inconsistent with feminism, Nellis says that she never considered them anything more than "silly," and she feels that Hefner was not worthy of feminist "demonization."[15] While many feminists considered them degrading, for women like Nellis the centerfolds were merely playful, if immature expressions of commercial sexuality. At the height of the women's movement, however, Nellis recalls that many of her liberal friends criticized her for working at *Playboy*, though she never thought of the magazine as sexist. Nellis simply viewed her job as a great opportunity to meet important people, including, as we will see, feminist leaders like Betty Friedan.[16]

The modern feminist movement had its popular roots in the 1963 publication of Betty Friedan's *The Feminine Mystique*. The bestselling book pointed to a malaise that gripped suburban women who, due to the limitations of traditional femininity, were unable to fulfill their intellectual and creative potential. That same year, the budding movement drew its legislative motivation from the Presidential Commission on the Status of Women, which found rampant gender discrimination within the American economic and labor systems. Inspired by the need for reform as uncovered by the commission's report, Freidan and others formed the National Organization for Women (NOW) in 1966, and focused on antidiscrimination.[17] By the late 1960s, the women's movement was still a relatively limited phenomenon, with activists working for legal reform through NOW, and college women in organizations like Students for a Democratic Society (SDS) developing a radical consciousness.

The year 1968 marked a change in the movement. That summer women protested the Miss America Pageant in Atlantic City. Lambasting the "ludicrous 'beauty' standards" that turned women into "[Degraded] Mindless-Boob-Girlie Symbol[s]," feminists threw consumer products like bras, makeup, and magazines such as *Cosmopolitan* and *Playboy* into a Freedom Trashcan.[18] With that protest, the push for women's rights took on a national character and gained increasing attention in the media and popular culture. At the same time, many activists began to embrace a more radical agenda focused on social, sexual, and cultural liberation. In November 1969, the first significant article on feminism to run in a major magazine appeared in *Time*.[19] The piece introduced the movement to America, citing the grievances of the "10,000 converts" to the cause, which included discrimination at work, in the home, in education, as well as criticisms targeting "*Playboy* as well as most women's magazines, which take an equally narrow view of women's role."[20] The article discussed the mainstream National Organization for Women, but focused on the more sensational radical organizations, like Cell-16 and Redstockings.

The article was primarily an instructional guide to the emerging movement, and acknowledged the real need for change. However, typical of much of the contemporary discussion of feminism at the time, the piece was marked by snide putdowns. For example, captions to photos belied support for feminism—the title "Collision with realities" accompanied Cell-16 leader Roxanne Dunbar's picture, while a photo of a busty woman bending over to toss away her bra was salaciously titled, "Anatomy need not be destiny."[21] As the women's movement grew, it fought an uphill battle to be taken seriously in the media. Some publications, like *Cosmopolitan*, expressed support for feminism.

In 1970, Helen Gurley Brown said in an editorial, "We're *for* many of the tenets (equal-with-men pay for women, equal job opportunities, inexpensive child-care centers) while being *against* the hostile-to-men . . . anti-sex aspects of the movement."[22] When *Esquire* asked about her position in 1973, Brown noted that she always supported women's liberation, but since the start of the movement she newly recognized the extent to which women as a class were oppressed: "I am now totally convinced of the rightness of this cause."[23] But much of the media coverage was less enthusiastic. After the massive women's strike for equality in August 1970, the *New York Times* dismissively announced, "For Most Women, 'Strike' Day Was Just a Topic of Conversation." The article gave the last word to a woman who had not participated, but spent the day doing laundry, "Women's liberation? . . . Never thought about it much, really."[24]

In 1971, *Esquire* published an essay by Helen Lawrenson that was critical of the movement. Deemed "The Feminine Mistake," Lawrenson called feminism "an unfortunate and fatuous . . . attempt at manipulated hysteria," based on "hatred for men. . . . It's a phony issue and a phony movement." Lawrenson argued that even the most liberated women wanted to be dominated and controlled by the men they love. For those individuals who wanted more out of life, she labeled them "neurotic, inadequate women [who are] appallingly selfish."[25] In 1973, *Esquire* devoted an entire issue to women, and particularly the women's movement. It included sensitive and reasonable commentary on feminism, much of it written by women. For instance, Sara Davidson outlined the history of the second wave, while Germaine Greer discussed women's sexuality.[26]

But the issue also belittled the movement and some of its leaders, particularly Gloria Steinem. One piece included a chart of feminist organizations and personalities, noting that feminism was "an idea whose time has come." But the article was condescendingly titled "302 Women Who Are Cute When They're Mad." It was paired with an illustration of Steinem and a sarcastic description of the defeat of an abortion platform at the 1972 Democratic convention. The caption said that Steinem was "disappointed and angry" and about "to burst into tears."[27] The same issue featured a caricature of Steinem that asked, "What if Gloria Steinem were Miss America?" The answers provided said she "would not have won Miss Congeniality" and "would still be a royal pain in the ass."[28] By 1973, feminism was a pervasive movement rapidly reforming the foundations of American society. But much of the media, including *Esquire*, continued to wrestle with its position on women's liberation.

Media scholar Susan Douglas has documented the ways in which the mainstream media challenged, or even ridiculed, feminism in the early 1970s. For instance, ABC News broadcaster Howard K. Smith admitted that women's liberation was an unworthy cause, and instead called for "man's lib." Family sitcoms, like *The Beverly Hillbillies* and *Green Acres*, poked fun at feminism; even comics were "a key repository of antifeminism." Additionally, as Douglas pointed out, women were both typecast and "severely underrepresented on television" in shows and commercials.[29] Douglas, as well as film scholar Molly Haskell, notes that films of those years were blatantly misogynist and portrayed extreme violence toward women, such as in *A Clockwork Orange* and *Last Tango in Paris*.[30]

Feminists protested much of the media's representations of women. *Playboy* was particularly targeted for the perceived objectification of its centerfolds. Hefner biographer Russell Miller writes, "[Feminists] infiltrated the Playboy Mansion in Chicago and plastered the paintings in the ballroom with anti-*Playboy* stickers. There were demonstrations outside Playboy Clubs and at Grinnell College in Iowa, half a dozen male and female students stripped during a visit by a *Playboy* representative."[31] One Grinnell woman declared, "We protest *Playboy*'s images of lapdog female playthings with idealized proportions. . . . The *Playboy* bunnies are an affront to human sexual dignity."[32] Journalist Thomas Weyr argues, "more than any other publication in America, *Playboy* was the target of feminist outrage."[33] No doubt the magazine's tremendous popularity, in spite of the growing feminist consciousness of the era, incensed many activists. Despite Hefner's perception that militant feminism was the thorn in his side, activists from various points on the feminist spectrum targeted *Playboy*.

The magazine reached a peak audience of seven million in the early 1970s, just as the women's movement attained critical mass. In 1970, the Congress to Unite Women met in New York City and was overtaken by lesbian activists protesting homophobia and heterosexism.[34] Several of the most influential feminist manifestos were published in that year, including Kate Millet's *Sexual Politics* and Shulamith Firestone's *The Dialectic of Sex*. The Boston Women's Health Collective published the initial version of what would become the iconic *Our Bodies, Ourselves*. Also in 1970, NOW marked the fiftieth anniversary of suffrage with the Women's Strike for Equality Day, which "focused on abortion rights, child care, and equal educational and economic opportunity."[35] Thousands of women walked off of their jobs, both in and out of the home. With the strike, "the new movement suddenly gained visibility, setting off another round of explosive growth. Women marched and demonstrated in cities across the country . . . Following the strike, new members flooded into NOW chapters."[36] Women's liberation had become a vast, diverse movement demanding the attention of the nation and of *Playboy*.

By 1970, Hefner's magazine had already established itself as an important journalistic vehicle for the times, and his editors saw the women's movement as a newsworthy issue that *Playboy* needed to discuss.[37] In fact, *Playboy* had already acknowledged the emancipated woman in "The New Girl," a playful essay by Beat writer John Clellon Holmes published in January 1968. Described as "an appreciative appraisal of the emergent modern female, . . . self-emancipated, unabashedly sexy, charmingly individualistic and a joy to the men in her life,"[38] Holmes favorably contrasted the new womanhood with the "masculinized" women of first-wave feminism and called this new movement "postfeminism."[39] As the country sat on the cusp of the exploding women's movement, he pronounced that "feminism . . . is dead."[40] Indeed, he wrote, the American woman had already "entered into an equality with men, psychic as well as legal, in which she can at last discover and develop a uniquely individual *and* a uniquely feminine personality."[41]

The emancipated woman that Holmes conceived was not his invention, and she actually had appeared in *Playboy* years earlier in the form of Helen Gurley Brown.[42] In 1962, Brown burst onto the contemporary scene with the bestselling *Sex and the Single Girl*, which celebrated traditional seduction, but also called for women's economic independence, and their sexual and reproductive freedom.[43] Touting her book as "The Unmarried Woman's Guide to Men, Careers, the Apartment, Diet, Fashion, Money and Men,"[44] Brown repackaged the *Playboy* lifestyle for women. Hefner says that after her book was published, Brown came to him and offered "to start a magazine that would be the female version of *Playboy*."[45] He says that his company was putting all its money into the Playboy Clubs that were springing up across the country, and he was struggling to keep his new magazine, *Show Biz Illustrated*, afloat, so he was unable to begin a new project.[46] Instead, Brown went on to become editor of *Cosmopolitan*, where she remade the magazine in the image of *Playboy*.

Through her book, and later through *Cosmopolitan*, Brown insisted upon women's economic independence and reproductive choice, she rejected the sexual double standard, yet still embraced heterosexual seduction and femininity. A year before Betty Friedan published her feminist call to arms, Brown challenged the traditional notions of feminine sexual passivity and financial dependence. Radical feminists critiqued her version of female emancipation a decade later, but in retrospect it was her vision of liberation—women's social, political, and economic emancipation coupled with heterosexual difference—that was ultimately embraced by the larger culture.

Brown's take on single femininity echoed the style of *Playboy*: "I think a single woman's biggest problem is coping with the people who are trying to marry her off! . . . [T]he single woman, far from being a creature to be pitied and patronized, is emerging as the newest glamour girl of our times."[47] Like Hefner, she celebrated the differences between the sexes: "I adore a woman to be feminine, to be female and to attract a man."[48] She focused on money, too, but took a particularly feminine approach that combined independence with traditional stereotypes, "Being smart about money is sexy. It is part of the attractive American career-girl image—being able to reconcile a checkbook, having something to *reconcile*, being able to pay your own way (only don't you dare!)."[49] America now had a female version of Hefner with which to contend.

Playboy's alliance with Brown was natural, and in April 1963, it published an interview with the newly famous author. Just as *Playboy* had styled its sexuality as an all-encompassing lifestyle including fashion, design, and fine dining, Brown agued, "part of a single girl's arsenal of sex appeal is her apartment and her clothes and the fact that she can give an intimate little dinner."[50] While her entire book was premised on sex, she noted, "I'm not for promiscuity . . . I just know what goes on. And I know it isn't the end of the world when a girl has an affair."[51] Many of her views reflected the attitude *Playboy* had been promoting for years: "I do think there's too much of this falling hopelessly, hideously, horribly in love because you've been to bed with a man. Because of our mores in this country and our conscience-stricken girls, they feel that any man they sleep with must be the . . . one that they marry."[52] Challenging the sexual double standard, Brown undoubtedly contributed to a changing culture that increasingly accepted women's active sexuality.

Brown told *Playboy* that she had hoped to include in her book a section on contraception and abortion, but her publisher refused: "I get a lot of mail about how to keep from having a baby . . . It shouldn't be that much of a problem. . . . [American abortion laws need] overhauling. . . . It's outrageous that girls can't be aborted here."[53] It would be two years before the Supreme Court would extend privacy rights to cover married women's use of contraceptives in *Griswold v. Connecticut*, and ten years before the same right was interpreted to include abortion, but these issues were being addressed in *Playboy* by a bestselling female author.

Brown treated female sexuality in much the same way *Playboy* did. She lauded independent, fun-loving femininity, while at the same time fell back on old stereotypes. Brown's womanhood centered on "bagging a man,"[54] but she insisted, "I'm all for equality, a single standard of wages. Women should pull their own weight." She discussed the use of female sexuality as a "very strong weapon" in manipulating men. But she attributed such a need to larger gender inequities in the world: "If all things were equal . . . if men and women held the same jobs and got the same things out of being married, then I think it would be wrong."[55] Brown said the purpose of her book was to convince women they were not powerless sexually, socially, or economically. "The girl is the underdog. The first thing I hoped to do was to convince her she was not . . . that way. . . . [S]ociety has put her in that position—i.e., if you don't have a husband you're some kind of schmuck."[56]

Brown's version of femininity—sexy but not clingy, independent but not remote—remained the preference of *Playboy* throughout the decade. The feeling was mutual, as Brown expressed enthusiastic support for *Playboy* in personal letters to its editorial director, A. C. Spectorsky. Brown repeatedly told Spectorsky that as editor-in-chief of *Cosmopolitan*, she valued the "training" she received from him and from *Playboy*,[57] and was "inspired and impressed"[58] by the magazine. Calling it one of "the good things of life,"[59] Brown submitted letters to the editor for publication in *Playboy*. She praised it for acknowledging, "women really *are* . . . as interested in sex as men are, if not more so."[60]

In 1968, five years after Brown's interview in *Playboy*, Holmes's piece on postfeminism was published. In the intervening years, Brown's Single Girl had been replaced by a new, politically charged version of emancipated womanhood. Though Holmes's article addressed feminism, it lacked any sense of political urgency and apparently ruffled few feathers. Celebrating modern womanhood as a "joy," Holmes, like Brown years earlier, presented a fantasy of nonthreatening, sexy, fun female liberation. Assuming that most sexual inequities had been relegated to history, there was little reason to worry about the changes that might accompany a gender revolution.

By 1970, *Playboy* could not afford such lightheartedness. Feminists picketed outside the *Playboy* offices and Hefner's mansion in Chicago, which was called "a bastion of male supremacy and commercial exploitation of women as 'sex objects.'"[61] "You think that Hugh Hefner and *Playboy* don't exploit women," asked one protester, "I'll believe that when I see Hefner walking the streets of Chicago with a bunny tail tied to his rump," she said, referring to the Playboy Club Bunny waitresses.[62] Radicals stormed the stage of

The Dick Cavett Show, disrupting Hefner's appearance with shouts of "Off the pig!"[63] Twenty-year-old California activist Meg McNelly said of the Playmates in a *Los Angeles Times* article, "It occurred to me this was the big male idea, that a girl is supposed to be beautiful and only for his pleasure, and that she shuts up for life."[64] Protesters at the 1968 Miss America Pageant targeted media like *Playboy*,[65] and in 1970, Hefner received a death threat from the militant women's group Women's International Terrorist Conspiracy from Hell (WITCH). The handwritten note read, "h.h.—Wherever you go; Whatever you do; The Black Hex of Death is upon you."[66] As the women's movement expanded, criticism of Hefner, the Playmates, and the Bunnies became an ever more common refrain. The seriousness of these complaints, death threats notwithstanding, showed that some feminists apparently saw *Playboy*'s portrayal of women as a problem on par with pay differentials and lack of reproductive rights.

At the same time, pressure from *Playboy*'s own readers to address the movement increased as Forum letters on feminism began to appear regularly. Readers like Michael Sharwood-Smith of Sweden demanded a serious consideration of feminism in the popular magazine. Sharwood-Smith said, "As a constant reader of your magazine . . . I believe that intelligent men must support [feminism]. I suspect that a lot of women read *Playboy* and I would like to hear their opinions on this issue."[67] Myra A. Josephs, a Ph.D. from New York, agreed, "I would like to see *Playboy* . . . discuss this subject . . . [Its] readers should be informed."[68] Such letters indicate that readers saw *Playboy* as an appropriate vehicle to "inform" its audience about the growing movement for women's liberation. The magazine still celebrated masculine hedonism and still contained naked centerfolds. Nonetheless, in an era of rising feminist consciousness, many readers thought that *Playboy* had a duty, and a right, to host a discussion of changing femininity.

In 1970, Hefner publicly articulated a position on feminism, though the stance was ultimately as controversial within the company as without,

Though we are opposed to the destructive radicalism and the anti-sexuality of . . . militant feminism, our position on women's rights . . . is as consistently liberal as our position on all human rights. We've been crusading for a long time for universal availability of contraceptives and birth control information, as well as for the repeal of restrictive birth control laws. . . . Likewise, we reject the Victorian double standard. . . . We are also opposed to the traditional stereotype that relegates women to domestic drudgery. We ... believe that any woman who wants to shun the homemaker's role for a career, or who wants to combine both, should have the opportunity to implement that decision. ... we believe women ought to be given equal pay for work of equal value. ... We believe that many distinctions, apart from the purely physical, do and should exist. ... This leads us to conclude that there should be distinct social roles for men and women.[69]

Hefner reduced the complexity of feminist thought to a divide between mainstream feminism that supported civil liberties and individual choice, and a radicalism that supposedly called for an overthrow of heterosexual norms; he fully supported the former, and was totally opposed to the latter. However, it was his hostility toward the militants rather than his support for the liberal platform that motivated him to speak out most boisterously in *Playboy*. His ego could not tolerate the challenge presented by the women's movement. Indeed, he felt personally betrayed by the ridicule and anger so many progressives hurled at him. Hefner believed that he and his magazine had been staunch allies of the left, and now felt that activists had "turned on their benefactor."[70]

An article by Julie Baumgold in *New York* magazine in June 1969 gave Hefner a model on which to base his magazine's approach to radical feminism.[71] The piece mocked the twelve ultraradical organizers that composed the Boston Female Liberation Movement. Baumgold noted the women's "denim workshirts ... schizoid language ... calloused heels,"[72] and characterized them as man- and baby-hating.[73] She argued that the women were working for "the destruction of the family,"[74] and called the organization a "revolt of damaged women."[75]

Hefner applauded the article. In July 1969, he requested for *Playboy* a "satirical piece" on militant feminism, which he referred to as the "superfeminist movement."[76] In the pages of *Playboy*, militant feminism meant the brand that shunned femininity and heterosexual seduction, including organizations like Female Liberation Cell-16, whose members were noted for wearing masculine clothes, heavy boots, and short hair, and who were ridiculed by *Playboy* for "[demonstrating] the karate blows and kicks designed to keep objectionable men in their place."[77] According to longtime editor Jim Petersen, *Playboy*'s staff felt "defensive and angry"[78] at what the magazine perceived as the "rage" of the militants who were thought to advocate female separatism, avoidance of heterosexual sex, the "abolition of marriage, the transfer of child rearing from the home to communal centers and the elimination of all sex differences in clothing, education, home life, politics, and manners."[79] A magazine whose existence depended upon heterosexual desire could not tolerate so radical a challenge to the traditional rules of seduction. *Playboy*'s support for feminism had its limits, but it was not just *Playboy* that celebrated femininity and sexual difference.

Though the women's movement was often stereotyped by the standards of the vociferous and the militant, many feminists embraced conventional feminine beauty and chose not to reject heterosexuality, sometimes creating tension among activists. *Playboy* critic Gloria Steinem, for example, was disparaged by some feminists as a "media-anointed, telegenic leader" and was resented for her "beauty and glamour," while other women felt ostracized from the feminist movement because they had relationships with men or, conversely, with women.[80] In contrast to feminists who criticized *Playboy*, activist Ellen Willis thought objectification had its benefits: "I didn't understand all the outrage about being treated like a sex object. I was angry because I'd always been rejected by men for being too smart, too intelligent. I *wanted* to be a sex object."[81]

So *Playboy*'s support for female beauty and heterosexuality was not inherently incompatible with some forms of feminism. The context of that support, however, through the promotion of nude female bodies in a men's magazine, tainted Hefner's version of liberation in the eyes of many feminists.

Several months after Hefner's request for an article on the superfeminists, editorial director A. C. Spectorsky expressed reservations about Hefner's preferred approach. Aware of the magazine's precarious position in an era of rising female consciousness, Spectorsky argued,

> I think it would be a grave error for our first piece on the subject to attack the irrational extremists, and to be satirical, unless we give a very fair shake to the real problems that intelligent, rational, thinking women are concerned with. I can imagine no publication that is in a more sensitive position in this matter. We get criticism enough, from young men as well as women, for what they claim is our anti-feminist, women-as-objects stance, and for our Playmates and Bunnies. If we just put down the whole feminist thing in a contemptuous, superior, amused, or one-sided way, it will make us look square and dated.[82]

Managing editor Jack Kessie agreed, calling the proposed satire "a disaster."[83] Ultimately, Hefner's appeal for a satirical piece gave way to a serious article commissioned to journalist Susan Braudy.

Braudy was chosen for the piece because Hefner and his editorial team believed that a woman would have better access than a man to feminist gatherings. Lehrman initially contacted other journalists to write the article, including Gloria Steinem, but he found no takers. Braudy was eventually approached through a New York agent with connections to a *Playboy* editor.[84] In the resulting essay, Braudy profiled the most extreme elements of the movement. She focused on organizations like Redstockings, whose members often embraced "no sex strike[s]" and female separatism,[85] and the equally radical Women's International Terrorist Conspiracy from Hell (WITCH). WITCH leader Robin Morgan helped to organize the infamous 1968 Miss America protest in Atlantic City, during which radical feminists "assaulted the seaside city" and threw "symbols of 'female oppression' . . . into a 'Freedom Trashcan.'"[86] Morgan pointed out that while WITCH had not yet advocated a separatist agenda—she herself was married and had a son—she was willing to confront men "with [her] karate-trained body and other deadly weapons."[87] Even more militant was Roxanne Dunbar, leader of Cell-16 of Boston, whom Braudy described as "[defining] the radical limits for feminists."[88] According to Braudy, Dunbar "read Simone de Beauvoir's *The Second Sex* and walked out on her husband and a child with a birth defect."[89] Cell-16 hoped to "[masculinize women] through karate lessons, masturbation, celibacy, and rejection of women's traditional roles."[90]

Though Braudy's piece focused on militant feminism, she included a brief mention of NOW as a "conservative and pragmatic" alternative to militancy whose leader, Betty Friedan, "[didn't] believe in fantasy radicalism."[91] While Braudy pointed out "divisions" among these various groups, she ultimately concluded, "what unites the feminists is stronger than what divides them. Although some feminists shrilly confuse sex with sexual roles, many of their criticisms of American society are serious."[92] Braudy warned that the revolution's "battleground will be the business, home, and bed of every man in the country."[93]

When Braudy filed the article in December, controversy erupted among *Playboy* editors. An unusual flurry of company memos documented the debate.[94] Concern centered on Braudy's treatment of the radical fringe of the movement. Some editors argued that the magazine needed to publish a balanced, objective report; supporters of the Braudy piece were not convinced that *Playboy*'s readers would be interested in anything less than a challenge to extreme feminism.

The article offended several women editors. Associate editor Julia Trelease was asked by Jack Kessie to comment not only on Braudy's piece, but also on whether she thought *Playboy* should print a report on the feminist movement at all. Trelease strongly believed that the magazine should only deal with the issue if it were "a serious piece, not a snide put-down, but what [the movement is] really all about. If we can't do it right, I'd rather not see us do it at all." She argued that Braudy "puts too much emphasis on radical groups rather than conservatively constructive associations such as Betty Freidan's NOW ... I think we should concentrate on the two most important causes of the modern female's inequality—conditioning from childhood, and our historically-male-dominated society."[95] Similarly, staffer Pat Pappas thought the piece was a sensational and dishonest account that ignored the "real problems" facing contemporary women.[96] Copy chief Arlene Bouras found the article "offensive," but thought that it would suffice for the pages of *Playboy*.[97] Associate cartoon editor Michelle Altman thought it "strange" that the magazine was publishing a piece on feminism: "every effort that is made in print to establish the fact that *Playboy* feels that women are not exploitable sex objects is methodically and automatically negated by the photo features we run (if nothing else); we seem to have a wide chasm of hypocrisy running down our backs. However, if we are going to run it, I think we should present the 'movement' more fairly than these first few paragraphs do."[98]

The men were split. A memo, probably from senior editor Michael Lawrence,[99] bluntly stated opposition to the piece. "I think the ... movement has serious, sweeping and legitimate grievances ... and a positive program for reform—but the way this author has handled the subject makes the whole thing sound quixotic, irrational, extremist and basically destructive."[100] In contrast, associate articles editor Arthur Kretchmer found the article "a good journalistic account of the doings and thinking of the new feminists. .... I don't think there is an ideological problem—we are accurately reporting, not supporting; and Braudy makes clear that these women are a minority ... I'm for the piece."[101] Senior editor Nat Lehrman considered himself a supporter of women's rights, but was hostile to militant feminism. He favored Braudy's arguments but felt certain changes in the essay were needed. He said that the basic premise of the piece was on target, but that

Braudy needed to include more analysis of radicalism, rather than merely reporting militant statements and allowing the "dykes" to "hang themselves." Lehrman argued, "If anybody should examine these premises, it's us." He later amended his original memo by pointing out that Braudy dealt only with the "radical fringe," not with the "really important issues of the movement." *Playboy*, Lehrman argued, simply needed to spell out this distinction to make the piece fair.[102]

By early January 1970, news of the debate reached Hefner, who for many years had isolated himself and worked almost exclusively from his nearby Chicago mansion. Reacting to the controversy with frustration, Hefner insisted he did not want an objective report, as several of the supporting memos deemed the article, but rather a "devastating piece that takes the militant feminists apart."[103] Hefner argued that it was the radical faction of the movement that was dominating the political discussion:

> What I'm interested in is the highly irrational, emotional, kookie trend that feminism has taken in the last couple of years. These chicks are our natural enemy—and there is . . . nothing we can say in the pages of *Playboy* that will convince them that we are not. It is time to do battle with them and I think we can do it in a devastating way. . . . [Militant feminists] are rejecting the overall [roles] that men and women play in our society. . . . Now this is something clearly to which we are unalterably opposed. . . . The society they want is an asexual one. We believe women should have truly human roles in society, and that each individual . . . should be able to explore the broadest aspects of their nature . . . We certainly agree that a woman's place is not in the home, that a woman should enjoy a career, that she should not be limited with many of the old-fashioned, traditional notions relative to a double standard in sex, etc. . . . It is an extremely anti-sexual, unnatural thing that [militant feminists] are reaching for. . . . all of the most basic premises of the extreme form of new feminism [are] unalterably opposed to the romantic boy-girl society that *Playboy* promotes.[104]

In the end, some changes to Braudy's article were requested but she ultimately declined to sell the piece to *Playboy*. Instead, Braudy published an article in *Glamour* magazine that lambasted *Playboy* for the incident, saying that Hefner's memo revealed "what [he] felt in his heart of hearts [about the women's movement]."[105] Further controversy ensued when a *Playboy* secretary sympathetic to the women's movement surreptitiously copied Hefner's irate memo and released it to the press.[106]

In the meantime, Spectorsky hired journalist Morton Hunt to write a new article.[107] Spectorsky reported to Hefner that Hunt's piece would "incorporate the more ludicrous antics and statements of the radical feminists. More significantly, the article will analyze the entire question of the shifting male and female roles . . . Hunt will also examine the existing evidence about male and female differences; and he'll spell out our beliefs, as suggested in your memo."[108] On January 30, Hefner responded, "I feel that we have here, potentially, an article of considerable importance to us . . . because it is a new area of social controversy in which *Playboy* can be a significant spokesman. . . . [W]e are not taking the wholly conservative, traditional position . . . We recognize that women have been an oppressed second-sex . . . [W]e want to play heavily on the asexual and actually anti-sexual aspects of the new-feminism, since that is an area that our own readers would find particularly interesting."[109]

Finally, in May 1970, nearly a year after Hefner first requested the article, *Playboy* published its major piece on the feminist movement, "Up Against the Wall, Male Chauvinist Pig," by Morton Hunt. The article was a critique of the women the magazine described as the "man haters [who are doing] their level worst to distort the distinctions between male and female."[110] Like Braudy's article, the piece began with a description of militants as aggressive, ugly, and mannish. Hunt seemed to throw his support to mainstream feminism in the first half of the essay. He provided a brief history of the American feminist movement, from its start in 1848, through the winning of the franchise, to the discontent articulated by Betty Friedan. He drew a distinction between the "millions" of women who supported the feminist movement to varying degrees, and the "few hundred extremists" who were supposedly mobilizing for a separatist revolution.[111] Hunt argued that radicals supported "the withering away of heterosexual desire and heterosexual intercourse."[112] He acknowledged the legitimacy of much of the historic sweep of the women's movement, and took seriously the debate over whether sex roles were culturally constructed or biologically determined, acknowledging that both factors played an important part in creating contemporary standards for women's behavior.

Even when Hunt cited what he considered to be the ridiculous ravings of militants, he occasionally treated them with respect, "One is tempted to dismiss such women too easily as frigid or Lesbian . . . one is tempted to say, condescendingly (and probably incorrectly), that all they really need is to get soundly laid. In any event, either way of dismissing them is only an *ad hominem* attack."[113] After describing a feminist meeting in which militants from Female Liberation Cell-16 cut off their long hair to protest female subordination, Hunt warned their critics, "While snickering at . . . the neofeminists, one is likely to underestimate both their seriousness of purpose and the legitimacy of many of their complaints. . . . No other recent struggle for human rights has been so frivolous and yet so earnest, so absurd and yet so justified, so obsessed on the one hand with trivia and, on the other, with the radical restructuring of male-female relationships, of family life and of society itself."[114] Granting that women were struggling for human rights, he went on to highlight various statistics on pay differentials, education discrimination, and the inequities of pink-collar labor, noting the movement was a "major drive by American women, the Labor Department and the Equal Employment Opportunity Commission to give women an even break in the job market."[115]

Ultimately, however, Hunt's piece on the "fiery feminists" ended as a celebration of traditional gender roles and sexual difference, "no matter how men and women share or trade their roles, there remains an underlying maleness and femaleness in us, as in all other animals."[116] He said that gender difference "feels good, and is productive of well-being" and was "deeply gratifying to male and female alike. It is complimentarity . . . that makes heterosexual love, both physical and emotional, so necessary and so fulfilling."[117] Though Hunt admitted that a woman was "quite capable of performing nearly all the kinds of work men do," he said, "As long as she's childless, there's no reason she should not do so and on equal terms with men."[118] He noted, however, that "it might not be the best thing" for a premenstrual woman to pilot a jet. Hunt assumed that most women did not prioritize work but rather "love and marriage."[119] He argued that "it is only reasonable" that men should be the heads of families and their primary breadwinners, and that women, as the primary caregivers, should accept "a secondary part in the world of work and achievement in order to have a primary part in the world of love and the home."[120] While the piece was framed as a critique of radical feminism, Hunt departed from his initial focus on militancy with a reaffirmation of separate spheres—men rule the public domain; women, the private—a stance that cut at the mainstream movement as well.

Hunt pronounced the greatest crime of militant feminists to be the total denial of the innate differences between men and women, ridiculing their rejection of feminine attire, hairstyles, makeup, and the "subtle cues and incitements men and women offer each other."[121] As longtime editor Jim Petersen maintains, *Playboy* was based on the difference between the sexes.[122] As such, a militant feminism that sought to eradicate those distinctions, at least as Hunt defined them, could not be supported in the pages of the magazine.

From the vantage point of the early twenty-first century, and considering the ultimate social rejection of the militant feminist agenda, Hunt's challenge to radical feminism was not unique to *Playboy*. Of course, the magazine had its very existence at stake in the differences between men and women, for what was the use of *Playboy* if women cannot be considered the sexual compliment to straight men? If women rejected long hair, makeup, and sexy clothing in favor of "polo shirts . . . mountain boots . . . [and] cropped locks,"[123] what would men find when they unfolded the center pages of the magazine each month?

Readers imagined various scenarios. In the fourteen letters chosen for publication in the following issue of *Playboy*, nine were from men, although the monthly readers' letter report stated that most of the responses to the article were from women.[124] The report noted, however, that "all" letters had "the conviction that the women's liberation movement merited the attention [*Playboy*] gave it." Outlining "highlights" from the letters, staffer Carole Craig noted that the majority of responses were critical of Hunt and supportive of the feminist movement. One reader said: "You pride yourselves on promoting progressive causes and individual freedom, but [why] do you stop short when it comes to an essential ingredient of the *Playboy* world—women?"[125]

Of the letters published, eight were critical of feminism and six supported it. So compared to the letters reflected in the report, *Playboy* chose to represent more evenly both detractors and supporters of feminism. The magazine's editors likely used the letters in this way to further articulate their own ambivalence about the movement. For example, reader Alan Stone's letter appeared in the magazine. "When the militant feminists start their guerrilla insurrection," he wrote, "I will have no trouble blasting them." Mary Weiner's letter likewise blamed feminist discontent on the women themselves: "If women would seize the challenge [of self-fulfillment], instead of sitting around and feeling sorry for themselves, they could have rich and happy lives."[126] Some published letters disagreed with Hunt's conclusions. Ed Gittelson argued that "letting a man write an article on women's liberation is just another example of *Playboy*'s male-dominated, sexist, family-based, militarist, capitalist philosophy that is expressed throughout the magazine."[127] Feminist sociologist Jesse Bernard wrote in to say that while Hunt recognized the economic inequalities endemic to society, he failed to grasp the underlying cause,

> Sexism is the unconscious, taken-for-granted, unquestioned, unexamined, unchallenged acceptance of the attitude that the world as it looks to men is the only world ... that the values of masculine culture are the only values; that the way men think about sex is the only way it can be regarded; and that what men believe about women is an accurate portrait of what all women are really like, all departures from that stereotype being perverse or abnormal. It is because Hunt is so unconscious of his own sexism and his own prejudices that he is able to regard women's liberation as both ridiculous and threatening.[128]

Bernard's reaction to Hunt's refusal to take seriously the feminist critique of established gender roles highlighted the dilemma facing *Playboy*. By 1970 it would have been difficult to argue against equal pay in a liberal magazine, and so Hunt's article supported that part of the feminist cause. Many individuals, however, including some of the women who wrote to *Playboy*, steadfastly clung to traditional notions of beauty, domesticity, and seduction. Like Hefner and Hunt, they refused to reject conventional femininity. Other magazines took a similar approach. For instance, a *Cosmopolitan* article on the movement in 1970 expressed enthusiastic support for feminism, but insisted that men and women are different by nature and should have complimentary roles, calling any other belief "utterly wrong-headed."[129] It is not hard to see why Hefner and his fans might feel this way—if such a rejection were taken up on a massive scale, the *Playboy* world would come crashing down.

The fact that such a lively debate could take place in the pages of *Playboy*, and that all sides of the debate were represented, even if skewed in favor of *Playboy*'s position, demonstrates that Americans on various points of the political spectrum saw *Playboy* as an appropriate place to debate women's liberation. Throughout its history, the letter columns were an important part of the magazine, occupying a number of pages each month. At least as important as the articles themselves, some letters acted as a teach-in on contemporary issues. Had many *Playboy* readers thought to question, examine, and challenge their own views on gender, as Bernard suggested? One cannot say for sure, but *Playboy* was bringing such issues to their attention. The lesson was an important one, for many Americans were apparently still unfamiliar with the cause, as a February 1970 *LA Times* article felt the need to define the movement for its readers, "[it's] the newest activist movement brewing . . . across the nation. It's called the New Feminism or Women's Liberation, but what it boils down to is Woman Power."[130] Likewise, a *Cosmopolitan* piece said of the growing movement, "the general population seems totally unaware of what is happening."[131] In these early days of the movement, a woman like Bernard, though no fan of the magazine, took it seriously enough to react and respond to important pieces like "Up Against the Wall."

Playboy's own editors reacted to the piece as well, causing more internal debate. Book editor Mary Ann Stuart sent a memo directly to Hugh Hefner to outline her objections to the piece. She argued that although Hunt appropriately acknowledged the tension between "socially prescribed" and "psychobiologically determined" gender roles, she pointed out that Hunt ultimately reinforced the primacy of traditional roles for the sexes. "While the article purports to put down extremists who are damaging an admittedly just cause, it instead manages to throw out the just cause." She added that while *Playboy* "has so diligently fought to free both men and women from sexual repressions, inhibitions and insecurities, it is disappointing to read . . . '[women] discover that in order to obey the desires of their bodies and emotions, they have to settle for second-rate careers.'"[132] Stuart, like Hefner and other editors, perceived a special place for *Playboy* in the changing culture: "To fulfill its role in the sexual revolution, I should hope to see *Playboy* encourage men and women to work together constructively in creating viable alternatives to the traditional sex roles—new roles that give them both . . . more freedom of choice and real human equality."[133] Stuart believed that *Playboy* had an important "role" to play in the shifting sexual landscape. Regardless of what the centerfolds may have represented, Stuart thought that the magazine had the potential to influence, for better or for worse, at least part of the dialogue surrounding the feminist movement. As one of the most widely read publications of its day, she was probably right.

Senior editor Nat Lehrman reacted to Stuart's memo with his own take on the Hunt piece. He disagreed with Stuart's assertion that Hunt "relegated women to the household." He understood Hunt as having said "essentially, that in this society in this day the most satisfying solution for most women is a combination of career and home."[134] Hefner played referee to Lehrman and Stuart's volley of opinions in another memo dated June 23, 1970, in which he put forth a drastically different view of feminism than the one he presented in the earlier memo. Hefner sought to clarify "*Playboy*'s official position on female emancipation." After months of controversy, Hefner said that he ultimately had "reservations" about Hunt's piece. He confessed that he agreed with Stuart's position. He disagreed with Lehrman's argument that Hunt merely pointed out that *most* women *want* to forego a top-rate career in favor of motherhood; Hefner supported Stuart's view that Hunt inappropriately presented this scenario as the most desirable option,

> [A]s Mary Ann suggests . . . he . . . implies that [that lifestyle] is necessarily superior and to be recommended (though *Playboy* has always emphasized the importance of individuality in other areas of activity). . . . Hunt . . . suggests . . . that women who choose one of the alternative life styles he has listed are not "normal." . . . We would never suggest that a man who preferred bachelorhood to marriage was abnormal; why treat a woman any differently in this regard? . . . I think we should have concluded our article with the recommendation that a more truly free, humanistic, rational, society should offer both sexes a wide range of choices in establishing their identities as individuals. I agree with Hunt that "the eradication of all sex-role differences would be disastrous for mankind" . . . but that doesn't mean that women shouldn't be allowed the same opportunity to explore their individuality. . . . *Playboy* should emphasize a wide variety of sexual roles that are compatible, complimentary and constructive, as an aid to establishing a more permissive, personally stimulating and rewarding society.[135]

Lehrman says that he was "furious" at Hefner's about-face.[136] When confronted with the conflicting memos over thirty-five years later, Hefner stands by his criticism of what he perceived to be the antisexualism of radical feminism, but says he "intentionally" used provocative words in his memos to make his point.[137] Regarding the second memo, in which he contradicted

Lehrman's view and expressed full support for liberal feminism, Hefner simply says, "I guess I was not the chauvinist pig I was supposed to be."[138]

Actually, Hefner was right, he was not the "pig" that many critics have made him out to be. But he was also not the feminist that *he* said he was. Throughout this period Hefner supported the political, reproductive, and economic rights of women, and he publicly argued against the sexual double standard. These were crucial issues for second-wave feminists; as Steven Watts points out, Hefner and modern feminists "shared more than they knew."[139] Still, Hefner supported the privilege of men to define narrow standards of feminine beauty and sexual availability. The contradictory memos reflected the tension not only in the magazine and among the staff, but within Hefner himself, over the competing visions of feminine emancipation with which the entire country was grappling.

Today, the traditional trappings of femininity of the sort promoted in *Playboy* still hold sway over most heterosexual men's conception of what is appealing in women, and over what many women find sexy in themselves. Hefner's fear that radical feminists would destroy all differences between the sexes and, according to him, all the fun of sex never came to pass. In fact, the tide of militant feminism that called for a radical restructuring of gender and sexual relations ebbed in the 1980s. American culture continues largely to embrace Hefner's version of seduction; it remains what he called the "romantic boy-girl society."[140] But *Playboy*'s conflicted relationship with feminism encompassed more than one article. In fact, *Playboy* articulated the interests of women in a variety of ways by the early 1970s. Furthermore, Hefner and his editors literally put their money where their mouths were in the form of charitable donations to women's causes, under the auspices of the Playboy Foundation.

6

Feminism, The Playboy Foundation, and Political Activism

The Foundation's mandate since its inception has been to preserve human rights and dignity.

PLAYBOY FOUNDATION PROMOTIONAL BROCHURE, 1985

Though the Morton Hunt article "Up Against the Wall, Male Chauvinist Pig" caused great controversy within *Playboy*, it was not the magazine's only attempt to deal with the topic of feminism. In March 1970 Barbara Nellis was hired at *Playboy* to work in their merchandising department. A recent graduate of Syracuse University, she was soon promoted to the editorial department, where she eventually became a director of research. Nellis had been politically active through the 1960s in the civil rights and antiwar movements. As such, she was put in charge of organizing a panel discussion among feminist leaders for the magazine. Since the early 1960s, *Playboy* had published a series of roundtables on various topics, and Nellis argues that while many male editors were "annoyed" by the feminist critique of *Playboy*, they saw the women's movement as a relevant journalistic subject that needed to be covered. Nellis maintains that Hefner "didn't get" the feminist anger over his centerfolds, and she argues that his inability to do so was linked to his isolation in the fantasyland that was the Chicago mansion, where he spent nearly every moment of his time. Nellis says, "in his world, no one was angry."[1]

In her attempt to put together a feminist panel for *Playboy*, Nellis contacted Betty Friedan, writer and activist Germaine Greer, Gloria Steinem, and several members of the radical Redstockings organization. The panel would have brought the women together to debate issues relevant to the movement, and it would have been published in *Playboy*. Nellis insists that the women had less objection to appearing in *Playboy* than they did to debating each other for the benefit of *Playboy*. She argues that many feminists she talked to were willing to appear on their own in the magazine, especially if they could debate Hefner, but were uncomfortable talking to each other in such a forum. Germaine Greer had this objection: "I am afraid that *Playboy*'s record vis-à-vis feminists does not inspire confidence. I am particularly uninterested in being contrasted with other feminists."[2] Nellis argues that "everybody's response" was the same. They appreciated the reach of *Playboy*, and many wanted to confront Hefner, but would only do so apart from other feminist leaders.[3] The panel never took place, although *Playboy* continued to acknowledge the women's movement. In July 1971, feminist leader Bella Abzug appeared in *Playboy*'s "On the Scene" feature, which profiled important or up-and-coming personalities.[4] Likewise, Nancy Friday's celebration of liberated feminine sexuality, *My Secret Garden*, was excerpted in *Playboy* in 1973.[5]

Eventually *Playboy* granted Germaine Greer a solo stage and "the ballsy author"[6] spoke to the magazine in an interview with Nat Lehrman in 1972. According to Lehrman, the pair remained friends for years; he notes with a broad smile, "I liked her."[7] Greer had made an international name for herself in 1970 with the bestselling feminist sexual manifesto *The Female Eunuch*. She represented neither the liberal feminism of NOW in its relatively conservative legal approach, nor the most extreme activists who rejected femininity and heterosexuality altogether. Greer was brash, sexy, and outspoken. Lehrman saw her as the "feminist who like[d] men."[8] The editorial remarks that accompanied the interview stated that men could read Greer's book and "not feel compelled to burden themselves with guilt for the crimes against women discussed therein. . . . She recognizes that the sexual polarities of society have been so locked in by economic, political and historical factors that it is pointless . . . to blame either sex."[9] This was a version of feminism that *Playboy* could support. Greer's appearance in *Playboy* was an important example of the ways in which the magazine engaged certain elements of the women's movement and brought feminism to its readers.

In the interview, Greer criticized strands of "antisexualism" in the women's movement. Lehrman noted, "She doesn't hide her randiness, often turning her head to look at a passing man and commenting about him in the way men generally do about women. This shouldn't be surprising, since she has described herself as a female chauvinist pig when it comes to sex." Greer's appearance in the magazine signaled that it was possible for *Playboy* and leading feminists to sit together at the same table and engage in debate. More importantly, it showed that some mainstream activists could see a silver lining around the cloud of *Playboy*'s chauvinism. Greer acknowledged that as a feminist she would be criticized for talking to *Playboy*, but wanted to reach out to the magazine's large readership and she felt that *Playboy* was "trying to go in a decent direction."[10] She criticized the centerfolds for being "excessively young," as well as unrealistic. She wondered what effect these pictures had on men's expectations of women: "Thanks to your youthful image of female sexuality, [a man is] not expected to fuck his seamy old wife anymore. . . . [I]t's not just the Centerfold I disapprove of. It's all the other images of women in *Playboy*. . . . There's no connection between the breasts you show and satisfactory sexual activity. And you display girls as if they were a commodity. . . . Why should women's bodies be this sort of physical fetish? Why can't their bodies just be an extension of their personalities, the way a man supposes *his* body is?"[11]

For the most part, published letters to the editor praised the interview. Sociologist Dan Stern of Ohio University applauded the magazine for its "courageous publishing venture, since most of her criticisms of [*Playboy*] are deeply insightful." A woman from the Buffalo Feminist Party criticized Greer for condemning *Playboy*'s "subliminal" sexist message, noting that Greer "has . . . overlooked the many positive steps *Playboy* and the Playboy Foundation have taken toward a re-evaluation of American society and mores."[12] This was a women's activist who embraced *Playboy*. The reader saw the sum of the magazine as greater than its (nude) parts.

Apparently Greer was agreeable to *Playboy* and its readers because she gave a repeat performance in 1973, contributing an article on rape. In "Seduction Is a Four-Letter Word," Greer argued that rape does not only happen on dark isolated streets, but in marriages, on dates, and at work. Calling rape a "national pastime," she lambasted the American justice system for neglecting and degrading victims while protecting perpetrators.[13] Notably—particularly for the pages of *Playboy*—Greer also labeled as rapists men who used "phony tenderness or false promises of an enduring relationship" to bed their dates.[14] Nat Lehrman suggested the piece to Greer, but admits that he did not intend the article to focus on such a provocative take on seduction.[15]

Greer pointed out that men are "supposed to seduce, to cajole, persuade, pressurize and eventually overcome" women, but in so doing men "are exploiting the oppressed and servile status of women."[16] With a not so subtle reference to *Playboy*, Greer blamed "commercial representations of the woman as sex object" for leaving men unprepared for the "discovery that women do not feel smooth and velvety all over . . . that a woman in heat does not smell like a bed of roses."[17] Careful to emphasize that casual, fleeting sexual encounters can be "perfect and satisfying," she insisted they must not be predicated on men's lies and abuses of power.[18] Greer railed against the misogyny that created rape and sexual exploitation. Speaking directly to *Playboy* readers, she declared, "*if you do not like us, cannot listen to our part of the conversation, if we are only meat to you, then leave us alone.*"[19] Carrying the banner of second-wave feminism, Greer pointed out that sex is political and public, and warned readers that the tide of the sex wars was changing.

The feminist antirape movement was just beginning in 1973, and with good reason. Some states, like New York, placed a great burden on victims to make their case. One New York City police detective admitted that many of his colleagues felt rape was "[no] big deal" unless the woman was a virgin.[20] In most states, a man could legally rape his wife. California senator Bob Wilson quipped, "If you can't rape your wife, then who can you rape?"[21] The cultural and legal prejudice against rape victims was increasingly challenged in the early seventies, but according to historian Ruth Rosen, the antirape movement would not be prioritized on the national political agenda until after the 1975 publication of Susan Brownmiller's book *Against Our Will: Men, Women and Rape.*[22] In 1973, though, *Playboy*'s readers were already being educated on the subject by a leading feminist.

Readers took up both sides of the fight. Colette Nijhof of the National Organization for Women wrote, "Congratulations for having published Greer's article on rape. . . . I believe the article can do much to help our work in revising all laws governing statutory and forcible rape." Jill Johnston, "'self-described 'Lesbian at large'" and writer for the *Village Voice* was puzzled. "I don't know why *Playboy* would encourage such an intelligent, enlightened and sophisticated view of rape and seduction in apparent contradiction to its own philosophy. . . . I guess the article is for women, really, so congratulations for printing it." Shawn Thomson of California was outraged: "If I wanted to read the militant rantings of a feminist bitch, I would buy feminist magazines. If *Playboy* is to become a sounding board for women's lib, say so and I will simply quit reading it."[23]

Regardless of the reaction of some of its readers, the editorial page declared Greer an "articulate and intelligent spokesman (-woman? -person?) for women's rights." The editors apparently gave their blessing to her views, noting, "she scores telling points in an argument that may be new to our readers."[24] But Greer's politicization of sex was not all that new to *Playboy*'s fans. While it may not have been described in such terms, Hefner had been politicizing sex for years. He had argued against repressive laws and moralities since before he founded *Playboy*, and there were positive implications of that appeal for both sexes.[25] As Thomas Weyr argued, "More than Kinsey, more than Masters and Johnson, more than the sex manuals of the day, [Hefner] made a mass audience aware of sex as a social issue . . . a matter of both individual and collective concern."[26] Of course, Greer and Hefner had different perspectives. Hefner campaigned for liberation, but Greer recognized the potentially damaging implications of Hefner's world—and, for that matter, of much of American culture—for women.

Readers continued to debate the women's movement through the early 1970s. Men and women, both in favor of and opposed to feminism, spoke out. Many letters focused on *Playboy*'s role in a changing society. The continual discussion of this topic showed that, despite editor Jack Kessie's concerns during the Susan Braudy controversy that feminism would be of little interest to *Playboy*'s readers, the changing status of women was indeed relevant to America's aspiring playboys.

Readers' letters spoke to the contradictions found in the magazine and showed that even many supporters of feminism saw *Playboy*'s treatment of femininity as complicated. Some readers felt that the greatest paradox was the magazine's espousal of liberal politics coupled with what many saw as its objectification of women. In 1972, New Yorker Joan Siegel wrote, "I'm a member of a women's lib organization, but I'm also a wife. I pick up my husband's copy of *Playboy* every month and regularly read one of the few departments I find morally acceptable: The *Playboy* 'Forum.'" She continued, "In spite of the subliminal sexist message that permeates the rest of your magazine, I must admit that your 'Forum' words on the subject of feminism are basically sound. . . . Bravo, *Playboy*."[27] Another female reader likewise admitted that she respected the politics of the *Playboy Philosophy* and Forum but wished the magazine would "[acknowledge] its bias where women's liberation is concerned."[28] Paul R. Freshwater of Cincinnati went further: "[Y]ou ... express a sane attitude on war, racism, law and abortion ... [but take] a reactionary position [on feminism], mindlessly continuing to portray women only as sexual objects." These letters showed that contemporary observers saw the potential in *Playboy* to offer a useable version of sexuality to both men and women. The magazine may not have lived up to that potential, but as the women's movement reached a critical mass, many progressive Americans saw *Playboy*'s gender politics as something more than sexist.

To charges of sexism, *Playboy* often recited the fact that their female readership—they claimed it was over three million by 1971—was "higher than that of most women's magazine's," and they listed the various feminist goals that they had actively supported. *Playboy* repeatedly argued that they only took issue with "that small, shrill faction of women's lib that believes equality cannot be achieved without destroying heterosexuality."[29] *Playboy* also argued that the "extreme segments [of the movement] try to divide progressive forces in this country, and thus weaken them."[30] In one case, the magazine noted, Hefner hosted a 1970 fundraiser for the Vietnam Moratorium Committee at his Chicago mansion. Feminists picketed outside, trying to stop guests from entering.[31]

Editor Nat Lehrman said that instead of battling each other, "all progressive people must work together on important issues, such as civil rights, war, ecology, women's rights, etc." He emphasized, "we *want* to be identified as crusaders for women's rights; our only quarrels with feminists are that they use *us* as a symbol of male 'chauvinism.'"[32] For *Playboy*, feminist rage against the magazine was a hysterical overreaction to what its editors saw as playful sexuality. Hefner and his associates believed they were freeing everyone, not just men, from the shackles of Puritan repression. They vehemently disagreed with the critics who accused them of fostering such repression.

Playboy's efforts to reach out to women did not go unnoticed by a number of readers. The Reverend Daniel Ross Chandler, Ph.D. of State University of New York College, New Paltz, argued against the feminist critique of *Playboy*, noting instead that the magazine "helped develop an authentic human sexuality ... *Playboy* has raised for public discussion and dialog the ethical issues of premarital and extramarital intercourse, the legalization of abortion and homosexuality and the viability of marriage and cohabitation."

Reverend Chandler went on to write, "*Playboy* has aided [the development of new lifestyles] by breaking down those traditional limitations that have tyrannized the human potential."[33]

Hefner put his money where his mouth was when it came to supporting many feminist causes. This was accomplished through The Playboy Foundation, which was founded in 1965 as the philanthropic arm of the magazine. The foundation's contributions focused on three areas, "the protection and extension of civil rights," "the modernization of laws pertaining to sex, drugs, contraception, abortion and censorship," and "support of research in the fields of human sexuality and population control."[34]

The foundation was created to enact the social and political philosophy that Hefner had laid out in his editorial series, the *Playboy* Philosophy. According to Burton Joseph, executive director of the foundation from 1969 through 1985, Playboy chose to fund organizations that had little alternative support and sought "groups and individuals that did not necessarily have a track record and were on the cutting edge of reform."[35] The foundation had a relatively modest operating budget, often around $250,000 in the early seventies, so it usually contributed to organizations that needed just enough support to establish themselves or to survive, thus enabling the recipients to make an impact and then attract the financial support of larger donors.[36] Not all grantees were little known startups, though. In 1971, for example, the foundation's top awards of $25,000 to $50,000, went to sex researchers William Masters and Virginia Johnson, to the Sexuality Information and Education Council of the United States (SIECUS), and to the National Committee for Prisoners' Rights.[37]

The Playboy Foundation did more than give money. When possible, it often provided other types of assistance to needy individuals or progressive organizations. The foundation offered its duplicating service, sponsored public services announcements, granted use of building spaces, organized retreats at Playboy-owned resorts for troubled teens, offered free reprints of useful *Playboy* articles, donated office equipment, set up hotlines and referral services, and volunteered staff time for activities like stuffing envelopes and making calls for organizations like the Midwest Population Center, Vietnam Veterans Against the War, National Organization for the Reform of Marijuana Laws (NORML), and Illinois Committee to Abolish Capital Punishment. The foundation also focused on networking with other likeminded organizations, with Burton Joseph on the board of the Midwest Population

Center, The National Committee for Prisoners' Rights, and the Chicago American Civil Liberties Union, and acting as referral attorney for groups like the Mattachine Midwest.[38]

The foundation contributed money to a variety of feminist causes. For instance, from 1970 to 1972, the foundation gave a total of $9,000 to local daycare centers such as the Evanston Child Care Center in Illinois, the Child Care Center Association, and the National Council of Negro Women for centers in Brooklyn and in Mississippi.[39] However, as did much of the feminist movement, the Playboy Foundation's support of women often focused on reproductive rights, giving "discreet but generous support to pro-choice groups."[40] The 1973 *Annual Report* noted that the foundation "assists in legal actions aimed at repealing restrictive abortion laws and it had aided individuals threatened with prosecution under state abortion statutes."[41] Further, the report noted that the foundation had assisted "research groups working on morning-after pills and once-a-month birth-control pills."[42]

One example included a contribution to Dr. Hilton A. Salhanick of Harvard Medical School. Salhanick was working to develop a safe, reliable abortifacient and requested financial support from the foundation. Editor Nat Lehrman, who was also one of the foundation's top administrators, felt the project was "the most fantastic Foundation proposal we've received yet . . . good, solid, sociological research of a real and valid feminist nature."[43] He argued, "From our point of view, this has got to be *the* scientific project of the decade. . . ." The foundation gave Salhanick $5,000.[44]

Some foundation money went to the support of legal cases. In one instance, the group assisted Shirley Wheeler of Florida, who was convicted of manslaughter after obtaining an abortion. In 1971 *Playboy* reported, "We are outraged at this act of sadistically vindictive moralism and we have pledged Playboy Foundation assistance to Mrs. Wheeler for as long as her case is in the courts."[45] The foundation contributed $3,500 to the case. Cyril Means, who was a leading constitutional expert on reproductive law, represented Wheeler, and with over $3,000 from the foundation later filed an amicus curiae brief in support of the Texas case that led to *Roe v. Wade* in 1973.[46]

Cases such Wheeler's became a political priority for *Playboy*, particularly as the movement for legalization expanded. Burton Joseph argues, "both as a matter of principle and due to the fact that there were virtually no other funding sources to support decriminalization" the Foundation focused much of its attention on abortion, particularly at the state level.[47] Like the larger women's movement, the abortion rights movement had reached a peak by the early 1970s, but had been active in a limited capacity since the early 1960s. Activists like Patricia Maginnis worked at the local, often underground level to educate women on how to obtain safe abortions. Maginnis and others printed homemade fliers on self-induced abortion and on where to find abortionists in Mexico. With no other means at her disposal, she distributed the fliers to women she passed on the street.[48]

By the mid-1960s, abortion was increasingly discussed in the popular American press, though the movement for abortion rights was still in its infant stages. Major magazines began presenting a variety of angles on the debate. For instance, a 1965 article in *Look* called illegal abortions a "growing tragedy," while *Ladies' Home Journal* followed with a piece from the perspective of a doctor, and *Time* included an article on the rising rate of illegal abortions in 1965.[49] Hefner's feminine counterpart, Helen Gurley Brown, had hoped to run in *Cosmopolitan* an article about abortion in the mid-1960s. But according to biographer Jennifer Scanlon, her publisher would not allow it. Nonetheless, Scanlon argues that Brown was always "vehement" about abortion rights, as Brown herself asserted in her interview with *Playboy*.[50]

Lawrence Lader, who with Pat Maginnis helped to found the National Abortion Rights Action League (NARAL) in 1969, was active in the nascent abortion rights movement in the mid-1960s. In spite of growing media attention, he said of national support, "There was almost nobody in the beginning, so it was lonely. . . . I couldn't even tell whether the incipient Women's Movement was interested in abortion."[51] He argued that the movement grew after his book *Abortion* was published in 1966, though there was still little institutional support for the cause.[52] Indeed there was a precipitous increase in media coverage of the subject in 1967.[53] For example, *Time* praised the liberalization of state laws in 1967, and later that year the magazine ran a piece critical of "archaic and hypocritical concepts and statutes" regarding abortion.[54]

If Lader believed he had few allies in the mid-sixties, he and Maginnis could count on *Playboy*. In January 1967, Maginnis wrote to the Forum and called on Americans to "force the government to change . . . brutal sectarian" abortion laws.[55] She appeared in the Forum again in January 1969, describing the "heavy . . . abortion traffic" flowing from the United States into Mexico, and thus the need for safe services in America.[56] In fact, *Playboy* had published its first statement in support of the legalization of abortion in its

December 1965 Forum, as readers increasingly contributed their thoughts on the issue. At least as early as April 1965, Hefner was planning to devote an entire installment to the topic of abortion (though the essay never materialized).[57] That same year the foundation began to make small donations, as low as $20, in support of reproductive rights, though the amounts increased rapidly. The first awards went to the Association for the Study of Abortion and to the Illinois Committee for the Medical Control of Abortion, with the latter organization receiving over $10,000 by 1969.[58] The foundation gave at least $140,000 to various reproductive rights organizations and in support of a variety of related legal cases from 1966 through 1977.[59]

With the conversation over abortion expanding in *Playboy* and in the culture, some readers like Janelle Lindsey opposed legalization. She decried the "pain and confusion" of abortion, and chastised men to take responsibility for contraception before pregnancy: "I . . . distrust any man running around trying to get abortion legalized—that's *me* he's tossing around like a political football. . . . For the female readers of *Playboy* who aren't taking birth-control pills . . . your subscriptions should be cancelled immediately!" Forum editors responded in December 1965, "We can't contradict your contention that the best birth-control method is a contraceptive used at the proper time. . . . We do feel, however, that the question of abortion is one of alternatives rather than absolutes. . . . [T]he legalization of abortion would simply increase the alternatives available to [a pregnant woman]. . . . We're not a woman . . . if we were, we would welcome the additional freedom of choice that legalized abortion would provide."[60] In 1967, *Time* noted that a mere public discussion of abortion was "virtually unthinkable . . . only a few years ago."[61] But in 1965, *Playboy* went beyond discussion and called for legalization. With letters submitted by activists like Maginnis, as well as progressive legislators, abortion providers, and *Playboy*'s own commentary, men and women alike received not only a political consciousness-raising in the Forum, but an education as well.

Many women wrote in to explain why they had sought abortions. In 1966, one anonymous woman wrote, "in desperation, I decided even possible death could not be worse, so went through with [the abortion]. The experience turned out to be even worse that I had anticipated . . . How different this might have been if laws had permitted me to go to a hospital where my own doctor could have attended me."[62] Another woman described her "horrid" experience in a home for unwed mothers and concluded, "Men make the laws and women suffer the consequences. I'm for letting the girl make her own choice—without legal interference."[63]

In May 1967, Playboy expanded its coverage of the movement to include practical information for readers. In the Forum, editors listed the states considering abortion reform, as well as the names of congressional representatives. Playboy called on readers to write to their congressmen and demand abortion reform. Readers responded with a flood of letters. Fully one-half of the twenty-four total Forum letters published in August 1967 were about abortion; the majority were in favor of reform.[64] To one letter from a woman who described her guilt and shame over an abortion she had as a teenager, Playboy replied, "It is our hope that a general increase of openness and honesty about sex, more adequate sex education for teenagers . . . and a liberalization of abortion laws will spare other girls from experiences such as yours."[65]

With growing public debate, as evidenced in Playboy and throughout the culture, the abortion rights movement became truly national in scope in the late 1960s and particularly by 1970. Various states, including Colorado and New York, began to expand access to abortion.[66] By that time, the Playboy Foundation had for several years been working in support of expanded access to birth control and abortion. One of the foundation's important causes was the legal defense of leading birth control and abortion rights advocate Bill Baird, director of the Hempstead, New York, Parents' Aid Society.[67] With "Hef's enthusiastic approval"[68] the Playboy Foundation gave Baird legal assistance when he was prosecuted for distributing birth control and abortion information, which was illegal in a number of states.

Playboy began reporting on Baird's crusade when Baird himself wrote a long letter to the Forum describing the legal trouble he ran into distributing contraceptives and abortion information in New York, New Jersey, Massachusetts, and later Wisconsin. Editors responded with an update on state contraceptive laws, and pledged their support to Baird.[69] Baird and others, like representatives of Planned Parenthood and various other activist organizations, used the Forum to publicize abortion services.[70] Phone numbers, costs of procedures, and other relevant facts were submitted to Playboy for publication. The Forum became such a prominent proponent of legalization of abortion that at least one organization, the California Committee to Legalize Abortion, claimed it was "formed in response to an appeal published in [the] 'Forum.'"[71] Though Playboy was officially a men's magazine, activists clearly thought it an appropriate place to address the reproductive needs of American women.

Throughout the late 1960s and early 1970s, the Forum acted as a clearinghouse for information on the evolving struggle for abortion rights. In August 1967, it featured letters from individuals around the country who reported on changes in state laws. For example, representative Arthur H. Jones of North Carolina praised the liberalization of abortion laws in his state, as did representative Charles P. Kelley of Rhode Island.[72] Calling not for liberalization, which in many states required a woman to get approval by a committee of doctors before having an abortion, Dr. Nathan H. Rappaport of New York trumpeted repeal of all abortion laws. Rappaport, who had just completed his seventh prison term for performing abortions, described his ordeal and pleaded, "Every pregnant woman, single or married, should be able to get an abortion on demand, without being compelled to give any reason whatsoever for her decision."[73] In July 1970, a clergyman who regularly counseled women with unwanted pregnancies asked the Forum for information to offer women. *Playboy* responded with an update on all existing state laws, as well as information on obtaining an abortion overseas. Some organizations, like the Abortion Counseling, Information, and Referral Services of New York, used the Forum to advertise their services, provide practical information on abortion procedures, and tell readers how to contact them.[74]

In March 1970, the foundation contributed $10,000 to the Chicago Clergy Consultation Service on Problem Pregnancies.[75] The consultation service was created to counsel "desperate" pregnant women. Women could contact the service via phone, where they would be greeted by a recorded message that told them the contact information of counselors. From that point, they could find out where to obtain a safe abortion.[76] Calling it a "humanitarian . . . project,"[77] the Playboy Foundation avoided prosecution for aiding in such illegal activity by specifying that the consultation service must not use their funds to "[violate] . . . existing abortion laws,"[78] but rather "only for research and/or lobbying, or anything . . . that is legal."[79] They included hotlines to the Clergy Consultation Service, which offered abortion provider information in various states.

The overall philosophy of Hefner and of *Playboy* was staunchly in favor of individual rights, so support for women's rights in this area was logical, but *Playboy* had an additional motivation to support reproductive choice. As historian Linda Gordon points out, the twentieth century saw a rapidly increasing world population, and by the 1960s concerns over global overpopulation became a common public refrain in the United States. Attempting to minimize the influence of communism on unstable regions, American foreign policy increasingly focused on overpopulation in the third world. Gordon writes that even Planned Parenthood took up the language of global population control—as opposed to the language of women's rights—and waged a propaganda campaign to convince Americans to support the cause. She says that "population control was the defining element in the politics of reproduction" at that time, and that until the feminist movement of the late sixties revived birth control as a women's rights issue, most people and organizations used the terms "birth control" and "population control" interchangeably.[80]

Playboy supported the campaign for population control. The January 1965 issue included an article on overpopulation by Sir Julian Huxley. *Playboy* called the essay "an ominous warning of an imminent crisis."[81] In July 1968 it reported on the issue in "Newsfront," a column devoted to reporting on legal, social, and political developments relevant to topics discussed in the Forum. Editors noted, "Mankind's disastrous overbreeding continues at an alarming rate." In response to a reader's letter on the subject in that same issue, *Playboy* wrote, "Fortunately [for] the problem of population control. . . . Modern science has provided nearly perfect contraceptive and abortion techniques. . . . Where these techniques have been made available and where the population is educated to their benefits, encouraging progress has . . . been made in solving the problem."[82] Additionally, population control advocacy groups like Zero Population Growth repeatedly wrote to the Forum to argue for greater abortion rights, and in August 1970 *Playboy* featured an interview with the organization's founder, Paul Ehrlich, bestselling author of *The Population Bomb*. Clearly, *Playboy* had reason to support reproductive rights, as the issue—in the form of population control—was on the minds of many Americans in the late sixties. Hefner's motivation may or may not have been solely based on the rights of women. But as Linda Gordon argues, "only the rare birth control advocate in the period continued the feminist, individual rights, and sexual freedom agenda associated with earlier [and later] birth control thinking."[83] Regardless, *Playboy* vociferously promoted the message of reproductive freedom to its readers.

By the early 1970s, as the debate over abortion reached a cultural peak, the issue claimed a significant number of pages in *Playboy*. In September 1970, the magazine ran a piece by Dr. Robert Hall entitled "The Abortion Revolution." Described as "a doctor's chronicle of the bitter and continuing battle to abolish our obsolete laws against terminating pregnancy," Hall was an outspoken advocate for legalization.[84] Calling abortion laws "absurd," Hall echoed the typical stance of the *Playboy* Philosophy when he wrote that the contemporary debate surrounding the rights of the fetus had no place in a country founded on the principle of separation of church and state.[85] Hall argued that the question was not whether and at what point a fetus has a soul, but "whether women have a fundamental right to bear or not to bear children and, incidentally, whether a church should be free to impose its beliefs on the state."[86] He traced the emergence of the abortion struggle, ultimately arguing that the "abortion revolution" would be won as the American revolution had—because a change in favor of legalization had already taken place within the minds of Americans, allowing laws to follow.[87]

Reader response to Hall's article included a letter from Mary S. Calderone, a leading activist for sex education in the United States and head of SIECUS, who thanked *Playboy* for publishing the piece. Similar praise came from representative Leland H. Rayson of Illinois, who sponsored state abortion-reform bills, and noted psychotherapist Albert Ellis. Like the Hall article, Forum letters reflected the questions surrounding the larger cultural debate. Men and women, for and against legalization, expressed their views in *Playboy*. A woman from Indianapolis, whose name was withheld, described her experience of obtaining an abortion in 1969: "I did not kill an infant. . . . What the abortionist took from my body was an organism . . . Far from feeling like a murderess, I believe I saved two lives—my own and that of the man who made me pregnant."[88] Another woman said she was abandoned by the father of her child, and was unable to travel to get an abortion in time. She wrote, "It breaks my heart to think what must happen to women without financial resources when they get into this predicament."[89]

Playboy's unwavering stance on abortion caused some readers to react with condemnation. James Nichols of Cincinnati wrote to describe a letter, published in the *Washington Post*, from a woman who had regretted her abortion. Nichols chastised *Playboy* and other supporters of legalization, "May you live to regret your words as much as this woman regrets her abortion."[90] Los Angeles resident Richard J. Green described the "evil in killing the human fetus. . . . Once a nation becomes callous and indifferent to the importance of human life . . . there may be no hope for human life."[91]

In September 1971, *Playboy* included "A Special '*Playboy* Forum' Report" to aid women in obtaining abortions. In the report, the magazine surveyed changing state abortion laws but ultimately concluded that recent progress had stalled: "The holy war to protect the 'right to life' of the fetus gets into high gear—and American women are the victims."[92] The piece provided contact information for pro-choice organizations such as NARAL, and offered guidance on how "to obtain an abortion," which included practical information such as phone numbers for abortion consultation services in various states and overseas, and for states without such hotlines, *Playboy* listed national organizations like Planned Parenthood.[93] Further, updates on legal battles surrounding abortion and other contemporary issues were featured monthly in a portion of the Forum called "Newsfront."

Organizations that appeared in the Forum enjoyed increased visibility, and were often able to expand their reach. For instance, Ruth Proskauer Smith, president of the Abortion Rights Association of New York, noted that after her organization was mentioned in a previous issue, it received "several hundred requests from *Playboy* readers" for informational pamphlets on abortion rights.[94] Smith's organization was later able to revise and reprint a pamphlet on abortion providers because the "response from [*Playboy*] readers was so great."[95] Likewise, Roberta Schneiderman of Zero Population Growth Abortion Referral Service thanked *Playboy* for publishing phone numbers for the service: "we received over 700 calls from persons who said they found us through *Playboy*. . . . Please keep up the good work. Elective abortion couldn't have a better friend and we are enormously grateful."[96] Attorney Harriet F. Pilpel, board member of Planned Parenthood-World Population and of the American Civil Liberties Union, called reproductive freedom "a necessary and fundamental freedom in a democratic society," and she praised the Forum "for its significant role in reporting developments and opinions in science, law, morality and sociology as they relate to sex, reproduction, civil liberties and human rights."[97]

In 1972, Bill Baird continued his struggle for expanded access to birth control and abortion, and continued to be prosecuted in various states. He appealed to *Playboy*'s readers once again, this time drawing the feminist establishment into the debate. Baird claimed that he was shunned by "people who should have been my allies. . . . Not one feminist group would respond to my request that it file an *amicus curiae* brief on my behalf. . . . The ultimate absurdity came when National Organization for Women founder Betty

Friedan told newspaper reporters, 'It's been rumored that Bill Baird is a CIA agent.' I am grateful to the Playboy Foundation and to many others who have helped."[98]

After the Supreme Court ruled in favor a woman's right to an abortion in the 1973 case *Roe v. Wade*, *Playboy* celebrated the decision and the role it saw itself as playing in changing the social dialogue surrounding the issue. An editorial published a few months after the ruling noted that "*Playboy* joined many national and local organizations in the effort that climaxed in the U.S. Supreme Court abortion decision" and that already "in 1965, 'The *Playboy* Forum' opened a dialog with *Playboy*'s readers on abortion" while "the Playboy Foundation began assisting the right-to-abortion movement in 1966." The editorial also spelled out clearly the relationship between abortion rights and the *Playboy* Philosophy more generally: "The Court's decision . . . holds out hope for changes in other areas in which the law infringes on individual rights and liberties."[99]

It was not just the issue of abortion that inspired *Playboy* to work toward feminist goals. Future Supreme Court justice Ruth Bader Ginsberg, then a representative for the American Civil Liberties Union's Women's Rights Project, acknowledged in the Forum her gratitude for the foundation's contribution to the fund, which eventually totaled $100,000.[100] The project focused on "research and litigation . . . in the areas of abortion, credit discrimination, sexual discrimination, divorce and child custody."[101] Echoing a growing concern in the culture, from 1973 to 1977 the foundation contributed nearly $13,000 to various organizations working for expanded rights and protections for rape victims. Recipients included the Center for Women Policy Studies, the Illinois Citizens Committee for Victim Assistance, the Midwest Women's Center, and the Joann Little Defense Fund, which was set up to aid a female prisoner who killed a prison guard when he attempted to rape her.[102] Ironically, the foundation paid $1,000 in legal expenses to the Iowa ACLU for their defense of the Grinnell College students whose nude campus protest against *Playboy* led to charges of public indecency.[103]

Additional contributions to women's causes and organizations included: $13,500 in support of Title VII equal employment legislation; $1,500 to the National Women's Education Fund, which encouraged "women to participate in the political process"; $3,000 to the American Women's Economic Development Corporation, which assisted "women in starting their own businesses and in job performance and advancement"; and $1,500 to the

Women's Labor History Film Project.[104] Other recipients of foundation support included the League of Women Voters, The National Conference of Woman and the Law, and the Equal Rights Amendment.[105]

For many feminists, however, Playboy's philanthropy could only go so far. Controversy erupted in 1971 when the foundation offered legal support to the National Organization for Women. Instead NOW asked for one night's profit from all Playboy Clubs. The organization publicized their request in order to put pressure on Playboy, but Hefner refused to go along, calling it "crude extortion." NOW went on to declare that "no amount of money 'would compensate for the low rating of the source. . . . [T]o accept money from the [Playboy Foundation] would only contaminate us."[106] The conflict caused Barbara A. Townley of New Orleans to write, "I'm wholeheartedly in favor of women's rights, but I don't think Hugh Hefner even remotely resembles the Antichrist. . . . Thanks for your offer to help. Perhaps when the women's movement . . . starts going after the real dragons, we can get together."[107]

If some feminists in the seventies rejected foundation money, others accepted it as reparations, or as a necessary evil in difficult economic times, or they simply accepted it. Noting that funding for women's projects was sparse in the early seventies, Marjorie Fine Knowles, writing for the Women's Studies Newsletter, promoted the Playboy Foundation among organizations that were willing to assist or work toward feminist goals.[108] Likewise, when the foundation paid the printing costs of the Dayton Women's Center's service directory, scholar Judith Ezekiel notes that there was "surprisingly little debate."[109] An ACLU board member said of foundation money, "How much is hand wash and how much is real, I don't know. . . . but I'll put up with it."[110] At the height of the women's movement, Playboy's money inspired debate. There was no consensus among feminists.[111]

Playboy's stance on abortion rights and feminism, in the magazine and through its foundation, paralleled the growth of the women's movement in the U.S. national consciousness. There can be no doubt that while Americans themselves were waking up to the demands being made by feminists, Playboy magazine served as a progressive channel of debate over women's liberation. Hefner believed, and still believes, that he was in the vanguard of sexual emancipation for both men and women. Though the politics of his magazine fell short of a truly feminist agenda, Playboy nonetheless contributed to the cultural negotiation of newly emerging femininities. Despite some critics' claims of sexism and sexual objectification, the magazine did not resist or even lag behind the liberal American mainstream in its support for women's rights. As debates within the movement demonstrated, feminists themselves questioned the appropriateness of traditional notions of femininity and cultural customs of sexuality in a changing social and domestic landscape. Regardless of Hefner's motivations for supporting feminist causes such as access to birth control and abortion, women's activists shared many of his goals, and those feminist causes were promoted to his readership along with the centerfolds.

Whatever the imprint *Playboy* has left on the collective memory of American culture, reducing its treatment of femininity to a discussion of objectification, as many critics have done, obscures the complexity and contradiction of the magazine. Certainly, much of the traditional critique is valid. In its insistence on conventional gender difference, *Playboy* refused to acknowledge the political challenge to its centerfolds. In fixating on the radical minority of feminists, as he often did, Hefner missed an opportunity to focus his readers' attention on his support for the broader liberal wing of the movement, which might have reduced the feminist rage against his magazine. But at the height of *Playboy*'s popularity, people looked to the magazine as an important journalistic vehicle of the times. Along with the visual messages of female objectification that Hefner may have sent, he also sent equally potent messages of liberal activism that could not have been lost on many readers. Letters that supported *Playboy*'s position as a progressive publication demonstrated that contemporaries often saw the magazine as a whole package, one that served up not only titillating centerfolds but also important political agendas. Indeed, as the women's movement emerged as a national force in the late 1960s, *Playboy* positioned itself as a supporter of civil liberties for all, regardless of gender. And as sexuality became part of the public debate, it also became political, in *Playboy* and in the larger culture.

Conclusion

We do live, now, in a *Playboy* world.[1]

HUGH HEFNER, 2006

*W*hen Gloria Steinem faced off with Hugh Hefner for Mc-Call's magazine in 1970, she got the opportunity that editor Barbara Nellis claims many feminists wanted—the chance to confront the founder of *Playboy*. Steinem criticized the magazine for its objectification of women and its relentless consumerism. She asserted that Hefner's rants against American Puritanism were merely "beating a dead horse." Steinem argued that the battle over censorship and repression was irrelevant: "People are getting killed in the streets, in Vietnam, and you're fighting the Post Office." But even she had a surprisingly complicated view of *Playboy*.

Though Steinem clearly did not support the magazine, she acknowledged Hefner's influence, calling him "one of the most powerful men in the country." Given his cultural reach, she charged Hefner with responsibility for better addressing the ills of the nation, saying, "I think the sexual revolution is going on fine without you. I'm just not sure the rest of the country is." In spite of her intense political opposition to *Playboy*, Steinem granted, "You're partly responsible for women's lib in a way. You supplanted brute strength as a symbol of maleness with sports cars and appliances. If men don't play their warrior role, women don't have to play their mother-of-warriors role."[2]

At the height of anti-Vietnam protest, a challenge to the warrior mentality was significant to progressives.

Regardless of Steinem's minor ideological concessions, she was certainly no fan of *Playboy*, calling it "boyish, undeveloped, anti-sensual, vicarious, and sad."[3] While her comments suggested that *Playboy* did more harm than good, her insight into Hefner's reformulation of masculinity was apt. Steinem knew that the magazine had offered the country a new standard of manhood, even if for her that ideal was based on shallow materialism. In retrospect, Hefner was also accurate in his summation of many contemporary sociopolitical trends during the interview. He presciently observed, "We've seen a remarkable shift toward the right in the past year [after the election of Richard Nixon] and there's been an immediate effect on the Supreme Court and on what kind of bills come up in Congress. Conservative is a very kind word for it. Antiracial, antisocial, antisexual—it goes across the whole spectrum."[4] With the domination of conservatism and the religious right in the last quarter of the twentieth century, it seems that Hefner was not as politically irrelevant as Steinem portrayed him.

As the 1970s came to a close, *Playboy* and much of the women's movement remained diametrically opposed. The emergence of the antiporn faction of the movement in the late seventies and early eighties, led by women like Andrea Dworkin and Catharine MacKinnon, exacerbated tensions between Hefner and some activists, as *Playboy* became associated with hardcore publications like *Hustler*. Antiporn activist Gail Dines describes Hefner as a sanitized version of the typical, sleazy pornographer. She argues that *Playboy* helps to "subordinate woman as a class" as it relegates Playmates to the status of commodities "to be used and discarded."[5] But for other feminists like Betty Friedan, a truce with *Playboy*, or at least a better understanding, eventually emerged.

In 1992, Friedan, who had likewise clashed with more radical segments of the movement over issues like sexuality, agreed to an interview with *Playboy*. Signaling just how far the magazine's relationship to the women's movement had come, *Playboy* called the godmother of liberal feminism "the perfect subject for the 30th anniversary of the *Playboy Interview*."[6] Friedan, one of the activists Barbara Nellis had unsuccessfully tried to recruit in the early seventies, had a nuanced view of *Playboy* twenty years later. Like so many feminists, she argued that historically the club Bunnies and the Playmates "denied the personhood of women" because they portrayed women as objects in the service of men. But Friedan also said that the magazine had come a long way since those days—surmising that she would not have agreed to an interview then—and noted that she found violence against women in modern popular culture much more problematic than the *Playboy* centerfolds.[7]

Friedan claimed, just as Hefner always had, that she saw nothing wrong with the sexual objectification of women: "I suppose sometimes women are sex objects—and men are too, by the way. It's the definition of women just as sex objects that bothers me. Women can celebrate themselves as sex objects . . . as far as I'm concerned." Additionally, she suggested that the Bunnies and Playmates of the earlier generation were harmful because they were part of an overall culture that dehumanized women: "the image came at us from everywhere—from *Playboy*, from the ads and programs on television. . . . That is why it was objectionable. . . . That was the feminine mystique, when women were second-class people. . . . The Playboy Bunny image of women's sexuality was an extreme Rorschach for a culture that completely denied the personhood of women."[8]

In what some have called the post-feminist era, Friedan developed an alternative view of *Playboy*'s brand of femininity: "[the] centerfold is fine. . . . it is not pornographic, though many of my sisters would disagree. It's harmless. . . . [T]here are things far worse than the centerfolds."[9] She called contemporary feminist protest against *Playboy* "a waste of time." Like Hefner, she prioritized "the liberation of human sexuality, not the repression of it. Most of all, I am for freedom of speech."[10] Years after *Playboy* and the women's movement clashed over the meaning of liberation, each side adamant that the other would destroy its sexual potential, one of the movement's most prominent leaders seemed to make peace with *Playboy*.

In spite of decades of feminist critique of the magazine, and regardless of any rapprochement, *Playboy* has become resonant with many young women—women of a generation highly suspicious of the label "feminist." It is unlikely that the largely young and female audience of the E! network's reality hit *The Girls Next Door* are familiar with *Playboy*'s history. They would not remember the magazine's complex mix of hedonistic bachelorism, consumerism, and quasi-feminism. Regarding *Playboy*'s modern popularity with women, writer Ariel Levy has a theory, and it has little to do with feminism. In *Female Chauvinist Pigs: Women and the Rise of Raunch Culture*, Levy argues that the modern ubiquity of porn culture is the result of women's

figure 11. Hefner and the original stars of the hit reality show *The Girls Next Door.* Reproduced by special permission of *Playboy* magazine. Copyright by Playboy.

embrace of their own objectification. Levy sees the popularity of *Playboy* among women as part of "the country's reinvigorated interest in all things bimbo."[11] Her assessment reflects the continued resentment many feminists feel toward Hefner and his magazine. That antagonism is based not only on the traditional feminist critique of *Playboy*, like the one offered by Steinem in 1970, but also on the lifestyle that Hefner continues to promote—that of a "septuagenarian babe-magnet . . . and the surreal world of celebrities, multiple 'girlfriends,' and the non-stop bikini parties [Hefner has] set up around himself."[12]

Complicating a feminist appraisal of *Playboy* is Hugh Hefner's daughter, Christie Hefner. From 1982 to 2009, she operated as the president, chair, and then CEO of Playboy Enterprises, Inc. (PEI).[13] Christie is a self-avowed feminist, and indeed has devoted much energy to promoting women's interests in business and politics. For some, this fact makes an all-out attack on *Playboy*'s gender politics more difficult. But there remain critics who are thoroughly unimpressed with Christie Hefner's success or her feminism. Like her father, his magazine, and his money—often perceived as tainted—Christie's politics do not necessarily make up for her promotion of hetero-male sexuality. Ariel Levy considers her a female chauvinist pig, while Steinem and Barbara Ehrenreich have likewise dismissed her, although *Ms.* magazine once admitted that Christie was a "tireless pro-choice campaigner."[14] Regardless of one's view of *Playboy*, though, Christie is undoubtedly one of the country's most successful women executives.

In 2008, *Forbes* magazine ranked Christie as one of the world's most powerful women.[15] Her many years as CEO of PEI is a record among women heads of publicly traded companies, and has made her one of the most sought-after speakers in the business world.[16] She is widely credited with bringing PEI "back from the brink of financial disaster" in the 1980s by streamlining the corporation, cutting costs, and refocusing company investments in burgeoning industries like cable television, video, and eventually the Internet.[17] Her father was delighted to entrust the company to Christie. Phi Beta Kappa at Brandeis University, she proved to have the discipline and leadership skills necessary to revive the company when it seemed that the world, and the sexual revolution, had passed it by. More than that, the rise of a powerful woman to head the quintessential men's magazine was a triumph for *Playboy*. The elder Hefner repeatedly said, "There is something fascinating and quite wonderful about the heir to *Playboy* being a woman, not a man. If it had at all been calculated, it couldn't have been better. . . . if she hadn't been born into this, the promotions department would have invented her."[18]

Christie is quite different from Hugh, in both style and substance. In contrast to her father's flamboyant sexual lifestyle, Christie is refined and private, and perceived by the business world as a shrewd, serious executive. Regularly donning conservative suits and pearls, she sees her aptitude for business as a compliment to Hefner's creative vision.[19] She grew up distant from her father, who left his young family in the 1950s to pursue the bachelor lifestyle he so enthusiastically articulated in the pages of *Playboy*. By the end of her college years in the mid-seventies, Christie came to accept the reality of Hefner's life and personality, and the two developed a close relationship. Christie said she "admired her father for his intelligence, kindness, and progressive social views."[20]

Hefner hired her as an assistant in 1975. She then became president of the company in 1982 and CEO in 1988. By that time, Hefner and his company were suffering in part from a conservative Reagan-era backlash against sexual and cultural liberation, and readership began to wane. As profits plunged,

figure 12.   Christie Hefner. Reproduced by special permission of *Playboy* magazine. Copyright by Playboy.

Christie took the helm and reoriented the company by successfully launching a softcore cable and video venture aimed primarily at heterosexual couples.[21] She then became a publishing pioneer in crossing over from print to the Internet in the mid-nineties.[22] One of the primary ways in which Christie hoped to update *Playboy* was through a vigorous appeal to women with the inclusion of more celebrities in the magazine and particularly through the marketing of *Playboy*-branded consumer items for women, which by 2008 raked in $800 million for the company in the United States and overseas.[23] Moreover, the Playboy Clubs Christie closed in the eighties due to financial drain reopened in Las Vegas and in international resorts like Macao after the turn of the millennium.

In spite of Christie's appeal to women, she has added fuel to the feminist anti-*Playboy* fire. In 2001, as PEI struggled to keep up in an increasingly raunchy market, father and daughter Hefner finally took up the business of hardcore video pornography. Hugh Hefner had long resisted this move—since the days of the pubic wars in the early seventies—but financial pressures convinced him of the utility of going hardcore. Apparently he had to persuade Christie, but ultimately the venture happened when PEI purchased three X-rated pay-per-view networks.[24]

As contradictory as the magazine in her charge, Christie Hefner has emerged as not just a successful businesswoman, making money by selling female sex, but also a prominent feminist activist and advocate for women in the workforce. Throughout her career, she has supported the Equal Rights Amendment and reproductive rights, helping to establish the pro-choice organization Emily's List.[25] She is a cofounder of the Committee of 200, a group that promotes women's business leadership, and has worked for the American Civil Liberties Union.[26] Over the years, some feminists, and indeed much of the mainstream media and business world, have come to celebrate her commitment to liberal causes.[27] Betty Friedan considered Christie a friend and declared her "marvelously supportive of many causes—not only free speech but of the rights of women."[28] Feminist attorney Gloria Allred has called Christie "one of the most articulate, committed, hardworking feminists in the country."[29] Journalist Catherine Flannery, writing for the *Toronto Star*, deemed her "true to [the] feminist cause," while the prominent television news program *60 Minutes* once described Christie as a "successful feminist businesswoman."[30] Even longtime *Playboy* critic Gloria Steinem "brought [Christie] onto the board of Voters for Choice."[31]

By the time of her retirement in 2009, many commentators could note without irony Christie's devotion to feminism and liberal activism. The decidedly unsexy American Library Association hosted her as keynote speaker at its annual conference, calling her "a passionate advocate of freedom of expression, social justice, equal rights and opportunities for women."[32] The organization Women on the Web looked to her for comment not on the role of the Playmates in a post-feminist world, but for her perspective on the *Lilly Ledbetter Fair Pay Act*.[33] In 2003, she received the University of Illinois at Chicago's Family Business Council Leadership Award and has recently become a regular commentator on the cable news circuit.[34] In the new millennium, it seems that Christie Hefner has become as mainstream as the magazine her father founded more than five decades ago.[35]

Fiercely loyal, Christie has rigorously affirmed the vision of gender and sexuality articulated by Hugh Hefner. When asked about the conflict that so many feminists see in *Playboy*'s centerfolds, Christie reiterates the party line. She, like her father, says that the Playmates merely demonstrated that "good girls like sex, too." She argues that one of *Playboy*'s important contributions to American social standards was its "departure [from] the prevailing Madonna/whore dichotomy" that placed women in two opposing, narrow sexual categories. Instead, she claims that *Playboy* told men they could "*both* admire and desire women.*" Christie Hefner argues that *Playboy*'s "[scrupulous] good taste" in presenting the Playmates was crucial to its construction of womanhood. She says that the magazine, "[attracted] the most beautiful woman, including the most famous women, [and] the best photographers. [*Playboy*'s] gone out of its way to present the models in a way that humanizes them . . . by telling their stories, by supporting them in promotional and charitable ways, where they are actually out there as individuals, talking about whatever it is they are interested in."[36] She points out, "the perspective of the photographer and the reader . . . is adoring and positive." There is no sense of shame, as if someone is "looking through a keyhole" at something "dirty and naughty." Rather, she insists, the attitude taken in, and toward, the centerfolds is "sun-lit . . . healthy and natural."[37]

Regarding feminism, however, Christie contradicts Hugh Hefner's self-characterization.[38] She says that she does not consider her father a feminist, which Christie defines as "someone committed to insuring equality of treatment and opportunity for women."[39] Rather, she says that he is a humanist, "someone who looks to people to build a better world, as opposed to waiting for the hereafter," and "who respects . . . people, regardless of what [their] differences might be."[40] She acknowledges that historically *Playboy* was a "progressive [political] ally of the women's movement, but [as] a men's magazine . . . it won't portray women as *Ms.* magazine would."[41] Christie Hefner recognizes that her father "worked to change that world" of the postwar years, "but was also a product of that world."[42] In other words, she believes that *Playboy* was, compared to the media and culture around it, ahead of the pack in terms of gender politics. But her statement also implies that her father did not exist outside the context of his time and in fact his magazine reflected some of the bias of that pre-feminist society.

Fifty years later, Hefner's magazine has gone from an ambitious kitchen table project to a successful magazine, from an empire to a cultural institution. Ultimately, its meaning has shifted from the hipster bachelor of the early sixties to the Carrie Bradshaw bachelorette of the new millennium.

Most of the young women who purchase bejeweled rabbit charms or go to movie theaters to see films like *The House Bunny* have no awareness of the early gender politics of the magazine. But from a consumer perspective, the contemporary popularity of *Playboy* among women makes sense, because it has grown from *Playboy*'s status as a consumer icon. Christie Hefner believes that the television show *The Girls Next Door* "[solidified] the relevance and appeal of the brand as a quality, stylish, sexy brand for women." In other words, she argues, "You see young women being very comfortable with their sexuality, and I actually think that's a very positive change."[43]

It is the legacy of the early decades of the magazine, when *Playboy* offered a thoughtful, if conflicted, renegotiation of gender and heterosexuality that provides the context within which the modern incarnation of Hefner's empire has become relevant to women. Regardless of the motivation of *Playboy*'s modern female fans, whether it is internalized objectification, as Levy argues, or it is a healthier attitude toward sex, as Christie Hefner insists, the link between *Playboy* and modern femininity is not surprising. From an editorial perspective, the appeal of the magazine to women is justified. The magazine supported liberal feminist goals like equal rights, reproductive freedom, and it challenged the double standard. But however adamant Christie Hefner or her father may be in claiming allegiance with women, the continued ire of feminists like Ariel Levy shows that whatever *Playboy* has done to advance women's issues has not been enough to overcome the perceived objectification of the centerfolds and the antiwoman rants of *Playboy*'s early years.

As is always the case regarding questions of gender, sexuality, and feminism, notions of power dictate one's perspective on *Playboy*. Critics of the magazine prioritize the power inherent in its creation, that is the authority claimed by Hugh Hefner to define standards of femininity, beauty, and male sexual desire. Likewise, some feminist observers lament the passivity of the frozen, photographed women in the hands of the male reader. Alternatively, supporters see the centerfold models as empowered and in control of their bodies and sexuality in a capitalist society. Each actor—the creator, the consumer, and the woman in between them—exerts a particular brand of authority. Determining which version reigns supreme depends on one's politics. Although as one journalist put it, "feminism and *Playboy* [are] one of the great arch-enemy pairings in American culture," this book makes clear that there is no unified feminist position on (or against) *Playboy*, and there probably never was.[44] Just as feminism itself has been a diverse movement made up of a variety of goals and perspectives, there are likewise disparate feminist impressions of Hefner's magazine and money, demonstrating the potential utility of Playboy not just for men, but for many women as well.

Playboy remains a top seller among men's magazines in the new century.[45] Furthermore, American culture has largely embraced the version of gender and heterosexuality promoted by Playboy in the postwar years, and the country continues its—and the magazine's—celebration of the rampant consumerism central to creating those identities. Men are no longer required to don gray flannel and commute to their office jobs in order to provide for wives and children. Today, men can take up the modern playboy existence—that of the metrosexual, an urban heterosexual who spends more time and money on fashion and facials than does his girlfriend. The sophisticated jet-setting lifestyle promoted in Playboy fifty years ago has become an acceptable standard for many American men.

The changes for women have been more dramatic. At the turn of the millennium, women have far outpaced the social, economic, and political status of midcentury Playmates. Women work outside the home, may remain single and childless, are economically independent, and can have active, hedonistic sex lives if they choose. In spite of Hefner's fears that feminism would destroy differences between the sexes, early twenty-first-century standards of beauty still promote sexy femininity. Indeed, if Hefner saw Sex and the City's celebration of his empire as a victory for him, as he declared in a recent interview, the show itself might be evidence of the extent to which American culture has embraced the type of femininity that Playboy promoted years ago. The program's characters, Carrie, Miranda, Samantha, and Charlotte, resembled manifestations of Hefner's ideal—beautiful, feminine, financially stable career women who were highly invested in exploring both their sexuality and consumer society.

In the midst of all this change, Playboy has survived the staid 1950s and the progressive political challenges of the sixties and seventies. And in spite of the triumph of conservatism and the religious right—among the very forces that Hefner perceived himself battling—in the eighties and nineties, Hefner and his empire have persisted. Biographer Steven Watts argues, "Hefner's vision of America as the land of self-fulfillment has been realized in many ways. His notions of sexual happiness and material comfort, pleasure and leisure, maleness and femaleness, of individuals freed from many of the restraints of family and religion have become commonplace."[46] *Playboy* has emerged more than fifty years from its founding as a cultural phenomenon. In the process, *Playboy* presented to America an inclusive sexual agenda. That agenda promoted liberation for all, both men and women alike, and offered its readers a useable guide to the rapidly changing postwar landscape. While gender antagonism was a part of the magazine from its inception, particularly in the form of antimarriage diatribes and the rantings of Philip Wiley, there were myriad other messages of compassion, respect, and equality in *Playboy*'s pages.

Not merely the "flight from commitment" commonly attributed to the magazine, *Playboy* advised readers to honor the commitments that they made to one another. Monogamy was not shunned in the magazine's advice columns. Rather, *Playboy* reinforced and promoted the obligations and responsibilities traditionally associated with romantic relationships. What was new in *Playboy*, however, was that these conventional values were updated with progressive views of sexuality. The double standard that shunned female sexual expression outside of marriage was condemned as unfair and inequitable. The Advisor and the Forum discussed sexual differences, including homosexuality, with respect.

Though *Playboy* held relationships in high esteem, one of the magazine's important points was that men should delay romantic commitments until they had a period of personal exploration and maturation—another trend that, fifty years later, has become accepted practice for many Americans. For that time of independence in men's lives, likely during their twenties, *Playboy* offered itself as a lifestyle guide. Regular columns on fashion, cooking, and decorating instructed men on how to navigate the continually rising waters of postwar consumerism. But in that process, the sophisticated ease with which the playboy was supposed to conduct his life was simultaneously undermined by the magazine's intense consumer drive, placing masculinity under harsh scrutiny. Not only women, but men as well were expected to self-consciously evaluate their bodies, their clothes, their hair, and their apartments with potential lovers in mind.

The other side of *Playboy*'s construction of gender was its famous centerfolds. Typical condemnation of *Playboy* deems them objectified and degraded, but what most observers have not taken into consideration is the challenge these images posed to postwar standards of sexuality. In the 1950s, women were expected to walk a fine line between attractiveness and healthy sexual development, but to do so only within the confines of marriage. The Playmates crossed that line with joyous enthusiasm. They, like the Advisor, told *Playboy*'s readers that women were just as sexual as men. Furthermore, the wholesome, all-American Playmates declared that it was acceptable for women, even the nice ones, to like sex.

No matter how compatible *Playboy* might have been with a version of liberated feminine sexuality in the fifties and early sixties, the feminist movement of the 1970s challenged Hefner's cultural relationship to women. *Playboy*'s central article on the movement, "Up Against the Wall, Male Chauvinist Pig," lambasted radicals, and swept liberal feminists into the critical heap as well. But Hefner's personal stance on the movement, as well as that of many of his editors, was in favor of much of the mainstream feminist platform. The magazine contributed thousands of dollars to women's causes, and was especially vocal in support of reproductive rights. But Hefner overreacted to the stance of militants who critiqued femininity and heterosexual seduction and thus helped to solidify his own misplaced reputation for antifeminism. As archival documents demonstrate, however, Hefner was actually an unlikely ally of liberal feminism.

In spite of traditional feminist criticism, *Playboy*'s gender politics defy easy categorization. Gender antagonism and sophomoric fears of commitment were certainly part of the *Playboy* universe, but there was more to that world than antimarriage rants and available women. A look at the whole of Hefner's product makes clear that *Playboy* was complex and contradictory. As Christie Hefner has argued, "The magazine presents women in a lot of different ways, depending on what pages you are reading."[47] Hefner's goal was to produce a sexy, consumer magazine for men. Therefore, as Christie admits, *Playboy* was never going to present women in the way a feminist magazine would have.[48] But, maybe in spite of himself, Hefner offered his readers a new, inclusive heterosexual agenda—one that included sexual pleasure for both men and women. It was a credo that was embraced by the American mainstream, and would come to dominate the American sexual scene for the next fifty years.

$\mathcal{N}$otes

INTRODUCTION

1. *Time*, "Think Clean," March 3, 1967.

2. Gloria Steinem, "What Playboy Doesn't Know about Women Could Fill a Book," *McCall's*, October 1970, 139.

3. Steinem, "What *Playboy* Doesn't Know," 140.

4. Katie Buitrago, "What Sort of Woman Reads *Playboy*," *Chicago Reader*, February 4, 2010.

5. James Gilbert, *Men in the Middle: Searching for Masculinity in the 1950s* (Chicago: University of Chicago Press, 2005), 191.

6. J. Robert Moskin, "Why Do Women Dominate Him?" in *The Decline of the American Male*, by the editors of *Look* magazine (New York: Random House, 1958), 4, 22.

7. Elaine Tyler May, *Homeward Bound: American Families in the Cold War Era* (New York: Basic Books, 1988), 94.

8. Susan Douglas, *Where the Girls Are: Growing Up Female with the Mass Media* (New York: New York Times Books, 1994) 61, 63.

9. For alternative readings of the 1950s, see Joel Foreman, *The Other Fifties: Interrogating Midcentury Icons* (Urbana: University of Illinois Press, 1997).

10. Bill Osgerby, *Playboys in Paradise: Masculinity, Youth and Leisure-Style in Modern America* (New York: Oxford, 2001), 149.

11. Brooks Barnes, "The Loin in Winter: Hefner Reflects, and Grins," *New York Times*, October 23, 2009.

12. John D'Emilio and Estelle Freedman, *Intimate Matters: A History of Sexuality in America* (New York: Harper and Row, 1988). For more on the role of the media in creating and perpetuating sexual standards, see Chrys Ingraham, *White Weddings: Romancing Heterosexuality in Popular Culture* (New York: Routledge, 1999).

13. Jonathan Ned Katz, *The Invention of Heterosexuality* (New York: Dutton, 1995), and George Chauncey, *Gay New York: Gender, Urban Culture, and the Making of the Gay Male World* (New York: Basic Books, 1994).

14. Because of the editorial focus of this research, the Playboy Club Bunnies are not extensively discussed here. For more on the Bunnies, see Gloria Steinem, "I Was a Playboy Bunny," reprinted in *Outrageous Acts and Everyday Rebellions* (New York: Henry Holt and Company, 1995); Kathryn Lee Scott, *The Bunny Years* (New York: Pomegranate Press, 1999); and Steven Watts, *Mr. Playboy: Hugh Hefner and the American Dream* (Hoboken: Wiley, 2008), chapters 8 and 12.

15. Bill Davidson, "Czar of the Bunny Empire," *Saturday Evening Post*, April 28, 1962, 34.

16. "The Chimes of the First Methodist Church," February 21, 1965. PRC, carton 2325, folder "Healthy Sex Society."

17. Digby Diehl, "Q&A Hugh Hefner," *Los Angeles Times*, February 27, 1972, W20.

18. *Time*, "Think Clean," March 3, 1967.

19. *Time*, "Hefner's Grandchild," August 28, 1972.

20. *Time*, "Adventures in the Skin Trade," July 30, 1973.

21. Watts, *Mr. Playboy*, 3, 83.

22. For more, see Thomas Weyr, *Reaching for Paradise: The Playboy Vision of America* (New York: New York Times Books, 1978), 248–311.

CHAPTER ONE

1. Author interview with Hugh M. Hefner, November 3, 2006, Los Angeles, CA. For more on Hefner's biography, see Russell Miller, *Bunny: The Real Story of Playboy* (New York: Holt, Rinehart, and Winston, 1984); Steven Watts, *Mr. Playboy: Hugh Hefner and the American Dream* (Hoboken: John Wiley and Sons, Inc., 2008); and Thomas Weyr, *Reaching for Paradise: The Playboy Vision of America* (New York: New York Times Books, 1978).

2. Author interview with Hefner.

3. Author interview with Hefner. Hefner is intensely focused on the issue of American sexual repression. In writing *Playboy*'s version of American sexual history, editor Jim Petersen says that he had to convince Hefner to focus on a "biography of sex" rather than a "history of repression." James R. Petersen, *The Century of Sex: Playboy's History of the Sexual Revolution, 1900–1999* (New York: Grove Press, 1999), 3.

4. Author interview with Hefner.

5. Author interview with Hefner.

6. Bill Davidson, "Czar of the Bunny Empire," *Saturday Evening Post*, April 28, 1962, 34.

7. Author interview with Hefner.

8. Author interview with Hefner.

9. Author interview with Jim Petersen, February 2, 2006, Evanston, IL.

10. Various historians have noted a recurring sense of identity crisis among Ameri-

can men, not just in the postwar years, but also especially in the 1890s, due to similarly shifting cultural, economic, and political winds. Gail Bederman, however, complicates this idea by arguing that masculine crisis can only be perceived if we accept the notion of manhood as a "fixed essence" rather than an "ongoing ideological process." Gail Bederman, *Manliness and Civilization: A Cultural History of Gender and Race in the United States, 1880–1917* (Chicago: University of Chicago Press, 1996), 11. Much work has been done on the topic of masculinity. For a few references, see also Harry Brod, ed., *The Making of Masculinities: The New Men's Studies* (Boston: Allen & Unwin, 1987); Barbara Ehrenreich, *The Hearts of Men: American Dreams and the Flight from Commitment* (Garden City, NY: Anchor Press/Doubleday, 1983); Susan Faludi, *Stiffed: The Betrayal of the American Man* (New York: William Morrow and Company, Inc., 1999); Lynne Segal, *Slow Motion: Changing Masculinities, Changing Men* (New Brunswick: Rutgers University Press, 1990).

11. For various women's challenges to the gender status quo, see Joanne Meyerowitz, *Not June Cleaver: Women and Gender in Postwar America, 1945–1960* (Philadelphia: Temple University Press, 1994), and Wini Breines, *Young, White, and Miserable* (Chicago: University of Chicago Press, 1992). For a discussion of women's changing economic status, see Alice Kessler-Harris, *In Pursuit of Equity: Women, Men, and the Quest for Economic Citizenship in 20th-Century America* (New York: Oxford University Press, 2001).

12. This term will be discussed later in this chapter.

13. Susan Douglas, *Where the Girls Are: Growing Up Female with the Mass Media* (New York: Random House, 1995), 47–48.

14. Beth L. Bailey, *From Front Porch to Back Seat: Courtship in Twentieth-Century America* (Baltimore: Johns Hopkins University Press, 1989), 34.

15. Bailey, *From Front Porch*, 38.

16. Bailey, *From Front Porch*, 38.

17. Bailey, *From Front Porch*, 38.

18. Bailey, *From Front Porch*, 41.

19. David Savran, *Taking It Like a Man: White Masculinity, Masochism, and Contemporary American Culture* (Princeton: Princeton University Press, 1998), 47.

20. Arthur Schlesinger, Jr., "The Crisis of American Masculinity," *Esquire*, November 1958, 63.

21. K. A. Cuordileone, *Manhood and American Political Culture in the Cold War* (New York: Routledge, 2005), 17.

22. The book presented three essays that had originally appeared in the magazine. J. Robert Moskin, "Why Do Women Dominate Him?" in *The Decline of the American Male*, by the editors of *Look* magazine (New York: Random House, 1958), 24.

23. David Riesman, *The Lonely Crowd* (New Haven: Yale University Press, 1950).

24. William H. Whyte, Jr., *The Organization Man* (New York: Anchor Books, 1957), 439.

25. K. A. Cuordileone, "'Politics in an Age of Anxiety: Cold War Political Culture and the Crisis in American Masculinity, 1949–1960," *Journal of American History* 87 (September 2000): 525.

26. See Elaine Tyler May, *Homeward Bound: American Families in the Cold War Era* (New York: Basic Books, 1999).

27. *New York Times*, "Virile Democracy Is Urged by the President as Protection against Perils from Abroad," December 12, 1948, 4.

28. Cuordileone, "Crisis in American Masculinity," 529.

29. May, *Homeward Bound*, 94.

30. Savran, *Taking It Like a Man*, 48.

31. James Gilbert, *Men in the Middle: Searching for Masculinity in the 1950s* (Chicago: University of Chicago Press, 2005), 2–3.

32. Gilbert, *Men in the Middle*, chapter 7.

33. In fact, Gilbert devotes a chapter in *Men in the Middle* to *Playboy*'s influential editorial director, A. C. Spectorsky, as an alternative version of postwar masculinity, 189–214 (chapter 9).

34. Cuordileone, *Manhood and American Political Culture*, 39.

35. Hugh Hefner, "Open Letter from California," *Playboy*, December 1953, 27.

36. Miller, *Bunny*, 22–31.

37. Watts, *Mr. Playboy*, 2.

38. Watts, *Mr. Playboy*, 58.

39. Editorial, *Playboy*, December 1953, 3.

40. Miller, *Bunny*, ix.

41. Editorial comment, *Playboy*, December 1953, n.p.

42. Editorial comment, *Playboy*, August 1954, 3.

43. This will be discussed further in chapter 2.

44. Bill Osgerby, "Muscular Manhood and Salacious Sleaze: The Singular World of the 1950s Macho Pulps," in *Containing America: Cultural Production and Consumption in 50s America*, ed. Nathan Abrams and Julie Hughes (New York: Continuum, 2005), 125.

45. Miller, *Bunny*, 17.

46. *Playboy*, "Miss Gold-Digger of 1953," December 1953, 7–8.

47. Burt Zollo, "Open Season on Bachelors," *Playboy*, June 1954, 37.

48. Letters to the editor, Dear *Playboy*, *Playboy*, January 1954, 3.

49. Letters to the editor, Dear *Playboy*, *Playboy*, August 1954, 3–4.

50. Jules Archer, "Don't Hate Yourself in the Morning," *Playboy*, August 1955, 48.

51. Archer, "Don't Hate Yourself," 21, 32, 48.

52. Archer, "Don't Hate Yourself," 32.

53. Letters to the editor, Dear *Playboy*, *Playboy*, December 1955, January 1956.

54. Joanne Meyerowitz, "Women, Cheesecake, and Borderline Material: Responses to Girlie Pictures in the Mid-Twentieth-Century U.S.," in *Sexual Borderlands: Constructing an American Sexual Past*, ed. Kathleen Kennedy and Sharon Ullman (Columbus: Ohio State University Press, 2003).

55. Meyerowitz, "Women, Cheesecake, and Borderline Material," 320.

56. Letters to the editor, Dear *Playboy*, *Playboy*, May 1956, 6.

57. Editorial response, Dear *Playboy*, *Playboy*, August 1954, 3.

58. Editorial, *Playboy*, February 1956, 3. According to *Playboy*, Pamela Moore also wrote a controversial coming-of-age novel, *Chocolates for Breakfast*.

59. Pamela Moore, "Love in the Dark," *Playboy*, February 1957, 55–58.

60. Letters to the editor, Dear *Playboy*, Playboy, May 1957, 6–7.

61. Ivor Williams, "The Pious Pornographers: Sex and Sanctimony in the Ladies' Home Jungle," *Playboy*, October 1957, 26.

62. William Iversen followed up his 1957 piece with "The Pious Pornographers Revisited" in September and October 1964, in which he reiterated his original conclusions with updated research. He was a favorite at *Playboy* and wrote "I Only Want a Sweetheart, Not a Buddy" in July 1960. The piece was "A lament for the passing of an American institution: the all-girl girl" (57).

63. William Iversen, "Love, Death and the Hubby Image," *Playboy*, September 1963, 194.

64. Letter to the editor, Dear *Playboy*, Playboy, December 1963, 9.

65. Letter from James Gardner, Dear *Playboy*, Playboy, December 1963, 9.

66. Letter from Cynthia Kolb Whitney, Dear *Playboy*, Playboy, January 1964, 16.

67. Editorial response to Elayne B. Nord, Forum, *Playboy*, December 1963, 54.

68. Editorial response to Mrs. Veronica Graeme, Forum, *Playboy*, December 1963.

69. Kenon Breazeale, "In Spite of Women: *Esquire* Magazine and the Construction of the Male Consumer," *Signs* 20, no. 1 (Autumn 1994).

70. George Frazier, "The Entrenchment of the American Witch," *Esquire*, February 1962, 100–103, 138.

71. Phyllis Battelle, "The Corruptible Male," *Cosmopolitan*, May 1963, 41.

72. Author interview with Hefner.

73. Wylie made his first appearance in *Playboy* in November 1956 with "The Abdicating Male, and How the Gray Flannel Mind Exploits Him through His Women." The piece argued that Madison Avenue's appeal to the feminine ego with sexuality was damaging to women, as well as men and the entire culture. This was because advertisers convinced women that they needed so many products to appeal to men that ultimately, as the breadwinners, men had to work themselves to death to support so much feminine consumption (50). Wylie struck again in January 1963 with "The Career Woman." Wylie warned, "the she-tycoon, [cares] only about herself and heedless of the damage she is doing to the national psyche. . . . The creep of this she-pox on all artifacts of civilization is insidious and all-pervading" (154).

74. Philip Wylie, "The Womanization of America," *Playboy*, September 1958, 51.

75. Wylie, "Womanization," 77.

76. Letter from Rose Marie Shelley, Dear *Playboy*, Playboy, January 1959, 8.

77. In response to the popularity of the Philosophy, Playboy republished it outside the magazine as a series of brochures. Hugh M. Hefner, "The *Playboy* Philosophy," originally published December 1964, quoted here from brochure part 4, installment 19, HMH Publishing Co., Inc., 1964–65, 166.

78. Author interview with Hefner.

79. According to biographer Steven Watts, Freud was "one of [Hefner's] idols." *Mr. Playboy*, 54.

80. "The *Playboy* Panel: The Womanization of America," June 1962, 46.

81. "Panel: Womanization," 46.

82. "Panel: Womanization," 134.

83. "Panel: Womanization," 144.

84. Telegram from Spectorsky to Wylie, November 29, 1961. Playboy Records Center (hereafter PRC), carton 2326, folder "Asexual Society and Womanization, Male vs. Female."

85. Telegram from Wiley to Spectorsky, November 30, 1961. PRC, carton 2326, folder "Asexual Society and Womanization, Male vs. Female."

86. Letter from Spectorsky to Wylie, December 7, 1961. PRC, carton 2326, folder, "Asexual Society and Womanization, Male vs. Female."

87. Letter from Wylie to Spectorsky, December 13, 1961. PRC, carton 2326, folder "Asexual Society and Womanization, Male vs. Female."

88. Letter from Wylie to Spectorsky, December 13, 1961. PRC, carton 2326, folder "Asexual Society and Womanization, Male vs. Female."

89. Letter from Wylie to Spectorsky, December 13, 1961. PRC, carton 2326, folder "Asexual Society and Womanization, Male vs. Female."

90. Letter from Wylie to Spectorsky, December 13, 1961. PRC, carton 2326, folder "Asexual Society and Womanization, Male vs. Female."

91. Letter from Spectorsky to Wylie, December 21, 1961. PRC, carton 2326, folder "Asexual Society and Womanization, Male vs. Female."

92. Letter from Wylie to Spectorsky, May 11, 1962. PRC, carton 2326, folder "Asexual Society and Womanization, Male vs. Female."

93. Based on author's archival research in the Hugh M. Hefner (hereafter HMH) Papers, PRC, Playboy Enterprises, Inc., Chicago, IL.

94. Letter from Michael Lawrence to Albert Ellis, March 26, 1965. PRC, carton 2326, folder "Asexual Society and Womanization, Male vs. Female."

95. According to Lehrman, the notion of a matriarchal society was an outdated anthropological term, while the "Matrist-Patrist" theory was a psychoanalytic idea. Memo from Nat Lehrman to Dick Rosenzweig, June 10, 1965. PRC, carton 2326, folder "Asexual Society and Womanization, Male vs. Female."

96. Memo from Nat Lehrman to Dick Rosenzweig, June 10, 1965. PRC, carton 2326, folder "Asexual Society and Womanization, Male vs. Female."

97. Author interview with Hefner.

98. Author interview with Petersen.

CHAPTER TWO

1. Lisa Baker, "Playmate Play-Off," *Playboy*, April 1967, 122.

2. Russell Miller, *Bunny: The Real Story of Playboy* (New York: Holt, Rinehart and Winston, 1984), 46.

3. Alexander Bloom and Wini Breines, eds., "No More Miss America," in *Takin' It to the Streets: A Sixties Reader* (New York: Oxford University Press, 1995), 483.

4. Robert Cross, "Standoff at the Pleasure Dome," *Chicago Tribune*, February 9, 1969.

5. Maria Elena Buszek, *Pin-Up Grrrls: Feminism, Sexuality, Popular Culture* (Durham: Duke University Press, 2006), 244.

6. Buszek, *Pin-Up Grrrls*, 236.

7. This will be discussed in greater detail in chapter 5.

8. Letter from William R. Moors and editorial response, Forum, *Playboy*, October 1965, 56–57.

9. Editorial response, Forum, *Playboy*, February 1968, 44.

10. Author interview with Christie Hefner, October 16, 2007, New York City, NY.

11. Editorial response to Judy Elder, Forum, *Playboy*, June 1973, 64. Scholars Anthony F. Bogaert, Deborah A. Turkovich, and Carolyn L. Hafer measured objectification in almost forty years of Playmates. According to them, objectification is the "deemphasis of personal characteristics (e.g. face not shown)," which includes "model's eye clarity, facial clarity, and body posture." Bogaert et al. concluded that incidents of objectification were very low. Anthony F. Bogaert, Deborah A. Turkovich, Carolyn L. Hafer, "A Content Analysis of *Playboy* Centerfolds from 1953 through 1990: Changes in Explicitness, Objectification, and Model's Age," *Journal of Sex Research* 30, no. 2 (May 1993): 135–39.

12. Letter from Marilyn Kiss and editorial response, Forum, *Playboy*, April 1968, 61.

13. Psychologists Mala L. Matacin and Jerry M. Burger suggested of *Playboy* in the mid-1980s, "a case can be made that *Playboy* should not be labeled 'pornography' at all, that the images of women it presents are not at all similar to those in more obviously 'pornographic' publications." Mala L. Matacin and Jerry M. Burger, "A Content Analysis of Sexual Themes in *Playboy* Cartoons," *Sex Roles* 17, nos. 3–4 (1987): 181.

14. Andre Bazin, "Entomology of the Pin-Up Girl," *What Is Cinema? Volume 2*, trans. Hugh Gray (Berkeley: University of California Press, 2004), 158–59.

15. Bazin, "Entomology," 159.

16. Mark Gabor, *The Pin-Up: A Modest History* (New York: Universe Books, 1972), 23–27.

17. Pictorial essays, June 1968 and April 1963, respectively.

18. Richard A. Kallan and Robert D. Brooks, "The Playmate of the Month: Naked but Nice," *Journal of Popular Culture* 8, no. 2 (Fall 1974): 334.

19. Kallan and Brooks, "Playmate of the Month," 330–34.

20. Elaine Tyler May, *Homeward Bound: American Families in the Cold War Era* (New York: Basic Books, 1988), 112.

21. For example, Hefner argues, "guilty feeling persists that there is something evil in the flesh of man—a carryover from a Puritanism of our forefathers . . . which still motivates us on subtler, emotional levels." In response to the popularity of the Philosophy, Playboy republished it outside the magazine as a series of brochures. Hugh M.

Hefner, "The *Playboy* Philosophy," originally published December 1962, quoted here from brochure part 1, installment 1, HMH Publishing Co., Inc., 1962, 1963, 4.

22. Miss February 1971, Willy Rey, "Home Body," *Playboy*, February 1971, 113.

23. Marjorie Rosen, *Popcorn Venus: Women, Movies & the American Dream* (New York: Avon Books, 1974). See also Molly Haskell, *From Reverence to Rape: The Treatment of Women in the Movies* (New York: Holt, 1974); Thomas Doherty, *Pre-Code Hollywood: Sex, Immorality, and Insurrection in American Cinema, 1930–1934* (New York: Columbia University Press, 1999). For examples of films that punish sexual female characters, in *A Place in the Sun* (1951), Shelley Winters's character has premarital sex, gets pregnant, and eventually dies. A similar fate befalls Elizabeth Taylor's character in *Butterfield 8* (1960).

24. Herbert W. Richardson, *Nun, Witch, Playmate: The Americanization of Sex* (New York: Harper & Row, Publishers, 1971), 89.

25. Richardson, *Nun, Witch, Playmate*, 90–92.

26. Susan Douglas, *Where the Girls Are: Growing Up Female with the Mass Media* (New York: New York Times Books, 1994), 53.

27. Alice Kessler-Harris, *In Pursuit of Equity: Women, Men, and the Quest for Economic Citizenship in 20th-Century America* (New York: Oxford University Press, 2001), 208.

28. May, *Homeward Bound*, 135. The birthrate, or baby boom, of the postwar years rose from an average 2.4 children for most women in the 1930s to 3.2 in the 1950s. Ellen Carol DuBois and Lynn Dumenil, *Through Women's Eyes: An American History with Documents* (Boston: Bedford/St. Martin's, 2005), 556.

29. Douglas, *Where the Girls Are*, 61, 63.

30. Rosen, *Popcorn Venus*, 283.

31. Kessler-Harris, *In Pursuit of Equity*, 206.

32. Douglas, *Where the Girls Are*, 55.

33. Author interview with Nat Lehrman, June 23, 2006, New York City, NY.

34. Letter from editor Mark Williams to Nedra Lutz, August 18, 1965. HMH Papers, folder 3 "*Playboy* General Mail—Reader Service" (no box).

35. *Playboy*, "Mike Wallace Interviews *Playboy*," December, 1957, 84.

36. *Playmate of the Month* promotional folder, document "*Playboy*'s Playmates," 3. HMH Papers, box 79, 1966 Playmates–Promotions, folder 2.

37. *Playmate of the Month* promotional folder, document "*Playboy*'s Playmates," 3, 1966. HMH Papers, box 79, 1966 Playmates–Promotions, folder 2. Folders containing a congratulatory letter, a brief history of the magazine, circulation statistics, and guidelines on how to conduct oneself in the public eye were given to each Playmate.

38. Author interview with Jim Petersen, February 2, 2006, Evanston, Illinois.

39. Letter from Janet Pilgrim to John M. Holmes, July 19, 1968. HMH Papers, folder 3 "*Playboy* General Mail—Reader Service" (no box).

40. Letter from Janet Pilgrim to John M. Holmes, July 19, 1968. HMH Papers, folder 3 "*Playboy* General Mail—Reader Service" (no box).

41. As for the photographers, they received a $500 finder's fee; $1,600 for the centerfold shot; $500–600 for accompanying photos; $750 for follow-up work such as for

the Playmate Calendar; $150 for promotional photos; and, finally, a bonus of $1,000 if the subject was chosen as Playmate of the Year. *Playmate of the Month* promotional folder, document "*Playboy*'s Playmates," 3–4. HMH Papers, box 79, 1966 Playmates–Promotions, folder 2.

42. U.S. Bureau of the Census, "Current Population Reports: Income in 1967 of Persons in the United States," series P-60, no. 60, U.S. Department of Commerce, 1969, 15.

43. Memo from Dick Rosenzweig to Dick Morton, October 14, 1966. HMH Papers, box 78, 1966 PB Clubs–Playmates, folder 9. The memo confirmed approval of the Hefner quote that would be used in "transmittal letters" that would accompany pictorial scrapbooks, which were given to new Playmates.

44. *Playmate of the Month* promotional folder, document "*Playboy*'s Playmates," 5. HMH Papers, box 79, 1966 Playmates–Promotions, folder 2.

45. Donald Spoto, *Marilyn Monroe: The Biography* (New York: Harper Collins Publishers, 1993), 150–52. Sarah Churchwell, *The Many Lives of Marilyn Monroe* (New York: Metropolitan Books, 2004), 37.

46. Thomas Weyr, *Reaching for Paradise: The Playboy Vision of America* (New York: New York Times Books, 1978), 14–15.

47. Author telephone interview with Dolores Del Monte, February 4, 2007.

48. Letter from Hefner to Keith Bernard, April 21, 1955. HMH Papers, box 1, 1954–55, folder 8.

49. Letter from Hefner to B. Bernard, February 9, 1955. HMH Papers, box 1, 1954–55, folder 8.

50. Memo from Hefner to Vince Tajiri, March 18, 1970. A. C. Spectorsky (hereafter ACS) Papers, box 61, 1970 H–K, folder 4.

51. "Playmate Date Sheet and Model Release Form," 1968. HMH Papers, box 142, 1970 Spectorsky–1340, folder 7.

52. Letter from Hefner to Keith Bernard, June 23, 1955. HMH Papers, box 1, 1954–55, folder 8.

53. Letter from Hefner to Hal Adams, May 10, 1955. HMH Papers, box 1, 1954–55, folder 7.

54. Letter from Hefner to Frances Brenner, November 19, 1954, HMH Papers, box 1, 1954–55, folder 4.

55. Letter from Hefner to Hal Adams, June 22, 1955. HMH Papers, box 1, 1954–55, folder 7.

56. Letter from Hefner to Keith Bernard, April 21, 1955. HMH Papers, box 1, 1954–55, folder 8.

57. Miller, *Bunny*, 51.

58. Letters to the editor, *Playboy*, October, 1955, 3–4.

59. Letter from Hefner to Hal Adams, November 10, 1955. HMH Papers, box 1, 1954–55, folder 7.

60. Letter from Hefner to Hal Adams, November 19, 1955. HMH Papers, box 1, 1954–55, folder 7.

61. Letter from Hefner to Hal Adams, November 10, 1955. HMH Papers, box 1, 1954–55, folder 7.

62. Letter from Hefner to Hal Adams, June 5, 1956. HMH Papers, box 3, 1955–56, folder 4.

63. Letter from Hefner to Carlyle Blackwell, Jr., December 29, 1955. HMH Papers, box 1, 1954–55, folder 8.

64. Miller, *Bunny*, 52.

65. *Playboy* online archive, The *Playboy* Cyber Club, Playmate Files, Betty Blue at http://cyber.playboy.com/members/playmates/files/1956/11/index.html.

66. *Playboy* online archive, The *Playboy* Cyber Club, Playmate Files, Sharon Cintron at http://cyber.playboy.com/members/playmates/files/1963/05/.

67. Memo from Hefner to Spectorsky and Jack Kessie, March 6, 1963. ACS Papers, box 22, folder 10, 1963 E–K.

68. "Playmate of the Month" promotional folder, 2. HMH Papers, box 79, 1966 Playmates–Promotions, folder 2.

69. Memo from Hefner to Vince Tajiri and Bev Chamberlain, December 2, 1963. ACS Papers, box 22, folder 13, 1963 E–K.

70. Editorial, *Playboy*, October, 1955, 2.

71. *Playboy*, "Playboy's Office Playmate," July 1955, 27.

72. Letter from Hefner to Herb Flatow, August 1, 1956. HMH Papers, box 3, 1955–56, folder 9.

73. *Playboy*, "Photographing Your Own Playmate," June 1958, 35.

74. *Playboy*, "Photographing Your Own Playmate," June 1958, 37.

75. Miller, *Bunny*, 52.

76. Linda Witt, "Women Do Matter at *Playboy*," *Chicago Daily News*, July 10, 1973, 23.

77. Letter from Bonnie Carroll to Hefner, January 26, 1959. HMH Papers, box 10, folder 8, 1959.

78. Letter from Hefner to Bonnie Carroll, March 6, 1959. HMH Papers, box 10, folder 8, 1959.

79. Email correspondence from Gale Morin to the author, February 4, 2007.

80. Letter from Carole Waite to Hefner, 1959 (month/day not specified). HMH Papers, box 10, 1959, folder 8.

81. Letter from Carole Waite to Hefner, 1959 (month/day not specified). HMH Papers, box 10, 1959, folder 8.

82. Letter from Hefner to Carole Waite, July 2, 1959. HMH Papers, box 10, 1959, folder 8.

83. Author phone conversations with Carole Waite, August 2008. Although Carole did not have the opportunity to pose for *Playboy*, as a former model, she did work briefly as a Playboy Club Bunny in Beverly Hills. Thanks to Julia Akoury Thiel for putting me in touch with Carole.

84. Alice Denham, *Sleeping with Bad Boys: A Juicy Tell-All of Literary New York in the 1950s and 1960s* (New York: Book Republic, 2006), 8.

85. Author interview with Alice Denham, November 27, 2006, New York City, NY.

86. Author interview with Denham, and Denham, *Sleeping with Bad Boys*, 8–9.

87. Author interview with Denham.

88. Denham, *Sleeping with Bad Boys*, 113–14.

89. Denham, *Sleeping with Bad Boys*, 116.

90. Author interview with Denham.

91. Denham, *Sleeping with Bad Boys*, 116.

92. Author interview with Denham.

93. Denham, *Sleeping with Bad Boys*, 131.

94. Denham, *Sleeping with Bad Boys*, 132.

95. Author interview with Denham.

96. Gretchen Edgren, *The Playmate Book: Six Decades of Centerfolds* (Los Angeles: Taschen, 2005), 59.

97. Author email interview with Joyce Nizzari, June 15, 2007.

98. Author interview with Nizzari.

99. It is unclear when these forms began to be used. They start appearing in the archive sometime in the 1960s, although they may have been used earlier. The famous "Data Sheets," which included personal facts about the Playmate as well as a signature, began being published along with the centerfolds beginning in 1977.

100. "Playmate Data Sheet and Model Release," Linda Allison, April 29, 1968. HMH Papers, box 142, 1970 Spectorsky–1340, folder 7. There is no Playmate by the name listed on this data sheet, but since some women used stage names in the magazine, it is possible that she posed under a different name. However, the data sheet does not indicate that she was accepted.

101. "Playmate Data Sheet and Model Release," Lynda Jean Veverka, August 13, 1965. HMH Papers, box 78, 1966 Playboy Clubs–Playmates, folder 9.

102. "Playmate Data Sheet and Model Release," Mary Eileen Chesterton (Mimi), undated. HMH Papers, box 142, 1970 Spectorsky–1340, folder 7.

103. *Playboy*, "Playmate of the Year," August 1965, 72.

104. Letters to the editor, *Playboy*, June 1962, 14.

105. Letters to the editor, *Playboy*, August 1963, 10.

106. Rosen, *Popcorn Venus*, 282.

107. Rosen, *Popcorn Venus*, 284.

108. Spoto, *Marilyn Monroe*, 333, 423.

109. Marilyn Yalom, *A History of the Breast* (New York: Ballantine Books, 1997), 148.

110. Yalom, *History of the Breast*, 153.

111. Yalom, *History of the Breast*, 185.

112. "Playmate Promotional Rating Sheet," Tish Howard; Dee Harris (evaluator), July 1966. HMH Papers, box 78, 1966 Playboy Clubs–Playmates, folder 9.

113. "Playmate Promotional Rating Sheet," Tish Howard; Lee Gottlieb (evaluator), July 1966. HMH Papers, box 78, 1966 Playboy Clubs–Playmates, folder 9.

114. "Playmate Data Sheet and Model Release," Gloria Root, undated. HMH Papers, box 142, 1970 Spectorsky–1340, folder 7.

115. *Playboy*, "Revolutionary Discovery—*Playboy*'s Playmate of the Month," December 1969, 170–72.

116. *Playboy*, "Revolutionary Discovery," 171.

117. Edgren, *The Playmate Book*, 96, and author email interview with Victoria Valentino, January 2007.

118. Author interview with Valentino.

119. Editorial comment, "Playbill," *Playboy*, August 1967, 3.

120. Author email interview with Martha Smith, May 2009.

121. Interview with Smith.

122. Interview with Smith.

123. Miles Davis and Quincy Troupe, *Miles: The Autobiography* (New York: Simon and Schuster, 1989), 260.

124. Edgren, *The Playboy Book*, 447.

125. Bill Osgerby, *Playboys in Paradise: Masculinity, Youth and Leisure-Style in Modern America* (Oxford: Berg, 2001), 109–13; Sheridan Prasso, *The Asian Mystique: Dragon Ladies, Geisha Girls and Our Fantasies of the Exotic Orient* (New York: Public Affairs, 2005); Christina Klein, *Cold War Orientalism: Asia in the Middlebrow Imagination, 1945–1961* (Berkeley: University of California Press, 2003).

126. Prasso, *The Asian Mystique*, 5.

127. *Playboy*, "Playmate Play-Off: Jo Collins, China Lee, Astrid Schulz," April 1965, 119.

128. *Playboy*, "China Doll," August 1964, 72.

129. For more on the history of African American pin-ups, see Megan E. Williams, "The *Crisis* Cover Girl: Lena Horne, the NAACP, and Representations of African-American Femininity, 1941–1945," *American Periodicals* 16, no. 2 (2006): 200–218; also bell hooks, "Selling Hot Pussy: Representations of Black Female Sexuality in the Cultural Marketplace," in *Writing on the Body: Female Embodiment and Feminist Theory*, ed. Katie Conboy et. al. (New York: Columbia University Press, 1997), 113–28.

130. *Playboy*, "Portrait of Jenny," March 1965, 89, 93.

131. Laila Haidarali, "Polishing Brown Diamonds: African American Women, Popular Magazines, and the Advent of Modeling in Early Postwar America," *Journal of Women's History* 17, no. 1 (2005): 12.

132. Haidarali, "Polishing Brown Diamonds," 33.

133. Steven Watts, *Mr. Playboy: Hugh Hefner and the American Dream* (Hoboken: John Wiley and Sons, Inc., 2008), 194, 50.

134. Weyr, *Reading for Paradise*, 133.

135. Weyr, *Reading for Paradise*, 142.

136. Weyr, *Reading for Paradise*, 142.

137. The only other Asian or African American Playmates until the mid-1970s appear to have been Gwen Wong (April 1967), Jean Bell (October 1969), and Julie Woodson (April 1973).

138. Blonde Playmates appeared roughly 40 percent of the time from 1953 to 1973. For a discussion of the midcentury idealization of blonde hair, see Lois Banner, "The

Creature from the Black Lagoon: Marilyn Monroe and Whiteness," *Cinema Journal* 47, no. 4 (Summer 2008): 4–29.

139. Author interview with Hugh Hefner, November 3, 2006, Los Angeles, CA.

140. Author interview with Hefner.

141. Watts, *Mr. Playboy*, 136, 194–95.

142. Author phone interview with Jennifer Jackson, December 12, 2008.

143. Author interview with Jackson.

144. Author interview with Jackson.

145. Author interview with Jackson.

146. Letters to the editor, *Playboy*, June 1965, 12.

147. Letters to the editor, *Playboy*, June 1965, 12.

148. Letters to the editor, *Playboy*, June 1965, 14.

149. Letters to the editor, *Playboy*, June 1965, 12.

150. Letters to the editor, *Playboy*, June 1965, 14.

151. Kwame Anthony Appiah and Henry Louis Gates, Jr., eds., *Civil Rights: An A–Z Reference of the Movement that Changed America* (Philadelphia: Running Press, 2004), 279.

152. David Allyn, *Make Love, Not War: The Sexual Revolution: An Unfettered History* (Boston: Little, Brown and Company, 2000), 55–60. For more on postwar obscenity and censorship, see Whitney Strub, "Black and White and Banned All Over: Race, Censorship and Obscenity in Postwar Memphis," *Journal of Social History* 40, no. 3 (Spring 2007): 685–715; Strub, "The Clearly Obscene and the Queerly Obscene: Heteronormativity and Obscenity in Cold War Los Angeles," *American Quarterly* 60, no. 2 (June 2008): 373–98.

153. Larry Flynt's *Hustler* magazine infamously had on a cover the image of a woman being fed into a meat grinder. Extensive work has been done on the politics of pornography. For both sides of the debate, see Drucilla Cornell, ed., *Feminism and Pornography* (Oxford: Oxford University Press, 2000); Lisa Duggan and Nan Hunter, *Sex Wars: Sexual Dissent and Political Culture* (New York: Routledge, 2006); Andrea Dworkin, *Pornography: Men Possessing Women* (London: Women's Press, 1981); Kate Ellis et al., eds., *Caught Looking: Feminism, Pornography and Censorship* (East Haven, CT: Long River Books, 1992); Laura Kipnis, *Bound and Gagged: Pornography and the Politics of Fantasy in America* (New York: Grove Press, 1996); M. G. Lord, "Pornutopia: How Feminist Scholars Learned to Love Dirty Pictures," *Lingua Franca* 7, no. 3 (March 1997); Catharine MacKinnon, *Only Words* (Cambridge, MA: Harvard University Press, 1996) and *Feminism Unmodified: Discourses on Life and Law* (Cambridge, MA: Harvard University Press, 1988); Ann Snitow et al., eds., *Powers of Desire: The Politics of Sexuality* (New York: Monthly Review Press, 1983); Nadine Strossen, *Defending Pornography: Free Speech, Sex and the Fight for Women's Rights* (New York: NYU Press, 2000); Linda Williams established much of the academic consideration of pornography in *Hard Core: Power, Pleasure, and the "Frenzy of the Visible"* (Berkeley: University of California Press, 1989), and *Porn Studies* (Durham: Duke University Press, 2004).

154. For a discussion of early American concepts of sexual regulation and erotic

representation, see Clare A. Lyons, *Sex among the Rabble: An Intimate History of Gender and Power in the Age of Revolution, Philadelphia, 1730–1830* (Chapel Hill: University of North Carolina, 2006), esp. chap. 3; Walter Kendrick, *The Secret Museum: Pornography in Modern Culture* (New York: Viking Penguin, 1987), 11; Nicola Kay Beisel, *Imperiled Innocents: Anthony Comstock and Family Reproduction in Victorian America* (Princeton: Princeton University Press, 1998); Donna Dennis, *Licentious Gotham: Erotic Publishing and Its Prosecution in Nineteenth-Century New York* (Cambridge, MA: Harvard University Press, 2009); Helen Lefkowitz Horowitz, *Rereading Sex: Battles over Sexual Knowledge and Suppression in Nineteenth-Century America* (New York: Vintage Books, 2002); on Europe, see Steven Marcus, *The Other Victorians: A Study of Sexuality and Pornography in Mid-Nineteenth-Century England* (New York: Basic Books, 1966).

155. Allyn, *Make Love*, 57.

156. See James Gilbert, *A Cycle of Outrage: America's Reaction to the Juvenile Delinquent in the 1950s* (New York: Oxford University Press, 1988); and Allyn, *Make Love*, 60–61.

157. Weyr, *Reaching for Paradise*, 35; *New York Times*, "Playboy Case Closed," November 6, 1958, 63.

158. Watts, *Mr. Playboy*, 140.

159. Allyn, *Make Love*, 62; *New York Times*, "Power to Censor Is Still Unclear," December 20, 1959, E8.

160. Collected *Playboy* Philosophy, installment 11, 75.

161. Collected *Playboy* Philosophy, installment 11, 75.

162. Collected *Playboy* Philosophy, installment 11, 76.

163. Collected *Playboy* Philosophy, installment 11, 76.

164. Letter to the editor, "Dear Playboy," *Playboy*, October 1963, 14.

165. "Report of Proceedings," *City of Chicago vs. Hugh M. Hefner*, Municipal Court of Chicago, December 4, 1963, vj1 pp 33 and d22-4. HMH Papers, box 37, City of Chicago vs. HMH, 1963, folders 12 and 13.

166. Memo from Hefner to *Playboy* ad staff, June 20, 1963. ACS Papers, box 22, 1963 E–K, folder 11.

167. Collected *Playboy* Philosophy, installment 11, 75.

168. Collected *Playboy* Philosophy, installment 11, 75.

169. See Thomas F. O'Connor, "The National Organization for Decent Literature: A Phase in American Catholic Censorship," *Library Quarterly* 65, no. 4 (October 1995): 386–414. For work on a similar organization, see Whitney Strub, "Perversion for Profit: Citizens for Decent Literature and the Arousal of an Antiporn Public in the 1960s," *Journal of the History of Sexuality* 15, no. 2 (May 2006): 258–91.

170. Collected *Playboy* Philosophy, installment 3, 18.

171. Collected *Playboy* Philosophy, installment 12, 83.

172. Collected *Playboy* Philosophy, Installment 12, 86.

173. Miller, *Bunny*, 170.

174. Miller, *Bunny*, 170–76.

175. Miller, *Bunny*, 79.

176. Miller, *Bunny*, 179.

177. Miller, *Bunny*, 176–83.

178. Miller, *Bunny*, 177.

179. Miller, *Bunny*, 178.

180. Miller, *Bunny*, 183.

181. Miller, *Bunny*, 183.

182. Miller, *Bunny*, 182.

183. Miller, *Bunny*, 179.

184. Author interview with Lehrman.

185. Author interview with Lehrman.

186. Author interview with Petersen.

187. Author interview with Petersen.

188. Letter to the editor, Forum, *Playboy*, February 1972, 52–54.

189. Author interview with Hefner, and Watts, *Mr. Playboy*, 116.

190. Quote from author interview with Christie Hefner, October 16, 2007, New York City, NY.

CHAPTER THREE

1. *Time*, "The Boss of Taste City," March 24, 1961.

2. Author interview with Jim Petersen, February 2, 2006, Evanston, IL.

3. Author interview with Hugh M. Hefner, November 3, 2006, Los Angeles, CA.

4. Letter from Karl D. Brown, Jr., Dear *Playboy*, *Playboy*, May 1963, 32.

5. Memo from Hefner to Spectorsky et al., March 18, 1968. ACS Papers, box 46, 1968 G–L, folder 4.

6. In the 1950s, sociologist David Riesman articulated a supposedly new form of American manhood that was "other-directed," seeking peer approval, as opposed to the "inner-directed" men of previous generations. See David Riesman, *The Lonely Crowd: A Study of the Changing American Character* (New Haven: Yale University Press, 1955).

7. J. Robert Moskin, "Why Do Women Dominate Him?" in *The Decline of the American Male*, by the editors of *Look* magazine (New York: Random House, 1958), 12.

8. Bill Osgerby, *Playboys in Paradise: Masculinity, Youth and Leisure-Style in Modern America* (Oxford: Berg, 2001), 145.

9. Harvey Cox, "*Playboy*'s Doctrine of the Male," *Christianity and Crisis*, April 17, 1961, 57.

10. Beth Bailey discusses the objectification of men in *Esquire* in a similar way. Regarding the ubiquitous image of the wealthy man paired with a young woman that populated the pages of *Esquire*, particularly in its cartoons, Bailey argues, "the man, too, is objectified. His value to her lies only in what he can buy. He is interchangeable with any other well-stuffed wallet. Their relationship is obviously mutually exploitative: the man is as much a commodity to the woman as she is a commodity to him." Beth L. Bailey, *From Front Porch to Back Seat: Courtship in Twentieth-Century America* (Baltimore: Johns Hopkins University Press, 1988), 57.

11. Quoted in Becky Conekin, "Fashioning the Playboy: Messages of Style and Masculinity in the Pages of *Playboy* Magazine, 1953–1963," *Fashion Theory* 4, no. 4 (2000): 448.

12. James K. Beggan and Scott T. Allison, "The Playboy Rabbit Is Soft, Furry and Cute: Is This Really the Symbol of Masculine Dominance of Women?" *Journal of Men's Studies* 9, no. 3 (Spring 2001): 346.

13. Author interview with Hefner.

14. Conekin, "Fashioning the Playboy," 456.

15. Beggan and Allison, "The Playboy Rabbit Is Soft," 344. See also James K. Beggan and Scott T. Allison, "What Do Playboy Playmates Want? Implications of Expressed Preferences in the Construction of the 'Unfinished' Masculine Identity," *Journal of Men's Studies* 10, no. 1 (Fall 2001): 1–38. Additionally Beggan and Allison conducted a study of Playmates from the years 1985–2001 to argue that the accompanying text demonstrated that the models were, contrary to popular belief, portrayed as "tough," strong, vibrant women. "Tough Women in the Unlikeliest Places: The Unexpected Toughness of the Playboy Playmate," *Journal of Popular Culture* 38, no. 5 (August 2005): 796–818.

16. The literature on consumerism is extensive. Suggestions for further reading include Gary Cross, *An All-Consuming Century: Why Commercialism Won in Modern America* (New York: Columbia University Press, 2000); Victoria de Grazia and Ellen Furlough, *The Sex of Things: Gender and Consumption in Historical Perspective* (Berkeley: University of California Press, 1996); Stuart Ewen, *Captains of Consciousness: Advertising and the Social Roots of the Consumer Culture* (New York: McGraw-Hill Book Company, 1976); Stuart Ewen and Elizabeth Ewen, *Channels of Desire: Mass Images and the Shaping of American Consciousness* (New York: McGraw-Hill Book Company, 1982); Richard Wightman Fox and T. J. Jackson Lears, eds., *The Culture of Consumption: Critical Essays in American History, 1880–1980* (New York: Pantheon Books, 1983); Lawrence B. Glickman, ed., *Consumer Society in American History: A Reader* (Ithaca: Cornell University Press, 1999); Jennifer Scanlon, ed., *The Gender and Consumer Culture Reader* (New York: New York University Press, 2000).

17. Lizabeth Cohen, *A Consumer's Republic: The Politics of Mass Consumption in Postwar America* (New York: Vintage Books, 2003), 121.

18. Cohen, *A Consumer's Republic*, 127.

19. J. Ronald Oakley, *God's Country: America in the Fifties* (New York: Dembner Books, 1986), 248.

20. Oakley, *God's Country*, 228–39.

21. Oakley, *God's Country*, 230.

22. Cohen, *A Consumer's Republic*, 150.

23. Cohen, *A Consumer's Republic*, 148.

24. For more on the history of American magazines, see Carolyn Kitch, *The Girl on the Magazine Cover: The Origins of Visual Stereotypes in American Mass Media* (Chapel Hill: University of North Carolina Press, 2001); Tom Pendergast, *Creating the Modern Man: American Magazines and Consumer Culture, 1900–1950* (Columbia: University of Missouri Press, 2000); Jennifer Scanlon, *Inarticulate Longings: The Ladies' Home Journal,*

Gender and the Promise of Consumer Culture (New York: Routledge, 1995); Christopher P. Wilson, "The Rhetoric of Consumption: Mass-Market Magazines and the Demise of the Gentle Reader, 1880–1920," in *The Culture of Consumption: Critical Essays in American History, 1880–1980*, ed. Richard Wightman Fox and T. J. Jackson Lears (New York: Pantheon Books, 1983).

25. David Abrahamson, *Magazine-Made America: The Cultural Transformation of the Postwar Periodical* (Cresskill, NJ: Hampton Press, Inc., 1996), 37, 31. See also John Tebbel and Mary Ellen Zuckerman, *The Magazine in America, 1741–1990* (New York: Oxford University Press, 1991), 358.

26. Abrahamson, *Magazine-Made America*, 17.

27. Abrahamson, *Magazine-Made America*, 38.

28. Abrahamson, *Magazine-Made America*, 49.

29. Abrahamson, *Magazine-Made America*, 55; Wilson, "Rhetoric of Consumption," 49.

30. Watts, *Mr. Playboy*, 62–63.

31. Watts, *Mr. Playboy*, 63, 87, 89, 97.

32. Steven Heller, "The Art [Paul] of Playboy," *Print* 54, no. 1 (January/February 2000): 41.

33. Heller, "Art [Paul]," n.p.

34. Gay Talese, *Thy Neighbor's Wife* (New York: Dell Publishing, 1980), 88–89.

35. Watts, *Mr. Playboy*, 127–28.

36. By contrast, most working-class men's magazines in the 1950s, like *True* or *Men*, focused not on consumption or lifestyle, but on adventure stories about war, hunting, and more traditional male pastimes. Thomas Weyr, *Reaching for Paradise: The Playboy Vision of America* (New York: New York Times Books, 1978), 4–8.

37. David Halberstam, *The Fifties* (New York: Villard Books, 1993), 576.

38. Historian Mark A. Swiencicki argues that in fact American men had been important consumers since the nineteenth century. Mark A. Swiencicki, "Consuming Brotherhood: Men's Culture, Style and Recreation as Consumer Culture, 1880–1930," in *Consumer Society in American History: A Reader*, ed. Lawrence B. Glickman (Ithaca: Cornell University Press, 1999), 207–40.

39. Osgerby, *Playboys in Paradise*, 79.

40. Pendergast, *Creating the Modern Man*, 206. Kenon Breazeale, "In Spite of Women: *Esquire* Magazine and the Construction of the Male Consumer," *Signs* 20, no. 1 (Autumn 1994): 3.

41. Breazeale, "In Spite of Women," 5.

42. Hugh Merrill, *Esky: The Early Years at Esquire* (New Brunswick: Rutgers University Press, 1995), 4.

43. Breazeale, "In Spite of Women," 4.

44. Pendergast, *Creating the Modern Man*, 218.

45. Merrill, *Esky*, 47.

46. Breazeale, "In Spite of Women," 6, 10.

47. Pendergast, *Creating the Modern Man*, 213, 217.

48. Weyr, *Reaching for Paradise*, 9.

49. Weyr, *Reaching for Paradise*, 8.

50. Breazeale, "In Spite of Women," 19.

51. Author interview with Hefner.

52. Author interview with Hefner.

53. Author interview with Hefner.

54. *Playboy*, "Mike Wallace Interviews *Playboy*," December, 1957, 83.

55. Merrill, *Esky*, 129.

56. Weyr, *Reaching for Paradise*, 4.

57. Letters to the editor, Dear *Playboy*, *Playboy*, April 1954, 3.

58. Editorial comment, *Playboy*, February 1955, 4.

59. Letters to the editor, *Playboy*, May 1954, 3.

60. *Playboy*, "The *Playboy* Reader: About the Man Who Buys the Magazine," September 1955, 36–37.

61. Letters to the editor, *Playboy*, May 1954, 2.

62. Editorial, *Playboy*, April 1955, 2.

63. Letter from Neil W. Fisher to Hefner, September 15, 1960. ACS Papers, box 10, 1960 A–H, folder 11.

64. Letter from Spectorsky to Neil W. Fisher, October 3, 1960. ACS Papers, box 10, 1960 A–H, folder 11.

65. Memo from Hefner to Spectorsky et al., March 20, 1967. ACS Papers, box 40, 1967 H–M, folder 1.

66. Thomas Mario, "How to Play with Fire," *Playboy*, July 1954, 22, 35.

67. Thomas Mario, "Playboy at the Salad Bowl," *Playboy*, July 1956, 32.

68. Joanne Hollows, "The Bachelor Dinner: Masculinity, Class and Cooking in *Playboy*, 1953–1961," *Continuum: Journal of Media and Cultural Studies*, 16, no. 2 (2002): 145.

69. Hollows, "Bachelor Dinner," 146, 151.

70. *Playboy*, "*Playboy*'s Penthouse Apartment," September 1956, 60.

71. Editorial, *Playboy*, April 1959, 3.

72. *Playboy*, "*Playboy*'s Penthouse Apartment," September 1956, 54–55.

73. *Playboy*, "*Playboy*'s Penthouse Apartment," September 1956, 54–7.

74. *Playboy*, "*Playboy*'s Penthouse Apartment," September 1956, 59.

75. Elizabeth Fraterrigo, *Playboy and the Making of the Good Life in Modern America* (New York: Oxford, 2009), 84.

76. Beatriz Preciado, "Pornotopia," in *Cold War Hothouses: Inventing Postwar Culture from Cockpit to Playboy*, ed. Annmarie Brennan, Beatriz Colomina, and Jeannie Kim (Princeton: Princeton Architectural Press, 2004), 252, 229.

77. Preciado, "Pornotopia," 237.

78. Memo from Hefner to A. C. Spectorsky, February 2, 1959. HMH Papers, box 11, 1959, folder 3.

79. *Playboy*, "The *Playboy* Bed," April 1965, 88, 184.

80. Letter from Miss B. S., Advisor, *Playboy*, September 1967, 67.

81. Kessie initially wrote the fashion columns under the pseudonym Blake Rutherford. Weyr, *Reaching for Paradise*, 33.

82. Jack Kessie, "The Well Dressed Playboy," *Playboy*, January 1955, 38.

83. Letters from Lionel Samuelson, Dear *Playboy*, *Playboy*, February 1955, 3.

84. Letters to the editor, *Playboy*, April, May, July 1955.

85. Jack Kessie, "*Playboy*'s Christmas Stocking," *Playboy*, November 1955, 28, 56.

86. Jack Kessie, "Summa Cum Style," *Playboy*, October 1955, 52.

87. Memo from A. C. Spectorsky to Kessie et al., July 29, 1960. ACS Papers, box 11, I–Si 1960, folder 3.

88. Robert L. Green, "Urbanity Afoot," *Playboy*, March 1961, 74–75, 125. Green was a noted fashionista of the time, and took over the column from Kessie in 1959. Weyr, *Reaching for Paradise*, 60.

89. *Playboy*, "The Grooming Game," March 1967, 104–7.

90. In response to the popularity of the Philosophy, Playboy republished it outside the magazine as a series of brochures. Hugh M. Hefner, "The *Playboy* Philosophy," originally published January 1963, quoted here from brochure part 1 installment 2, HMH Publishing, Co., Inc., 1962, 1963, 13.

91. Robert L. Green, "Gifting the Guys: A Guide to Guiding the Girls toward Making You Happy Come Christmas," *Playboy*, December 1960, 37.

92. Green, "Gifting the Guys," 38.

93. Green, "Gifting the Guys," 40.

94. Green, "Gifting the Guys," 42.

95. Green, "Gifting the Guys," 44.

96. Green, "Gifting the Guys," 37.

97. Green, "Gifting the Guys," 44.

98. Green, "Gifting the Guys," 37.

99. Robert L. Green, "*Playboy*'s Fall and Winter Fashion Forecast," *Playboy*, October 1964, 97–99.

100. Green, "*Playboy*'s Fall and Winter Fashion," 101.

101. Green, "*Playboy*'s Fall and Winter Fashion," 97.

102. Advertisement for Dickies clothing, *Playboy*, September 1965, 202–5. Additionally, *Playboy* featured a regular series of subscription ads that began running in 1958 called "What Sort of Man Reads *Playboy*?" The ads typically featured a handsome, dapper man participating in some sort of classy cultural or professional activity, usually with one or more beautiful women looking on with approval or desire. These ads and others for *Playboy* have been analyzed in Beggan and Allison, "The *Playboy* Rabbit Is Soft."

103. Osgerby, *Playboys in Paradise*, 45. Osgerby made this observation about *Esquire*'s treatment of fashion in the 1930s, but it applies to *Playboy* as well.

104. Jay Sebring, "Topping Off the Well-Groomed Man," *Playboy*, April 1965, 125–26, 172–76.

105. Sebring, "Topping Off," 174.

106. Letter from F. H., Advisor, *Playboy*, April 1967, 43.

107. Letter from R. C., Advisor, *Playboy*, May 1970, 60.

108. Richard Dyer, "Don't Look Now: The Male Pin-up," in *Sexual Subject: A Screen Reader in Sexuality*, ed. Mandy Merck (New York: Routledge, 1992), 274.

109. Memo from Hefner to Spectorsky et al., May 23, 1968. ACS Papers, box 46, 1968 G–L, folder 4.

110. *Playboy*, "Hair Today, Gone Tomorrow," September 1968, 119–21.

111. *Playboy*, "Hair Today, Gone Tomorrow," 120–21.

112. Robert L. Green, "Super Skivvies!" *Playboy*, February 1972, 123–25.

113. Robert L. Green, "Clint Eastwood: Pushover for Pullovers," *Playboy*, March 1972, 123–25.

114. Robert L. Green, "So It's a Bracelet. What's It to Ya?" *Playboy*, July 1972, 106–7.

115. Reynolds's centerfold appeared in the April 1972 issue of *Cosmopolitan*.

116. *Playboy*, "*Playboy*'s Playmate of the Month," August 1972, 110–12.

117. *Playboy*, "Student Bodies," September 1972, 99–103.

118. Arthur Knight and Hollis Alpert, "Sex Stars of 1972," *Playboy*, December 1972, 206. Apparently not everyone agreed with *Playboy*'s decision to feature Reynolds as a sexy star. Patty Ness of South Dakota wrote a letter to the editor: "somehow the photo you ran of [Burt Reynolds] in *Sex Stars of 1972* . . . really turned me off. Next time, instead of showing his hairy ass, you might try rolling him over." Letter from Patty Ness, Dear *Playboy*, *Playboy*, March 1973, 14. Other pictorials that showed male nudity included "Porno Chic," which was about the growing popularity of adult films and had a full frontal of porn star Harry Reems. Bruce Williamson, "Porno Chic," *Playboy*, August 1973, 141. Another article about a *Playboy*-produced film based on a Desmond Morris book, "The Naked Ape," showed a nude man. *Playboy*, "The Naked Ape," September 1973, 159.

119. Memo from Hefner to Jack Kessie, December 21, 1967. ACS Papers, box 40, 1967 H–M, folder 3.

120. *Esquire*, fashion feature, August 1968, 107; "A Season of Silk Shirts, Fine Fur Coats, Other Old Elegances," *Esquire*, November 1968, 133.

121. Memo from Hefner to Jack Kessie, December 21, 1967. ACS Papers, box 40, 1967 H–M, folder 3.

122. Before publication, Hefner apparently only objected to the title of the piece, "Let Yourself Goo." Spectorsky defended the title, describing it as fun and irreverent. According to memos, Hefner did not comment on the piece again until after it was published, when he criticized both the title and accompanying photo spread. Memos between Hefner and Spectorsky, October 30, 1967, through January 11, 1968. ACS Papers, box 46, 1968 G–L, folder 3.

123. Memo from Hefner to A. C. Spectorsky et al., January 3, 1968. ACS Papers, box 46, 1968 G–L, folder 3.

124. Memo from Hefner to A. C. Spectorsky and Jack Kessie, October 30, 1967. ACS Papers, box 46, 1968 G–L, folder 3.

125. Memo from Hefner to A. C. Spectorsky et al., January 11, 1968. ACS Papers, box 46, 1968 G–L, folder 3.

126. Memo from Spectorsky to Hefner, October 31, 1967. ACS Papers, box 46, 1968 G–L, folder 3.

127. Memo from Tajiri to Hefner, January 9, 1968. ACS Papers, box 46, 1968 G–L, folder 3.

128. Memo from Spectorsky to Hefner, January 5, 1968. ACS Papers, box 46, 1968 G–L, folder 3.

129. Weyr, *Reaching for Paradise*, 57.

130. Robert L. Green, "The New Edwardian," *Playboy*, March 1967, 88.

131. Weyr, *Reaching for Paradise*, 61.

132. Robert L. Green, "Avant-Garb," *Playboy*, August 1969, 88–89.

133. Memo from Spectorsky to Robert L. Green, February 17, 1970. HMH Papers, box 142, 1970 Spectorsky–1340, folder 1.

134. Memo from A. C. Spectorsky to Green, November 19, 1970. HMH Papers, box 141, 1970 Reader Service–Spectorsky, folder 7.

135. Letter from Gary Reed and editorial response, Forum, *Playboy*, September 1970, 82, 212.

136. Letter to Advisor, *Playboy*, January 1968, 51–52.

137. Letter from L. F. and editorial response, Advisor, *Playboy*, January 1971, 51.

138. Author interview with Hefner.

CHAPTER FOUR

1. Letter from Mrs. Veronica Graeme, Forum, *Playboy*, December 1963, 54.

2. Author interview with Hugh M. Hefner, November 3, 2006, Los Angeles, CA.

3. Thomas Weyr, *Reaching for Paradise: The Playboy Vision of America* (New York: New York Times Books, 1978), 197.

4. Weyr, *Reaching for Paradise*, 11.

5. Rollo May, *Love and Will* (New York: W. W. Norton & Company, Inc., 1969), 58.

6. Author interview with Nat Lehrman, June 23, 2006, New York City, NY.

7. Biographer Steven Watts affirms this view by saying that Hefner "updated the erotic game of enticement and pursuit between men and women that was as old as humankind. But it also encouraged men to see women primarily as sexually alluring creatures to be bedded and enjoyed serially." Watts, *Mr. Playboy: Hugh Hefner and the American Dream* (Hoboken: John Wiley and Sons, Inc., 2008), 231.

8. Watts refers repeatedly to Hefner's pursuit of romance in *Mr. Playboy*.

9. In response to the popularity of the Philosophy, Playboy republished it outside the magazine as a series of brochures. Hugh M. Hefner, "The *Playboy* Philosophy," originally published March 1963, quoted here from brochure part 1, installment 4, HMH Publishing Co., Inc., 1962, 1963, 20.

10. Author interview with Hefner; Weyr, *Reaching for Paradise*, 15–16; Russell Miller, *Bunny: The Real Story of Playboy* (New York: Plume, 1984), 18–21.

11. Hefner, "Philosophy (March 1963)," brochure part 1, installment 4, 21.

12. Hefner, "Philosophy (March 1963)," brochure part 1, installment 4, 21.

13. This notion of the column acting as a brother or trusted confidant was emphasized by Jim Petersen in an interview with the author, February 2, 2006, Evanston, IL.

14. Lehrman made this point in a collection of notes he compiled for an autobiography of Hefner that was never completed. Lehrman gave the notes to the author via email on June 18, 2006.

15. Lehrman autobiographical notes; and he reiterated this point in an interview with the author.

16. Author interview with Jim Petersen, September 1, 2005, Evanston, Illinois.

17. While the reports did not keep track of how many letters were from men or from women, it was noted when certain features elicited a particularly strong response from women, such as in the case of an article on feminism in 1970. Regarding overall numbers, one report noted that *Playboy* received on average four thousand letters a month in 1970, nearly a quarter of which were addressed to the Advisor. "May 1970 Editorial Mail" Report, compiled by Carole Craig, ACS Papers, box 1970 R–S, folder 4.

18. Joanne Meyerowitz, "Women, Cheesecake and Borderline Material: Responses to Girlie Pictures in the Mid-Twentieth-Century United States," in *Sexual Borderlands: Constructing an American Sexual Past*, ed. Kathleen Kennedy and Sharon Ullman (Columbus: Ohio State University Press, 2003), 320–45.

19. James K. Beggan, Scott T. Allison, and Patricia Gagné. "An Analysis of Stereotype Refutation in *Playboy* by an Editorial Voice: The Advisor Hypothesis," *Journal of Men's Studies* 9, no. 1 (Fall 2000): 1–21.

20. Barbara Ehrenreich, *The Hearts of Men: American Dreams and the Flight from Commitment* (Garden City, NY: Anchor Press/Doubleday, 1983), chapter 4.

21. Editorial response to J. K., Advisor, *Playboy*, June 1967, 43.

22. Editorial response to Miss J. M., Advisor, *Playboy*, May 1970, 59.

23. Editorial response to H. S., Advisor, *Playboy*, September 1971, 64.

24. Anne S. Lombard, *Making Manhood: Growing Up Male in Colonial New England* (Cambridge, MA: Harvard University Press, 2003); Ruth Rosen, *The Lost Sisterhood: Prostitution in America, 1900–1918* (Baltimore: Johns Hopkins University Press, 1982); E. Anthony Rotundo, *American Manhood: Transformations in Masculinity from the Revolution to the Modern Era* (New York: Basic Books, 1993); Christine Stansell, *City of Women: Sex and Class in New York, 1789–1860* (Urbana: University of Illinois Press, 1987).

25. Rotundo, *American Manhood*, 125.

26. Hefner, "Philosophy (December 1962)," brochure part 1, installment 1,1. For further discussion of the Philosophy, see Watts, *Mr. Playboy*, chapter 9.

27. Watts, *Mr. Playboy*, 186.

28. Weyr, *Reaching for Paradise*, 207.

29. Hefner, "Philosophy (March 1964)," brochure part 3, installment 16,128.

30. Editorial response, Forum, *Playboy*, August 1969, 48.

31. For more on midcentury psychiatric views of sexuality, see John D'Emilio, *Sexual Politics, Sexual Communities: The Making of a Homosexual Minority in the United States, 1940–1970* (Chicago: University of Chicago Press, 1983); Beth Bailey, *Sex in the Heartland* (Cambridge, MA: Harvard University Press, 1999); Joanne Meyerowitz, *How*

Sex Changed: A History of Transsexuality in the United States (Cambridge, MA: Harvard University Press, 2002).

32. Letter from Hefner to Mr. John Goldston, May 20, 1955. HMH Papers, box 3, 1955–56, folder 3.

33. Kinsey found that 37 percent of men and 13 percent of women admitted to having a sexual experience with a member of their own sex. D'Emilio, *Sexual Politics*, 35.

34. Jonathan Katz, *The Invention of Heterosexuality* (New York: Dutton, 1995), 66, 96.

35. David Allyn, *Make Love, Not War: The Sexual Revolution: An Unfettered History* (Boston: Little, Brown, 2000), 19, 21.

36. Author interview with Hefner.

37. Allyn, *Make Love, Not War*, 179.

38. Allyn, *Make Love, Not War*, 179. The American Psychiatric Association classified homosexuality as a mental illness until 1973.

39. Letter from Hefner to Ray Bradbury, July 11, 1955. HMH Papers, box 1, 1954–55, folder 8.

40. Letters to the editor, *Playboy*, November 1955, 5–6.

41. D'Emilio, *Sexual Politics*, 134.

42. D'Emilio, *Sexual Politics*, 138.

43. Response to M. M., Advisor, *Playboy*, July 1964, 25.

44. Response to R. W., Advisor, *Playboy*, September 1964, 62.

45. Hefner, "Philosophy (March 1964)," brochure part 3, installment 16, 128.

46. Hefner, "Philosophy (March 1964)," brochure part 3, installment 16,128.

47. Kevin White, *The First Sexual Revolution: The Emergence of Male Heterosexuality in Modern America* (New York: New York University Press, 1993), 9.

48. This incident is discussed in Steven Watts's biography, *Mr. Playboy*, 58.

49. George Chauncey, *Gay New York: Gender, Urban Culture and the Making of the Gay Male World, 1890–1940* (New York: Basic Books, 1994).

50. Hefner, "Philosophy (March 1964)," brochure part 3, installment 16,128.

51. Letter from Gerald C. Davison, Forum, *Playboy*, April 1967, 51.

52. Letter from David H. Barlow, Forum, *Playboy*, August 1968, 37.

53. Editorial response to Davison, Forum, *Playboy*, April 1967, 51.

54. Letter from anonymous, Forum, *Playboy*, December 1967, 83.

55. Editorial response, Forum, *Playboy*, July 1968, 51. The term "inversion" was originally used in the late nineteenth century to describe individuals who adopted the gender characteristics of the opposite sex. Here it is used interchangeably with "homosexuality."

56. Editorial response to Kameny, Forum, *Playboy*, March 1969, 46, 48.

57. Letter from Rita Laporte, Forum, *Playboy*, June 1969, 69.

58. Letter from William Edward Glover, Forum, *Playboy*, August 1969, 48.

59. Editorial response to L. G., Advisor, *Playboy*, August 1970, 38.

60. Letter and editorial response to J. P., Advisor, *Playboy*, May 1971, 56, 58.

61. Beggan et. al., "The Advisor Hypothesis," 13.

62. Editorial response to Rita Laporte, Forum, *Playboy*, June 1969, 69.

63. *Time*, "Coming to Terms," October 24, 1969.

64. Letter from Charles Philips, Forum, *Playboy*, October 1964, 64.

65. Letter from anonymous, Forum, *Playboy*, June 1964, 53.

66. Letter from anonymous, Forum, *Playboy*, February 1967, 38.

67. Letter from M. W., Advisor, *Playboy*, September 1972, 52.

68. Letter from anonymous, Forum, *Playboy*, February 1968, 46.

69. Letter from Lew Norton, Forum, *Playboy*, October 1967, 56.

70. Police harassment of gay men was a popular topic in the Advisor because of the political sympathy the magazine offered to gay men, but also because the issue intersected with the question of appropriate use of state power. In the Philosophy, Hefner repeatedly spoke out against governmental abuse of power in post office attempts to censor mail, regarding the right to privacy, and other similar issues.

71. Out of thirty-three letters published, nine discussed homosexuality.

72. Letter from James P. Wittenberg, Forum, *Playboy*, December 1967, 84.

73. Letter from anonymous, Forum, *Playboy*, December 1967, 84.

74. Letter from anonymous and editorial response, Forum, *Playboy*, May 1968, 61.

75. Author interview with Hefner.

76. Editorial response to J. F., Advisor, *Playboy*, January 1969, 46, and response to A. H., September 1969, 66.

77. Editorial response to T. B., Advisor, *Playboy*, January 1969, 46.

78. Letter from A. C. and editorial response, Advisor, *Playboy*, October 1965, 44.

79. Editorial response to J. V., Advisor, *Playboy*, July 1972, 46.

80. Editorial response to K. N., Advisor, *Playboy*, April 1964, 39. This response also emphasized that forestalling marriage was "especially essential" for men, because their lives and personalities would evolve so much through their twenties. It is unclear why *Playboy* believed men changed more as they matured than did women.

81. Editorial response to Charles Porter, Forum, *Playboy*, January 1973, 55.

82. Author interview with Petersen.

83. Editorial response to Miss G. M., Advisor, *Playboy*, December 1969, 64.

84. Editorial response to S. H., Advisor, *Playboy*, December 1969, 68.

85. Editorial response to G. B., Advisor, *Playboy*, February 1968, 34–35.

86. Editorial response to J. R. P., Advisor, *Playboy*, October 1968, 62.

87. Editorial response to E. F., Advisor, *Playboy*, June 1968, 50.

88. Editorial response to M. G., Advisor, *Playboy*, December 1961, 47.

89. Editorial response to W. L. H., Advisor, *Playboy*, March 1968, 40.

90. Letter from Mrs. C. S., and editorial response, Advisor, *Playboy*, June 1968, 47.

91. Letter from Mrs. M. L. and editorial response, Advisor, *Playboy*, July 1969, 39.

92. Editorial response to T. B., Advisor, *Playboy*, November 1968, 64.

93. Editorial response to Mrs. A. M., Advisor, *Playboy*, September 1971, 64.

94. Editorial response to Miss G. M., Advisor, *Playboy*, December 1969, 64.

95. Editorial response to B. Z., Advisor, *Playboy*, February 1969, 42.

96. Editorial response to Miss P. S., Advisor, *Playboy*, March 1969, 38.

97. Editorial response to Miss E. V., Advisor, *Playboy*, June 1970, 45.

98. This statistic was provided to the author by *Playboy* publicist Lauren Melone, in an email dated November 1, 2007. Melone noted that Mediamark Research, Inc. (MRI), a leading industry research group, began tracking the demographics of *Playboy*'s readership, including women, in 1970. She had no official information on women readers prior to 1970. Measuring readership is notoriously difficult, but various sources, both inside and outside of *Playboy*, agree on an estimated 20–25 percent female readership prior to 1970 (author interviews), and an article in *Time* magazine cited this statistic in 1967 ("Think Clean," March 3, 1967). For more on MRI, see John Tebbel and Mary Ellen Zuckerman, *Magazine in America, 1741–1990* (New York: Oxford University Press, 1991), 360.

99. Beggan et al., "The Advisor Hypothesis," 14.

100. Letter from Miss. L. R., Advisor, *Playboy*, November 1970, 50.

101. Bailey, *Sex in the Heartland*, 105.

102. Letter from anonymous and editorial response, Advisor, *Playboy*, July 1970, 50. Similar information was provided in July 1971, 48.

103. Letter from Miss C. T., Advisor, *Playboy*, May 1971, 58.

104. Editorial response to C. N., Advisor, *Playboy*, September 1971, 64.

105. Letter from Miss R. Hansen, Forum, *Playboy*, October 1973, 62.

106. Ruth Rosen, *The World Split Open: How the Modern Women's Movement Changed America* (New York: Penguin, 2001), 150.

107. Letter from Miss O. C. and editorial response, Advisor, *Playboy*, March 1971, 48.

108. Editorial response to L. M., Advisor, *Playboy*, August 1973, 43.

109. Letter from Mrs. B. E. and editorial response, Advisor, *Playboy*, August 1968, 35.

110. Editorial response to D. A., Advisor, *Playboy*, March 1969, 37.

111. Editorial response to B. S., Advisor, *Playboy*, February 1966, 40.

112. Editorial response to B. C., Advisor, *Playboy*, November 1968, 63.

113. Editorial response to G. L., Advisor, *Playboy*, April 1967, 46.

114. Allyn, *Make Love, Not War*, 166.

115. Allyn, *Make Love, Not War*, 168, and Nat Lehrman, *Masters and Johnson Explained* (Chicago: Playboy Press, 1970), 17.

116. Allyn, *Make Love, Not War*, 166–68.

117. Memo from Hefner to Nat Lehrman, March 18, 1970. HMH Papers, box 135, 1970 Lehrman–L misc., folder 4.

118. Lehrman autobiographical notes.

119. Hefner autobiography notes written by Lehrman. Lehrman was an early Playboy Foundation executive. Also from statistics provided to the author by the current executive director of the foundation, Cleo Wilson, "Playboy Foundation Grants, 1964–1970."

120. Nat Lehrman, "*Playboy* Interview: William Masters and Virginia Johnson," *Playboy*, May 1968, 102.

121. Lehrman, *Masters and Johnson Explained*, 16.

122. Lehrman, *Masters and Johnson Explained*, 17.

123. Lehrman autobiographical notes; and memo from Lehrman to Hefner, July 7, 1970. HMH Papers, box 135, 1970 Lehrman–L misc., folder 4.

124. Masters's initial work on sexuality began in 1954 with a study of behavior and arousal in prostitutes. Allyn, *Make Love, Not War*, 167.

125. Allyn, *Make Love, Not War*, 168–73.

126. Lehrman, "*Playboy* Interview: Masters and Johnson," 103.

127. Memo from Spectorsky to Hefner, January 9, 1970. ACS Papers, box 61, 1970 H–K, folder 3; and editorial, "Playbill," *Playboy*, May 1970, 3.

128. This article will be examined in detail in chapter 5.

129. Morton Hunt, "The Future of Marriage," *Playboy*, August 1971, 118.

130. Hunt, "Future of Marriage," 168.

131. Hunt, "Future of Marriage," 171.

CHAPTER FIVE

1. Wil S. Hylton, "Hugh Hefner," *Esquire*, June 2002, 100. This chapter was first published as "The Battle in Every Man's Bed: *Playboy* and the Fiery Feminists," *Journal of the History of Sexuality* 17, no. 2 (2008): 259–89.

2. Gloria Steinem, "I Was a Playboy Bunny," in *Outrageous Acts and Everyday Rebellions* (New York: Henry Holt and Company, 1995), 32. For more on the Bunny experience see, Kathryn Lee Scott, *The Bunny Years* (New York: Pomegranate Press, 1999), and Steven Watts's discussion of the Steinem story in *Mr. Playboy: Hugh Hefner and the American Dream* (Hoboken: John Wiley and Sons, Inc., 2008), 237–39.

3. No author, "No More Miss America," in *Takin' It to the Streets: A Sixties Reader*, ed. Alexander Bloom and Wini Breines (New York: Oxford University Press, 1995), 483.

4. With the growth of hardcore publications in the 1970s and the parallel growth of the feminist antiporn movement, *Playboy* was increasingly lumped together with those magazines that promoted harsh or even violent treatment of women. However, scholars Joseph E. Scott and Steven J. Cuvelier conducted a study of images of violence in *Playboy* and found them almost totally lacking. Joseph E. Scott and Steven J. Cuvelier, "Sexual Violence in *Playboy* Magazine: A Longitudinal Content Analysis," *Journal of Sex Research* 23, no. 4 (November 1987): 534–39. Alternatively, psychologists Mala L. Matacin and Jerry M. Burger analyzed *Playboy* cartoons from 1985 and concluded that "subtle" negative sexual stereotypes of women were portrayed in cartoons from that year, though not in the majority of cases. Mala L. Matacin and Jerry M. Burger, "A Content Analysis of Sexual Themes in *Playboy* Cartoons," *Sex Roles* 17, nos. 3–4 (1987): 179–86.

5. Watts, *Mr. Playboy*, 230.

6. Watts, *Mr. Playboy*, 210.

7. Author interview with Hugh M. Hefner, November 3, 2006, Los Angeles, CA.

8. Lehrman worked at *Playboy* from 1963 to 1987 in various capacities, including as

senior editor and president of publishing, and he helped to found and operate the Play-boy Foundation. As editor, Lehrman was in charge of all articles that dealt with human sexuality. The quotation is from Nat Lehrman, taken from personal notes and recollec-tions that he had drawn up for an autobiography of Hugh Hefner that was never com-pleted. The notes were given to the author in an email dated June 19, 2006. Lehrman repeated this statement in an interview with the author on June 23, 2006.

9. Author interviews with longtime *Playboy* editors Jim Petersen, February 2, 2006, Evanston, IL; Barbara Nellis, May 4, 2006, Chicago, IL; Arlene Bouras, June 22, 2006, New York City, NY; Nat Lehrman, June 23, 2006, New York City, NY.

10. The women's movement grew to include activists and organizations that had various and often competing agendas, including the politics of race, sexual orienta-tion, class, motherhood, etc. There has been extensive writing on the topic. For a good overview, see Ruth Rosen, *The World Split Open: How the Modern Women's Movement Changed America* (New York: Viking, 2000).

11. Author interview with Hefner.

12. Author interview with Hefner.

13. Thomas Weyr, *Reaching for Paradise: The Playboy Vision of America* (New York: New York Times Books, 1978), 173.

14. Author interview with Hefner.

15. Author interview with Nellis.

16. Author interview with Nellis.

17. Sara M. Evans, *Born for Liberty: A History of Women in America* (New York: Free Press, 1989), 277.

18. Bloom and Breines, *Takin' It to the Streets*, 482.

19. Susan J. Douglas, *Where the Girls Are: Growing Up Female with the Mass Media* (New York: New York Times Books, 1994), 167.

20. *Time*, "The New Feminists: Revolt against 'Sexism,'" November 21, 1969, 53.

21. *Time*, "The New Feminists," 54, 56.

22. Helen Gurley Brown, "Step Into My Parlor," *Cosmopolitan*, April 1970, 4.

23. *Esquire*, "When Did You Begin to Take the Women's Movement Seriously?" July 1973, 102.

24. Grace Lichtenstein, "For Most Women,'Strike' Day Was Just a Topic of Conver-sation," *New York Times*, August 27, 1970, 30.

25. Helen Lawrenson, "The Feminine Mistake," *Esquire*, January 1971, 83, 154.

26. Sara Davidson, "Foremothers," *Esquire*, July 1973, 71; Germaine Greer, "What Turns Women On?" *Esquire*, July 1973, 88.

27. *Esquire*, "302 Women Who Are Cute When They're Mad," July 1973, 81, 80.

28. *Esquire*, "What If . . . Gloria Steinem were Miss America?" July 1973, 132.

29. Douglas, *Where the Girls Are*, 193–203. For more on feminism and television in the 1970s, see Alana Levine, *Wallowing in Sex: The New Sexual Culture of 1970s American Television* (Durham: Duke University Press, 2007), esp. chapter 4.

30. Douglas, *Where the Girls Are*, 201–2; Molly Haskell, *From Reverence to Rape: The Treatment of Women in the Movies* (New York: Penguin Books, 1974), 323.

31. Russell Miller, *Bunny: The Real Story of Playboy* (New York: Holt, Rinehart, and Winston, 1984), 180.

32. Rosen, *The World Split Open*, 163. Thanks to Sarah Lindsley for information on this protest.

33. Thomas Weyr, *Reaching for Paradise*, 225.

34. Alice Echols, *Daring to Be Bad: Radical Feminism in America, 1967–1975* (Minneapolis: University of Minnesota Press, 1989), 214–15.

35. Ellen Carol DuBois and Lynn Dumenil, eds., *Through Women's Eyes: An American History* (Boston: Bedford/St. Martin's, 2005), 638, 644.

36. Evans, *Born for Liberty*, 288.

37. Author interview with Nellis.

38. John Clellon Holmes, "The New Girl," *Playboy*, January 1968, 178–81.

39. Holmes, "The New Girl," 182.

40. Holmes, "The New Girl," 182.

41. Holmes, "The New Girl," 186.

42. For more on Gurley Brown, see Jennifer Scanlon, *Bad Girls Go Everywhere: The Life of Helen Gurley Brown* (New York: Oxford University Press, 2009).

43. In *Make Love, Not War*, David Allyn sees *Playboy*'s inclusion of Wylie's writings, particularly in "The Career Woman," as an indication that *Playboy* and thus Hefner did not support Helen Gurley Brown's version of financially independent womanhood. Reflecting the magazine's often contradictory approach to femininity, however, there is also evidence to the contrary. For example, *Playboy* featured an article on women and employment by Brown, "Sex and the Office," in July 1964. While James Gilbert shows a "literary friendship" between Spectorsky and Wylie, archival evidence suggests a similar relationship between Spectorsky and Brown (letters from Brown to Spectorsky dated from 1963 to 1972, from a collection of letters that were auctioned by Christie's, December 2003, copy in possession of Playboy Enterprises, Inc., Chicago, IL, no box or other identifying number). In support of Brown and *Cosmopolitan*, Spectorsky shared *Playboy*'s prized list of "profile writers" and fees with her in 1967, some of the highest in the industry (letter from Brown to Spectorsky, January 31, 1967, from letters auctioned by Christie's). Hefner confirms an alliance with Brown (author interview with Hefner).

44. Helen Gurley Brown, *Sex and the Single Girl* (New York: Random House, 1962), front cover.

45. Author interview with Hefner.

46. Author interview with Hefner.

47. Brown, *Single Girl*, 4–5.

48. *Playboy*, "*Playboy* Interview: Helen Gurley Brown," April 1963, taken from *Playboy* online archive, The *Playboy* Cyber Club, http://cyber.playboy.com/members/magazine/interviews/196304/.

49. Brown, *Single Girl*, 105.

50. Brown interview, online archive.

51. Brown interview, online archive.

52. Brown interview, online archive.

53. Brown interview, online archive.

54. Brown interview, online archive.

55. Brown interview, online archive.

56. Brown interview, online archive.

57. Letter from Helen Gurley Brown to A. C. Spectorsky, January 31, 1967. From collection of letters that were auctioned by Christie's, December 2003. Copy in possession of Playboy Enterprises, Inc., Chicago, IL. No box.

58. Letter from Helen Gurley Brown to A. C. Spectorsky, February 10, 1971, auctioned letters.

59. Letter from Helen Gurley Brown to A. C. Spectorsky, March 11, 1966, auctioned letters.

60. Letter to the editor from Helen Gurley Brown, re: "Venus Defiled," June 1966, auctioned letters.

61. Bryce Nelson, "Antibunnies Jeer at Hefner Peace Bash," *Los Angeles Times*, April 17, 1970, 20.

62. Nelson, "Antibunnies."

63. *New York Times*, "Women Militants Disrupt Cavett Show with Hefner," May 27, 1970, 95.

64. Scott Moore, "New Front in Battle of Sexes: Campus Women Want to Liberate Betty Coed," *Los Angeles Times*, February 16, 1970, 3.

65. No author, "No More Miss America," in Bloom and Breines, *Takin' It to the Streets*, 483.

66. From the private archive of Hugh M. Hefner, housed at the Playboy Mansion West, Los Angeles, CA. My thanks to Hefner's historian and archivist, Steve Martinez, for making a copy available to me.

67. Letter from Michael Sharwood-Smith, Forum, *Playboy*, January 1970, 64.

68. Letter from Myra A. Josephs, Forum, *Playboy*, April 1970, 60.

69. Editorial response to Myra A. Josephs, Forum, *Playboy*, April 1970, 60.

70. Watts, *Mr. Playboy*, 236, 243.

71. Memo from Hefner to Spectorsky, January 30, 1970. ACS Papers, box 61, 1970 H–K, folder 3.

72. Julie Baumgold, "You've Come a Long Way, Baby," *New York*, June 9, 1969, 27–29.

73. Baumgold, "You've Come a Long Way," 27.

74. Baumgold, "You've Come a Long Way," 28.

75. Baumgold, "You've Come a Long Way," 32.

76. Memo "Articles for *Playboy*," from Hefner to Spectorsky, July 17, 1969. ACS Papers, box 61, 1970 H–K, folder 3.

77. Morton Hunt, "Up Against the Wall, Male Chauvinist Pig!" *Playboy*, May 1970, 95–96.

78. Author interview with Petersen.

79. Hunt, "Up Against the Wall," 96, 102.

80. Rosen, *The World Split Open*, on Steinem see 216, on sexuality see 164–75. While these were legitimate issues among feminists, the media often focused on attractiveness and sexual orientation as a way of trivializing the movement; see Douglas, *Where the Girls Are*, 227–28.

81. Allyn, *Make Love, Not War*, 166.

82. Memo "Feminist Article," from Spectorsky to Dick Rosensweig, December 15, 1969. ACS Papers, box 61, 1970 H–K, folder 3.

83. Memo "Super-feminist Movement," from Jack Kessie to Spectorsky, December 12, 1969. ACS Papers, box 61, 1970 H–K, folder 3.

84. Steinem did not respond to Lehrman's request. Braudy had been working as a freelance writer for *New York* magazine and the *New York Times* when *Playboy* contacted her (Weyr, *Reaching for Paradise*, 226).

85. Susan Braudy, "Women's Liberation Movement" manuscript, 16. ACS Papers, box 61, 1970 H–K, folder 3.

86. Braudy manuscript.

87. Braudy manuscript.

88. Braudy manuscript.

89. Braudy manuscript.

90. Braudy manuscript.

91. Braudy manuscript.

92. Braudy manuscript.

93. Braudy manuscript.

94. I describe the reaction as "unusual" because I found no other article in the company's archive from the period of the 1960s and '70s to have elicited so much editorial discussion.

95. Memo from Julia Trelease to Jim Goode, December 11, 1969. ACS Papers, box 61, 1970 H–K, folder 3.

96. Memo from Pat Pappas to Jack Kessie, December 11, 1969. ACS Papers, box 61, 1970 H–K, folder 3.

97. Memo from Arlene Bouras to Jack Kessie, December 11, 1969. ACS Papers, box 61, 1970 H–K, folder 3.

98. Memo from Michelle Altman to Pat Pappas (undated, but probably from December 11, 1969). ACS Papers, box 61, 1970 H–K, folder 3.

99. The memo is simply signed "M," but was most likely from Lawrence.

100. Memo from Michael Lawrence to Jim Goode, December 5, 1969. ACS Papers, box 61, 1970 H–K, folder 3.

101. Memo from Arthur Kretchmer to Jim Goode, December 11, 1969. ACS Papers, box 61, 1970 H–K, folder 3.

102. Memo from Nat Lehrman to Jack Kessie, December 16, 1969. ACS Papers, box 61, 1970 H–K, folder 3.

103. Memo from Hefner to Spectorsky, January 6, 1970. ACS Papers, box 61, 1970 H–K, folder 3.

104. Memo from Hefner to Spectorsky, January 6, 1970. ACS Papers, box 61, 1970 H–K, folder 3.

105. Susan Braudy, "The Article I Wrote on Women That *Playboy* Wouldn't Publish," *Glamour*, May 1971, 246. In fact, Hefner's view was not all that hidden in the darkness of his heart. Views like the one expressed in the memo were articulated publicly in *Playboy*. In August 1970, *Playboy* elaborated on the Braudy controversy, after a reader asked why they had not used a woman journalist for the feminism piece. Editorial comment in the Forum admitted that Hefner asked for a "devastating" piece on feminism in which militants are once again called "kookie." *Playboy*, August 1970, 52.

106. Watts, *Mr. Playboy*, 242.

107. Memo from Spectorsky to Hefner (apparently unsent), January 7, 1970. ACS Papers, box 61, 1970 H–K, folder 3.

108. Memo from Spectorsky to Hefner, January 9, 1970. ACS Papers, box 61, 1970 H–K, folder 3.

109. Memo from Hefner to Spectorsky, January 30, 1970. ACS Papers, box 61, 1970 H–K, folder 3.

110. Hunt, "Up Against the Wall," 95.

111. Hunt, "Up Against the Wall," 96.

112. Hunt, "Up Against the Wall," 206.

113. Hunt, "Up Against the Wall," 104.

114. Hunt, "Up Against the Wall," 96.

115. Hunt, "Up Against the Wall," 96.

116. Hunt, "Up Against the Wall," 206.

117. Hunt, "Up Against the Wall," 207–8.

118. Hunt, "Up Against the Wall" 208.

119. Hunt, "Up Against the Wall," 208.

120. Hunt, "Up Against the Wall," 209.

121. Hunt, "Up Against the Wall," 206.

122. Author interview with Petersen. In September 1970, *Playboy* explained, "By 'female sexual characteristics,' we [do] not mean any specific artificial beauty aids (such as false eyelashes) nor such culturally learned behavior patterns as submissiveness. We meant the kind of behavior that serves . . . to signal one's femaleness and distinguish it from maleness—in other words, sex appeal. . . . We can't give you a detailed list of these signals, but we know them when we see them" (214).

123. Hunt, "Up Against the Wall," 95.

124. The readers' letters report was compiled each month and distributed to *Playboy* editors as a summary of reader response to the elements of each issue.

125. Of the fourteen letters published, only five were from women. This proportion is in contrast to the readers' letters report, which states that "a predominantly female, very vocal, readership responded" to the article. The quotation is from page 6 of report, unattributed. HMH, Reader Services, 1970 (box number missing).

126. Letters to the editor, *Playboy*, August 1970, 7–8.

127. Letters to the editor, *Playboy*, August 1970, 8.

128. Letters to the editor, *Playboy*, August 1970, 8.

129. Vivian Gornick, "The Women's Liberation Movement!" *Cosmopolitan*, April 1970, 144.

130. Moore, "New Front in Battle of Sexes," A1.

131. Gornick, "Women's Liberation," 140.

132. Memo from Stuart to Hefner and Lehrman, April 8, 1970. HMH Papers, box 135, 1970 Lehrman–L Misc., folder 4.

133. Memo from Mary Ann Stuart to Hefner and Lehrman, April 8, 1970. HMH Papers, box 135, 1970 Lehrman–L Misc., folder 4.

134. Memo from Lehrman to Stuart, April 8, 1970. HMH Papers, box 135, 1970 Lehrman–L Misc., folder 4.

135. Memo from Hefner to Lehrman and Stuart, June 23, 1970. HMH Papers, box 135, 1970 Lehrman–L Misc., folder 4. The right of women to work was articulated in the magazine. The March 1972 Advisor, for example, chastised a man for wanting his wife to stay at home. The Advisor said, "we can't see why you'd object to your wife's finishing her education and experimenting with a career. To deprive her of a chance to feel valuable to herself and society about and beyond the roles of wife and mother would be not only selfish but cruel. . . . [Y]ou should look forward to gaining a wife, who . . . will be infinitely more interesting—and challenging." *Playboy*, March 1972, 41.

136. Author interview with Lehrman.

137. Author interview Hefner.

138. Author interview with Hefner.

139. Watts, *Mr. Playboy*, 246.

140. Memo from Hefner to Spectorsky, 6 January 1970, ACS Papers, box 61, 1970 H–K, folder 3.

CHAPTER SIX

1. Author interview with Barbara Nellis, May 4, 2006, Chicago, IL. This chapter was first published as "The Battle in Every Man's Bed: *Playboy* and the Fiery Feminists," *Journal of the History of Sexuality* 17, no. 2 (2008): 259–89.

2. Correspondence from Greer to Nellis, dated 1971. From the personal collection of Nellis.

3. Author interview with Nellis.

4. *Playboy*, "On the Scene," July 1971, 159.

5. *Playboy*, "Fleshing Out the Sex-Fantasy Quiz," February 1973, 150.

6. *Playboy*, "*Playboy* Interview: Germaine Greer," January 1972, taken from the *Playboy* online archive, The *Playboy* Cyber Club, http://cyber.playboy.com/members/magazine/interviews/ 197201/.

7. Author interview with Lehrman, June 23, 2006, New York City, NY.

8. Author interview with Lehrman.

9. Greer interview, online archive.

10. Greer interview, online archive.

11. Greer interview, online archive.

12. Letters to the editor, *Playboy*, April 1972, 12–14.

13. Germaine Greer, "Seduction Is a Four-Letter Word," *Playboy*, January 1973, 82.

14. Greer, "Seduction," 164.

15. Author interview with Lehrman.

16. Greer, "Seduction," 178.

17. Greer, "Seduction," 226.

18. Greer, "Seduction," 228.

19. Greer, "Seduction," 228 (emphasis in the original).

20. Martha Weinman Lear, "Q: If You Rape a Woman and Steal Her TV, What Can They Get You for in New York? A: Stealing Her TV," *New York Times*, January 30, 1972, 11, 55.

21. Ruth Rosen, *The World Split Open: How the Modern Women's Movement Changed America* (New York: Viking, 2000), 183.

22. Rosen, *The World Split Open*, 182.

23. Letters to the editor, *Playboy*, April 1973, 11–12.

24. Playbill, *Playboy*, January 1973, 3.

25. Hefner spent one semester studying sociology in graduate school at Northwestern University in 1950 (Thomas Weyr, *Reaching for Paradise: The Playboy Vision of America* [New York: New York Times Books, 1978], 19). He wrote a paper entitled "Sex Behavior and the U.S. Law," in which he argued that if all sex laws still on the books were enforced, most Americans would be prosecuted (copy of paper from Hefner's personal archive at Playboy Mansion West, provided by Steve Martinez).

26. Weyr, *Reaching for Paradise*, 207.

27. Letter from Joan Siegel, Forum, *Playboy*, January 1972, 48.

28. Letter from Mrs. Jack Rubin, Forum, *Playboy*, December 1970, 88.

29. Editorial response, Forum, *Playboy*, July 1971, 45–46.

30. Letter from Nat Lehrman to Shirley Katzander, August 19, 1970. HMH Papers, box 135, 1970 Lehrman–L Misc., folder 4.

31. Bryce Nelson, "Antibunnies Jeer at Hefner Peace Bash," *Los Angeles Times*, April 17, 1970, 20.

32. Letter from Nat Lehrman to Shirley Katzander, August 19, 1970. HMH Papers, box 135, 1970 Lehrman–L Misc., folder 4.

33. Letter from Daniel Ross Chandler, Forum, *Playboy*, April 1971, 54.

34. *Playboy*, "The Playboy Foundation 'Annual Report,'" January 1973, 57.

35. Author email interview with Burt Joseph, December 20, 2006.

36. Budget allocation for fiscal year 1971–72 gives a sense of the foundation's modest scope. The largest grants of $50,000 went to sex researchers Masters and Johnson; a voter registration project and a "pilot program in medical sex education at the University of Minnesota" each got $15,000; the National Committee for Prisoner's Rights and SIECUS received $25,000; Firearms Education and Information Council got $10,000; IUD Research Project got $2,900; NORML received $2,500; United Farm Workers Right

to Work Legal Defense Fund received $2,500. Smaller donations of $500 to $1,500 were made to other cases and organizations dealing with marijuana, Civil Service discrimination, and public housing, among other things, for a total of $154,400 in existing commitments. In addition, the foundation operated a crisis intervention telephone service, adding $100,000 to the budget. The recommended budget for 1971–72 was set at $750,000, plus the phone service. Memo from Burton Joseph to board of directors of the Playboy Foundation, June 29, 1971. ACS Papers, box 70, 1971 M–P, folder 10. In an email to the author dated September 23, 2009, Joseph confirmed overall budget estimate.

37. Details for the year 1970–71. Typically, most grants went to "sex research and sex related cases." In the fiscal year 1970–71, the foundation received approximately one thousand proposals, about half of which were "referred to another organization or supplied with the information requested or helped in some other way." Approximately one-quarter of proposals were rejected, and the last quarter received grant money. Memo from Burton Joseph to board of directors of the Playboy Foundation, June 29, 1971. ACS Papers, box 70, 1971 M–P, folder 10.

38. Memo from Burton Joseph to board of directors of the Playboy Foundation, June 29, 1971. ACS Papers, box 70, 1971 M–P, folder 10.

39. Statistics provided by Playboy Foundation director Cleo Wilson, "Playboy Foundation Grants," 1970–72. Information collected in a binder in the possession of Ms. Wilson, given to the author on November 14, 2007.

40. Mary Joe Neitz, review of *Abortion and the Politics of Motherhood*, by Kristin Luker, *Journal for the Scientific Study of Religion* 24, no. 4 (December 1985): 446.

41. *Playboy*, "The Playboy Foundation 'Annual Report,'" January 1973, 57.

42. *Playboy*, "The Playboy Foundation 'Annual Report,'" January 1973, 57.

43. Memo from Lehrman to Dick Rosenzweig, June 17, 1970. HMH Papers, box 135, 1970 Lehrman–L misc., folder 4.

44. Memo from Lehrman to Dick Rosenzweig, Bob Preuss, and Bob Gutwillig, July 30, 1970. HMH Papers, box 135, 1970 Lehrman–L misc., folder 1. Statistic taken from a list of foundation grants provided to the author by Cleo Wilson, executive director of the foundation, November 14, 2007.

45. Letter from Shirley Wheeler and editorial response, Forum, *Playboy*, December 1971, 77.

46. Memo from Cleo Wilson to Murray Fisher, "History of Reproductive Rights Giving," July 18, 1991. Document included in a binder in the possession of Ms. Wilson, given to the author on November 14, 2007.

47. Author interview with Joseph.

48. Ellen Messer and Kathryn E. May, eds., *Back Rooms: Voices from the Illegal Abortion Era* (Buffalo: Prometheus Books, 1994), 193.

49. J. Star, "Growing Tragedy of Illegal Abortion," *Look*, October 19, 1965, 149–50; Dr. X, "Doctor's Dilemma," *Ladies' Home Journal*, May 1966, 98–99; *Time*, "More Abortions: Reasons Why," September 17, 1965, 82.

50. Jennifer Scanlon, *Bad Girls Go Everywhere: The Life of Helen Gurley Brown* (New York: Oxford University Press, 2009). This information was provided by Scanlon to the author in emails dated January 15–18, 2008.

51. Messer and May, *Back Rooms*, 199.

52. Messer and May, *Back Rooms*, 199.

53. Based on a search of abortion articles in the online database *Readers' Guide Retrospective*.

54. *Time*, "Proof of Abortion's Value," May 26, 1967; *Time*, "The Desperate Dilemma of Abortion," October 13, 1967.

55. Letter from Patricia Maginnis, Forum, *Playboy*, January 1967, 54. Lader also appeared in Forum in May 1972, 67.

56. Letter from Patricia T. Maginnis, Forum, *Playboy*, January 1969, 50.

57. Memo from Hefner to Michael Laurence, April 30, 1965. HMH Papers, box 54, 1965 D–Editorial, folder 6. In this memo, Hefner explicitly states that he plans to devote a Philosophy installment exclusively to the issue of abortion, but there are other references to this intent, though slightly less explicit, at least as early as February 1964.

58. Statistics provided by Playboy Foundation director Cleo Wilson, "Playboy Foundation Grants," 1964–70. Information collected in a binder in the possession of Ms. Wilson, given to the author on November 14, 2007.

59. Statistics provided by Playboy Foundation director Cleo Wilson, "Playboy Foundation Grants," 1966–77.

60. Letter from Janelle Lindsey and editorial response, Forum, *Playboy*, December 1965, 227–28.

61. *Time*, "Disease of Unwanted Pregnancy," September 15, 1967.

62. Letter from anonymous, Forum, *Playboy*, November 1966, 66.

63. Letter from anonymous, Forum, *Playboy*, May 1967, 149.

64. Letters, Forum, *Playboy*, August 1967, 35–37.

65. Editorial response, Forum, *Playboy*, August 1967, 37.

66. Ellen Carol DuBois and Lynn Dumenil, *Through Women's Eyes: An American History with Documents* (Boston: Bedford/St. Martin's, 2005), 647.

67. Messer and May, *Back Rooms*, 207.

68. Memo from Nat Lehrman to Dick Rosenzweig, March 27, 1969. HMH Papers, box 135, 1970 Lehrman–L Misc., folder 4.

69. Letter from William R. Baird, Forum, *Playboy*, February 1968, 48, 174.

70. Letter from Bill Baird, Forum, *Playboy*, June 1971, 185.

71. Letter from Pamela Wright, Forum, *Playboy*, April 1967, 172.

72. Letters from Arthur H. Jones and Charles P. Kelley, Forum, *Playboy*, August 1967, 35.

73. Letter from Nathan H. Rappaport, Forum, *Playboy*, November 1967, 169.

74. Letter from John Alden Settle, Jr., Forum, *Playboy*, September 1970, 214.

75. Letter from Lehrman to Rev. E. Spencer Parsons, March 5, 1970. HMH Papers, box 135, 1970 Lehrman–L Misc., folder 4.

76. Messer and May, *Back Rooms*, 214.

77. Memo from Lehrman to Dick Rosenzweig, January 27, 1970. HMH Papers, box 135, 1970 Lehrman–L Misc., folder 4.

78. Letter from Lehrman to Rev. E. Spencer Parsons, March 5, 1970. HMH Papers, box 135, 1970 Lehrman–L Misc., folder 4.

79. Memo from Lehrman to Dick Rosenzweig, January 27, 1970. HMH Papers, box 135, 1970 Lehrman–L Misc., folder 4.

80. Linda Gordon, *The Moral Property of Women: A History of Birth Control Politics in America* (Chicago: University of Illinois Press, 2007), 279–86.

81. Sir Julian Huxley, "The Age of Overbreed," *Playboy*, January 1965, 103.

82. Forum Newsfront, *Playboy*, July 1968, 47, and editorial response to anonymous letter, Forum, *Playboy*, July 1968, 51.

83. Gordon, *Moral Property*, 282.

84. Robert Hall, "The Abortion Revolution," *Playboy*, September 1970, 112.

85. Hall, "Abortion," 112.

86. Hall, "Abortion," 114.

87. Hall, "Abortion," 276.

88. Letter from anonymous, Forum, *Playboy*, December 1970, 86.

89. Letter from anonymous, Forum, *Playboy*, March 1971, 53.

90. Letter from James Nichols, Forum, *Playboy*, November 1972, 84.

91. Letter from Richard J. Green, Forum, *Playboy*, September 1972, 60.

92. *Playboy*, "The Abortion Backlash: A Special *Playboy* 'Forum' Report," September 1971, 77.

93. "Abortion Backlash," 77. The information provided was for legal services based on state law. A similar guide had been published in *New York* magazine on September 28, 1970.

94. Letter from Ruth Proskauer Smith, Forum, *Playboy*, May 1971, 73.

95. Letter from Ruth Proskauer Smith, Forum, *Playboy*, September 1972, 58.

96. Letter from Roberta Schneiderman, Forum, *Playboy*, April 1972, 195.

97. Letter from Harriet F. Pilpel, Forum, *Playboy*, January 1969, 51.

98. Letter from Bill Baird, Forum, *Playboy*, July 1972, 57.

99. Editorial response, Forum, *Playboy*, May 1973, 71.

100. Letter from Ruth Bader Ginsberg, Forum, *Playboy*, August 1973, 52.

101. Statistics provided by Playboy Foundation director Cleo Wilson, "Playboy Foundation Grants," 1972–76.

102. Statistics provided by Playboy Foundation director Cleo Wilson, "Playboy Foundation Grants," 1973–77.

103. Memo from Burton Joseph to board of directors of the Playboy Foundation, June 29, 1971. ACS Papers, box 70, 1971 M–P, folder 10.

104. Statistics provided by Playboy Foundation director Cleo Wilson, "Playboy Foundation Grants," 1973–77.

105. Weyr, *Reaching for Paradise*, 241.

106. Editorial response to Joan Siegel, Forum, *Playboy*, January 1972, 48. A similar incident occurred in the early 1980s when *Ms.* magazine returned over $11,000 from the Playboy Foundation. Lois Romano, "Cristie [*sic*] Hefner, Daughter of the Revolution," *Washington Post*, December 4, 1983.

107. Letter from Barbara A. Townley, Forum, *Playboy*, June 1972, 70–72.

108. Marjorie Fine Knowles, "Foundation Grants to Women's Groups," *Women's Studies Newsletter*, no. 5 (Fall 1973): 10.

109. Judith Ezekiel, *Feminism in the Heartland* (Columbus: Ohio State University Press, 2002), 151.

110. Lally Weymouth, "The Princess of Playboy," *New York Magazine*, June 21, 1982, 38.

111. Feminist hostility toward Playboy Foundation money intensified amid the rising antipornography movement of the early 1980s. For an articulation of this position, see Catharine A. MacKinnon, *Feminism Unmodified: Discourses on Life and Law* (Cambridge: Harvard University Press, 1988), 134–45. Even at this point, though, a debate over the issue of accepting foundation money occurred at a women's studies conference and "generated much controversy." Deborah Chalfie and Sarah McKinley, "The Politics of Funding the Women's Movement," in "Selected Abstracts from the Second National Conference of the National Women's Studies Association, May 16–20, 1980, Bloomington, Indiana," *Frontiers: A Journal of Women Studies* 6, nos. 1–2, (Spring–Summer 1981): 71.

CONCLUSION

1. Author interview with Hugh Hefner, November 3, 2006, Los Angeles, CA.

2. Gloria Steinem, "What *Playboy* Doesn't Know about Women Could Fill a Book," *McCall's*, October 1970, 139–40.

3. Steinem, "What *Playboy* Doesn't Know," 76.

4. Steinem, "What *Playboy* Doesn't Know," 139.

5. Gail Dines, "'I Buy It for the Articles': *Playboy* Magazine and the Sexualization of Consumerism," in *Gender, Race and Class in Media*, ed. Gail Dines and Jean M. Humez (Thousand Oaks, CA: Sage Publications, 1995), 260–61.

6. *Playboy*, "*Playboy* Interview: Betty Friedan," September 1992, taken from *Playboy* online archive, The Playboy Cyber Club, at http://cyber.playboy.com/members/magazine/interviews/199209/.

7. "*Playboy* Interview: Betty Friedan."

8. "*Playboy* Interview: Betty Friedan."

9. "*Playboy* Interview: Betty Friedan."

10. "*Playboy* Interview: Betty Friedan."

11. Ariel Levy, *Female Chauvinist Pigs: Women and the Rise of Raunch Culture* (New York: Free Press, 2005), 36.

12. Levy, *Female Chauvinist Pigs*, 35.

13. Biographical sheet of Hefner, provided by Linda Marsicano, Playboy Enterprises, Inc., via email to the author, September 27, 2007.

14. Levy, *Female Chauvinist Pigs*, 35–43; Lois Romano, "Cristie [*sic*] Hefner, Daughter of the Revolution," *Washington Post*, December 4, 1983, L1.

15. Mary Ellen Egan and Chana R. Schoenberger, "The World's 100 Most Powerful Women," *Forbes*, August 27, 2008.

16. Biography of Christie Hefner, Washington Speakers Bureau, www.washingtonspeakersbureau.com; the Washington Speakers Bureau, a leading booking agency, lists her as one of their most requested speakers.

17. Quote from CBS News transcripts, "Christie Hefner, CEO of Playboy, Successful Feminist Businesswoman," *60 Minutes*, January 24, 1993.

18. Romano, "Daughter of the Revolution."

19. Susan Kastner, "Think Playboy Demeans Women?" *Toronto Star*, March 19, 1995, C4.

20. Steven Watts, *Mr. Playboy: Hugh Hefner and the American Dream* (Hoboken: John Wiley and Sons, Inc., 2008), 343.

21. For more see Watts, *Mr. Playboy*, chap. 16.

22. Greg Burns, "Adventures in the Skin Trade," *Chicago Tribune Magazine*, October 16, 2005, 18.

23. Wendy Bounds, "Can Aging Playboy Bunny Lure Women?" *Wall Street Journal*, November 10, 1998, B1. Mark Hansel, "In Business Q and A: Christie Hefner," *In Business Las Vegas*, June 13–19, 2008, page unknown.

24. Brian McCormick, "Playboy Testing the XX Factor," *Crain's Chicago Business*, October 2001; Burns, "Adventures," 13–14.

25. Watts, *Mr. Playboy*, 344; Levy, *Female Chauvinist Pigs*, 6.

26. Biographical sheet of Hefner, provided by Linda Marsicano.

27. On Steinem, see Bounds, "Can Aging Playboy"; on Ehrenreich, see Roger Cohen, "Ms. Playboy," *New York Times*, June 9, 1991, section 6, 2.

28. "*Playboy* Interview: Betty Friedan."

29. Watts, *Mr. Playboy*, 344.

30. Catherine Flannery, "Playboy Boss True to the Feminist Cause," *Toronto Sun*, March 26, 1995, M5; CBS News transcripts, "Christie Hefner, CEO of Playboy, Successful Feminist Businesswoman," *60 Minutes*, January 24, 1993.

31. Michael Winerip, "No Silk Jammies for Her," *New York Times*, September 27, 2009, Sunday Styles section, 2.

32. Press release, "Conference Opening Session to Feature Advocate Christie Hefner," *American Library Association*, June 22, 2009, www.ala.org/ala/newspresscenter/news/pressreleases2009/june2009/christiehefner_confsvcs.cfm.

33. "Ex-Playboy CEO Christie Hefner on Lilly Ledbetter, Women in the Workforce and Political Aspirations," *wowOwow, The Women on the Web*, www.wowowow.com.

34. ABC News transcripts, "Playboy at 50 Hugh Hefner," *20/20*, November 28, 2003.

35. For some modern journalistic appraisals of *Playboy* and its history, see Joan Acocella, "The Girls Next Door," *New Yorker*, March 20, 2006; David Carr, "Can an Old Leopard Change Its Silk Pajamas?" *New York Times*, April 21, 2003; Jennifer Harper, "Buy *Playboy* for the Articles—Really," *Washington Times*, October 3, 2002; Laura Kipnis, "Meet *Playboy* Sr.," *Slate.com*, October 30, 2003; Jennifer Pellet, "Pulling Rabbits out of Hats—Playboy Enterprises Chairman, President and CEO Christie Hefner," *Chief Executive*, September 1999.

36. Author interview with Christie Hefner, October 16, 2007, New York City, NY.

37. Author interview with Christie Hefner.

38. Biographical sheet of Hefner, provided by Linda Marsicano.

39. Author interview with Christie Hefner; and email correspondence from Christie Hefner to author, via Lauren Melone, Playboy Enterprises, Inc., October 17, 2007.

40. Author interview with Christie Hefner.

41. Author interview with Christie Hefner.

42. Author interview with Christie Hefner.

43. Mark Hansel, "Q and A: Christie Hefner."

44. Nicole Nolan, "Playboy Goes Limp without Feminist Vice Grip," *Salon.com*, September 30, 1998.

45. David Carr, "Can an Old Leopard Change Its Silk Pajamas?"

46. Watts, *Mr. Playboy*, 8.

47. Romano, "Daughter of the Revolution."

48. Author interview with Christie Hefner.

Works Cited

ARCHIVES

Hugh M. Hefner Scrapbook Collection, Playboy Mansion, Los Angeles, CA.
Hugh M. Hefner Papers (HMH), Playboy Enterprises, Inc., Chicago, IL.
A. C. Spectorsky Papers (ACS), Playboy Enterprises, Inc., Chicago, IL.
Playboy Records Center (PRC), Playboy Enterprises, Inc., Chicago, IL.

ORAL HISTORY INTERVIEWS

Arlene Bouras, June 22, 2006, New York City, NY.
Dolores Del Monte, February 4, 2007, via telephone.
Alice Denham, November 27, 2006, New York City, NY.
Christie Hefner, October 16, 2007, New York City, NY.
Hugh M. Hefner, November 3, 2006, Los Angeles, CA.
Jennifer Jackson, December 12, 2008, via telephone.
Nat Lehrman, June 23, 2006, New York City, NY.
Gale Morin, February 4, 2007, via email.
Barbara Nellis, May 4, 2006, Chicago, IL.
Joyce Nizzari, June 15, 2007, via email.
Jim Petersen, February 2, 2006, Evanston, IL.
Dick Rosenzweig, November 3, 2006, Los Angeles, CA.
Martha Smith, May 2009, via email.
Victoria Valentino, January 11, 2007, via email.
Carole Waite, August 2008, via telephone.

BIBLIOGRAPHIC SOURCES

ABC News Transcripts. "Playboy at 50 Hugh Hefner." 20/20, November 28, 2003.

Abrahamson, David. *Magazine-Made America: The Cultural Transformation of the Postwar Periodical*. Cresskill, NJ: Hampton Press, Inc., 1996.

Acocella, Joan. "The Girls Next Door." *New Yorker*, March 20, 2006.

Allyn, David. *Make Love, Not War: The Sexual Revolution: An Unfettered History*. Boston: Little, Brown, 2000.

American Library Association. "Conference Opening Session to Feature Advocate Christie Hefner." Press release, June 22, 2009.

Appiah, Kwame Anthony, and Henry Louis Gates, Jr., eds. *Civil Rights: An A–Z Reference of the Movement That Changed America*. Philadelphia: Running Press, 2004.

Bailey, Beth L. *From Front Porch to Back Seat: Courtship in Twentieth-Century America*. Baltimore: Johns Hopkins University Press, 1988.

———. *Sex in the Heartland*. Cambridge, MA: Harvard University Press, 1999.

Banner, Lois. "The Creature from the Black Lagoon: Marilyn Monroe and Whiteness." *Cinema Journal* 47, no. 4 (Summer 2008): 4–29.

Barnes, Brooks. "The Loin in Winter: Hefner Reflects, and Grins." *New York Times*, Media and Advertising section, October 23, 2009.

Battelle, Phyllis. "The Corruptible Male." *Cosmopolitan*, May 1963.

Baumgold, Julie. "You've Come a Long Way, Baby." *New York*, June 9, 1969.

Bazin, Andre. "Entomology of the Pin-Up Girl." In *What is Cinema? Volume 2*. Translated by Hugh Gray. Berkeley: University of California Press, 2004.

Bederman, Gail. *Manliness and Civilization: A Cultural History of Gender and Race in the United States, 1880–1917*. Chicago: University of Chicago Press, 1996.

Beggan, James K., and Scott T. Allison. "The Playboy Rabbit Is Soft, Furry and Cute: Is This Really the Symbol of Masculine Dominance of Women?" *Journal of Men's Studies* 9, no. 3 (Spring 2001): 341–70.

———. "Tough Women in the Unlikeliest Places: The Unexpected Toughness of the Playboy Playmate." *Journal of Popular Culture* 38, no. 5 (August 2005): 796–818.

———. "What Do Playboy Playmates Want? Implications of Expressed Preferences in the Construction of the 'Unfinished' Masculine Identity." *Journal of Men's Studies* 10, no. 1 (Fall 2001): 1–38.

Beggan, James K., Scott T. Allison, and Patricia Gagné. "An Analysis of Stereotype Refutation in *Playboy* by an Editorial Voice: The Advisor Hypothesis." *Journal of Men's Studies* 9, no. 1 (Fall 2000): 1–21.

Beisel, Nicola Kay. *Imperiled Innocents: Anthony Comstock and Family Reproduction in Victorian America*. Princeton: Princeton University Press, 1998.

Bloom, Alexander, and Wini Breines, eds. "No More Miss America." In *Takin' It to the Streets: A Sixties Reader*. New York: Oxford University Press, 1995.

Bogaert, Anthony F., Deborah A. Turkovich, and Carolyn L. Hafer. "A Content Analysis of *Playboy* Centerfolds from 1953 through 1990: Changes in Explicitness, Objectification, and Model's Age." *Journal of Sex Research* 30, no. 2 (May 1993): 135–39.

Bounds, Wendy. "Can Aging Playboy Bunny Lure Women?" *Wall Street Journal*, November 10, 1998.

Braudy, Susan. "The Article I Wrote on Women That *Playboy* Wouldn't Publish." *Glamour*, May 1971.

Breazeale, Kenon. "In Spite of Women: *Esquire* Magazine and the Construction of the Male Consumer." *Signs* 20, no. 1 (Autumn 1994): 1–22.

Breines, Wini. *Young, White, and Miserable*. Chicago: University of Chicago Press, 1992.

Brod, Harry, ed. *The Making of Masculinities: The New Men's Studies*. Boston: Allen & Unwin, 1987.

Brown, Helen Gurley. *Sex and the Single Girl*. New York: Random House, 1962.

———. "Step Into My Parlor." *Cosmopolitan*, April 1970.

Buchwald, Art. "Much Ado for Nothing." *Los Angeles Times*, November 9, 1967.

Buckley, William F., Jr. "A Playboy's Philosophy." *Los Angeles Times*, October 3, 1966.

Buitrago, Katie. "What Sort of Woman Reads *Playboy*." *Chicago Reader*, February 4, 2010.

Burns, Greg. "Adventures in the Skin Trade." *Chicago Tribune Magazine*, October 16, 2005.

Buszek, Maria Elena. *Pin-Up Grrrls: Feminism, Sexuality, Popular Culture*. Durham: Duke University Press, 2006.

Carr, David. "Can an Old Leopard Change Its Silk Pajamas?" *New York Times*, April 21, 2003.

CBS News Transcripts. "Christie Hefner, CEO of Playboy, Successful Feminist Businesswoman." *60 Minutes*, January 24, 1993.

Chalfie, Deborah, and Sarah McKinley. "The Politics of Funding the Women's Movement," from "Selected Abstracts from the Second National Conference of the National Women's Studies Association, May 16–20, 1980, Bloomington, Indiana." *Frontiers: A Journal of Women Studies* 6, no. 1/2 (Spring–Summer 1981): 71.

Chauncey, George. *Gay New York: Gender, Urban Culture, and the Making of the Gay Male World*. New York: Basic Books, 1994.

Churchwell, Sarah. *The Many Lives of Marilyn Monroe*. New York: Metropolitan Books, 2004.

Cohen, Lizabeth. *A Consumer's Republic: The Politics of Mass Consumption in Postwar America*. New York: Vintage Books, 2003.

Cohen, Roger. "Ms. Playboy." *New York Times*, June 9, 1991.

Conekin, Becky. "Fashioning the Playboy: Messages of Style and Masculinity in the Pages of *Playboy* Magazine, 1953–1963." *Fashion Theory* 4, no. 4 (2000): 447–66.

Corliss, Richard. "That Old Feeling: Your Grandfather's *Playboy*." *Time*, January 3, 2004.

Cornell, Drucilla, ed. *Feminism and Pornography*. Oxford: Oxford University Press, 2000.

Cox, Harvey. "*Playboy*'s Doctrine of the Male." *Christianity and Crisis*, April 17, 1961.

Cross, Gary S. *An All-Consuming Century: Why Commercialism Won in Modern America*. New York: Columbia University Press, 2000.

Cross, Robert. "Standoff at the Pleasure Dome." *Chicago Tribune*, February 9, 1969.

Cuordileone, K. A. *Manhood and American Political Culture in the Cold War*. New York: Routledge, 2005.

———. "'Politics in an Age of Anxiety': Cold War Political Culture and the Crisis in American Masculinity, 1949–1960." *Journal of American History* 87 (September 2000): 515–45.

D'Emilio, John. *Sexual Politics, Sexual Communities: The Making of a Homosexual Minority in the United States, 1940–1970*. Chicago: University of Chicago Press, 1983.

D'Emilio, John, and Estelle Freedman. *Intimate Matters: A History of Sexuality in America*. New York: Harper and Row, 1988.

Davidson, Bill. "Czar of the Bunny Empire." *Saturday Evening Post*, April 28, 1962.

Davidson, Sara. "Foremothers." *Esquire*, July 1973.

Davis, Miles, and Quincy Troupe. *Miles: The Autobiography*. New York: Simon and Schuster, 1989.

De Grazia, Victoria, and Ellen Furlough. *The Sex of Things: Gender and Consumption in Historical Perspective*. Berkeley: University of California Press, 1996.

Denham, Alice. *Sleeping with Bad Boys: A Juicy Tell-All of Literary New York in the 1950s and 1960s*. New York: Book Republic, 2006.

Dennis, Donna. *Licentious Gotham: Erotic Publishing and Its Prosecution in Nineteenth-Century New York*. Cambridge, MA: Harvard University Press, 2009.

Diehl, Digby. "Q&A Hugh Hefner." *Los Angeles Times*, February 27, 1972.

Dines, Gail. "'I Buy It for the Articles': *Playboy* Magazine and the Sexualization of Consumerism." In *Gender, Race and Class in Media*, edited by Gail Dines and Jean M. Humez. Thousand Oaks, CA: Sage Publications, 1995.

Doherty, Thomas. *Pre-Code Hollywood: Sex, Immorality, and Insurrection in American Cinema, 1930–1934*. New York: Columbia University Press, 1999.

Douglas, Susan J. *Where the Girls Are: Growing Up Female with the Mass Media*. New York: New York Times Books, 1994.

Dr. X. "Doctor's Dilemma." *Ladies' Home Journal*, May 1966.

DuBois, Ellen Carol, and Lynn Dumenil. *Through Women's Eyes: An American History with Documents*. Boston: Bedford/St. Martin's, 2005.

Duggan, Lisa, and Nan Hunter. *Sex Wars: Sexual Dissent and Political Culture*. New York: Routledge, 2006.

Dworkin, Andrea. *Pornography: Men Possessing Women*. London: Women's Press, 1981.

———. *Woman Hating*. New York: Dutton, 1974.

Dyer, Richard. "Don't Look Now: The Male Pin-up." In *Sexual Subject: A Screen Reader in Sexuality*, edited by Mandy Merck. New York: Routledge, 1992.

Echols, Alice. *Daring to Be Bad: Radical Feminism in America, 1967–1975*. Minneapolis: University of Minnesota Press, 1989.

Economist. "Real Men Get Waxed." July 3, 2003.

Edgren, Gretchen. *The Playboy Book: Six Decades of Centerfolds*. Los Angeles: Taschen, 2005.

———. *The Playmate Book: Six Decades of Centerfolds*. Los Angeles: Taschen, 2005.

Egan, Mary Ellen, and Chana R. Schoenberger. "The World's 100 Most Powerful Women." *Forbes*, August 27, 2008.

Ehrenreich, Barbara. *The Hearts of Men: American Dreams and the Flight from Commitment.* Garden City, NY: Anchor Press/Doubleday, 1983.

Ellis, Kate, et al., eds. *Caught Looking: Feminism, Pornography and Censorship.* East Haven, CT: Long River Books, 1992.

Esquire. "302 Women Who Are Cute When They're Mad." *Esquire*, July 1973.

———. Fashion feature. August 1968.

———. "A Season of Silk Shirts, Fine Fur Coats, Other Old Elegances." November 1968.

———. "What If . . . Gloria Steinem Were Miss America?" July 1973.

———. "When Did You Begin to Take the Women's Movement Seriously?" July 1973.

Evans, Sara M. *Born for Liberty: A History of Women in America.* New York: Free Press, 1989.

Ewen, Stuart. *Captains of Consciousness: Advertising and the Social Roots of the Consumer Culture.* New York: Basic Books, 2001.

Ewen, Stuart, and Elizabeth Ewen. *Channels of Desire: Mass Images and the Shaping of American Consciousness.* New York: McGraw-Hill, 1982.

Ezekiel, Judith. *Feminism in the Heartland.* Columbus: Ohio State University Press, 2002.

Faludi, Susan. *Stiffed: The Betrayal of the American Man.* New York: William Morrow and Company, Inc., 1999.

Flannery, Catherine. "Playboy Boss True to the Feminist Cause." *Toronto Sun*, March 26, 1995.

Foreman, Joel. *The Other Fifties: Interrogating Midcentury American Icons.* Urbana: University of Illinois Press, 1997.

Fox, Richard Wightman, and T. J. Jackson Lears, eds. *The Culture of Consumption: Critical Essays in American History, 1880–1980.* New York: Pantheon Books, 1983.

Fraterrigo, Elizabeth. *Playboy and the Making of the Good Life in Modern America.* New York: Oxford University Press, 2009.

Frazier, George. "The Entrenchment of the American Witch." *Esquire*, February 1962.

Gabor, Mark. *The Pin-Up: A Modest History.* New York: Universe Books, 1972.

Gilbert, James. *A Cycle of Outrage: America's Reaction to the Juvenile Delinquent in the 1950s.* New York: Oxford University Press, 1988.

———. *Men in the Middle: Searching for Masculinity in the 1950s.* Chicago: University of Chicago Press, 2005.

Glickman, Lawrence B. *Consumer Society in American History: A Reader.* Ithaca: Cornell University Press, 1999.

Goldsborough, Robert. "Inside the House that Hef Built." *Chicago Tribune*, December 20, 1964.

Gordon, Linda. *The Moral Property of Women: A History of Birth Control Politics in America.* Urbana: University of Illinois Press, 2007.

Gornick, Vivian. "The Women's Liberation Movement!" *Cosmopolitan*, April 1970.

Greer, Germaine. "What Turns Women On?" *Esquire*, July 1973.

Haidarali, Laila. "Polishing Brown Diamonds: African American Women, Popular Magazines, and the Advent of Modeling in Early Postwar America," *Journal of Women's History* 17, no. 1 (2005): 10–37.

Halberstam, David. *The Fifties*. New York: Villard Books, 1993.

Hansel, Mark. "Q and A: Christie Hefner." *In Business Las Vegas*, June 13–19, 2008.

Harper, Jennifer. "Buy *Playboy* for the Articles—Really." *Washington Times*, October 3, 2002.

Haskell, Molly. *From Reverence to Rape: The Treatment of Women in the Movies*. New York: Holt, 1974.

Hefner, Hugh. "The *Playboy* Philosophy." Parts 1–4, 1962–65, collected version. Chicago: HMH Publishing Co., Inc.

Heller, Steven. "The Art [Paul] of Playboy." *Print* 54, no. 1 (January/February 2000): 41–49.

Hollows, Joanne. "The Bachelor Dinner: Masculinity, Class and Cooking in *Playboy*, 1953–1961." *Continuum: Journal of Media and Cultural Studies* 16, no. 2 (2002): 143–55.

hooks, bell. "Selling Hot Pussy: Representations of Black Female Sexuality in the Cultural Marketplace." In *Writing on the Body: Female Embodiment and Feminist Theory*, edited by Katie Conboy et al. New York: Columbia University Press, 1997.

Horowitz, Helen Lefkowitz. *Rereading Sex: Battles over Sexual Knowledge and Suppression in Nineteenth-Century America*. New York: Vintage Books, 2003.

Hylton, Wil S. "Hugh Hefner." *Esquire*, June 2002.

Ingraham, Chrys. *White Weddings: Romancing Heterosexuality in Popular Culture*. New York: Routledge, 1999.

Kallan, Richard A., and Robert D. Brooks. "The Playmate of the Month: Naked but Nice." *Journal of Popular Culture* 8, no. 2 (Fall 1974): 328–36.

Kaplan, Don. "Why Women Love 'Girls Next Door.'" *New York Post*, August 6, 2007.

Kastner, Susan. "Think Playboy Demeans Women?" *Toronto Star*, March 19, 1995.

Katz, Jonathan. *The Invention of Heterosexuality*. New York: Dutton, 1995.

Kendrick, Walter. *The Secret Museum: Pornography in Modern Culture*. New York: Viking Penguin, 1987.

Kessler-Harris, Alice. *In Pursuit of Equity: Women, Men, and the Quest for Economic Citizenship in 20th-Century America*. New York: Oxford University Press, 2001.

Kipnis, Laura. *Bound and Gagged: Pornography and the Politics of Fantasy in America*. New York: Grove Press, 1996.

———. "Meet *Playboy* Sr." *Slate.com*, October 30, 2003.

Kitch, Carolyn. *The Girl on the Magazine Cover: The Origins of Visual Stereotypes in American Mass Media*. Chapel Hill: University of North Carolina Press, 2001.

Klein, Christina. *Cold War Orientalism: Asia in the Middlebrow Imagination, 1945–1961*. Berkeley: University of California Press, 2003.

Knowles, Marjorie Fine. "Foundation Grants to Women's Groups." *Women's Studies Newsletter*, no. 5 (Fall 1973).

Lawrenson, Helen. "The Feminine Mistake," *Esquire*, January 1971.

Lear, Martha Weinman. "Q: If You Rape a Woman and Steal Her TV, What Can They Get You for in New York? A: Stealing Her TV." *New York Times*, January 30, 1972, 11, 55.

Lehrman, Nat. *Masters and Johnson Explained*. Chicago: Playboy Press, 1970.

Levine, Alana. *Wallowing in Sex: The New Sexual Culture of 1970s American Television*. Durham: Duke University Press, 2007.

Levy, Ariel. *Female Chauvinist Pigs: Women and the Rise of Raunch Culture*. New York: Free Press, 2005.

Lewis, J. Anthony. "The 'Alternative Life-Style' of Playboys and Playmates." *New York Times*, June 11, 1972.

Lichtenstein, Grace. "For Most Women, 'Strike' Day Was Just a Topic of Conversation." *New York Times*, August 27, 1970.

Lombard, Anne S. *Making Manhood: Growing Up Male in Colonial New England*. Cambridge, MA: Harvard University Press, 2003.

Lord, M. G. "Pornutopia: How Feminist Scholars Learned to Love Dirty Pictures." *Lingua Franca* 7, no. 3 (March 1997).

Lyons, Clare A. *Sex among the Rabble: An Intimate History of Gender and Power in the Age of Revolution, Philadelphia, 1730–1830*. Chapel Hill: University of North Carolina, 2006.

MacKinnon, Catharine A. *Feminism Unmodified: Discourses on Life and Law*. Cambridge, MA: Harvard University Press, 1988.

———. *Only Words*. Cambridge, MA: Harvard University Press, 1996.

Marcus, Steven. *The Other Victorians: A Study of Sexuality and Pornography in Mid-Nineteenth-Century England*. New York: Basic Books, 1966.

Matacin, Mala L., and Jerry M. Burger. "A Content Analysis of Sexual Themes in *Playboy* Cartoons." *Sex Roles* 17, nos. 3–4 (1987): 179–86.

May, Elaine Tyler. *Homeward Bound: American Families in the Cold War Era*. New York: Basic Books, 1999.

May, Rollo. *Love and Will*. New York: W. W. Norton & Company, Inc., 1969.

McCormick, Brian. "Playboy Testing the XX Factor." *Crain's Chicago Business*, October 2001.

Merrill, Hugh. *Esky: The Early Years at Esquire*. New Brunswick: Rutgers University Press, 1995.

Messer, Ellen, and Kathryn E. May, eds. *Back Rooms: Voices from the Illegal Abortion Era*. Buffalo: Prometheus Books, 1994.

Meyerowitz, Joanne. *How Sex Changed: A History of Transsexuality in the United States*. Cambridge, MA: Harvard University Press, 2002.

———. *Not June Cleaver: Women and Gender in Postwar America, 1945–1960*. Philadelphia: Temple University Press, 1994.

———. "Women, Cheesecake, and Borderline Material: Responses to Girlie Pictures in the Mid-Twentieth-Century U.S." In *Sexual Borderlands: Constructing an American Sexual Past*, edited by Kathleen Kennedy and Sharon Ullman. Columbus: Ohio State University Press, 2003.

Miller, Russell. *Bunny: The Real Story of Playboy*. New York: Holt, Rinehart and Winston, 1984.

Moore, Scott. "New Front in Battle of Sexes: Campus Women Want to Liberate Betty Coed." *Los Angeles Times*, February 16, 1970.

Moskin, J. Robert. "Why Do Women Dominate Him?" In *The Decline of the American Male*, by the editors of *Look* magazine. New York: Random House, 1958.

Neitz, Mary Joe. Review of *Abortion and the Politics of Motherhood*, by Kristin Luker. *Journal for the Scientific Study of Religion* 24, no. 4 (December 1985): 446–47.

Nelson, Bryce. "Antibunnies Jeer at Hefner Peace Bash." *Los Angeles Times*, April 17, 1970.

Newsweek. "The *Playboy* Bust." October 18, 1971.

New York Times. "*Playboy* Case Closed." November 6, 1958.

———. "Power to Censor Is Still Unclear." December 20, 1959.

———. "Virile Democracy Is Urged by the President as Protection against Perils from Abroad." December 12, 1948.

———. "Women Militants Disrupt Cavett Show with Hefner." May 27, 1970.

Nolan, Nicole. "Playboy Goes Limp without Feminist Vice Grip." *Salon.com*, September 30, 1998.

Oakley, J. Ronald. *God's Country: America in the Fifties*. New York: Dembner Books, 1986.

O'Connor, Thomas F. "The National Organization for Decent Literature: A Phase in American Catholic Censorship." *Library Quarterly* 65, no. 4 (October 1995): 386–414.

Osgerby, Bill. "Muscular Manhood and Salacious Sleaze: The Singular World of the 1950s Macho Pulps." In *Containing America: Cultural Production and Consumption in 50s America*, edited by Nathan Abrams and Julie Hughes. New York: Continuum, 2005.

———. *Playboys in Paradise: Masculinity, Youth and Leisure-Style in Modern America*. Oxford: Berg, 2001.

Pellet, Jennifer. "Pulling Rabbits Out of Hats—Playboy Enterprises Chairman, President and CEO Christie Hefner." *Chief Executive*, September 1999.

Pendergast, Tom. *Creating the Modern Man: American Magazines and Consumer Culture, 1900–1950*. Columbia, MO: University of Missouri Press, 2000.

Petersen, James R. *The Century of Sex: Playboy's History of the Sexual Revolution, 1900–1999*. New York: Grove Press, 1999.

Pitzulo, Carrie. "The Battle in Every Man's Bed: *Playboy* and the Fiery Feminists." *Journal of the History of Sexuality* 17, no. 2 (2008): 259–89.

Prasso, Sheridan. *The Asian Mystique: Dragon Ladies, Geisha Girls and Our Fantasies of the Exotic Orient*. New York: Public Affairs, 2005.

Preciado, Beatriz. "Pornotopia." In *Cold War Hothouses: Inventing Postwar Culture from Cockpit to Playboy*, edited by Annmarie Brennan, Beatriz Colomina, and Jeannie Kim. New York: Princeton Architectural Press, 2004.

Richardson, Herbert W. *Nun, Witch, Playmate: The Americanization of Sex*. New York: Harper & Row, Publishers, 1971.

Riesman, David. *The Lonely Crowd: A Study of the Changing American Character*. New Haven: Yale University Press, 1955.

Romano, Lois. "Cristie [sic] Hefner, Daughter of the Revolution." *Washington Post*, December 4, 1983.

Rosen, Marjorie. *Popcorn Venus: Women, Movies & the American Dream*. New York: Avon Books, 1974.

Rosen, Ruth. *The Lost Sisterhood: Prostitution in America, 1900–1918*. Baltimore: Johns Hopkins University Press, 1982.

———. *The World Split Open: How the Modern Women's Movement Changed America*. New York: Penguin, 2001.

Rotundo, E. Anthony. *American Manhood: Transformations in Masculinity from the Revolution to the Modern Era*. New York: Basic Books, 1993.

Savran, David. *Taking It Like a Man: White Masculinity, Masochism, and Contemporary American Culture*. Princeton: Princeton University Press, 1998.

Scanlon, Jennifer. *The Gender and Consumer Culture Reader*. New York: New York University Press, 2000.

———. *Inarticulate Longings: The Ladies' Home Journal, Gender and the Promise of Consumer Culture*. New York: Routledge, 1995.

———. *Men Are Not the Enemy: The Life of Helen Gurley Brown*. New York: Oxford University Press, 2009.

Schlesinger, Arthur, Jr. "The Crisis of American Masculinity." *Esquire*, November 1958.

Scott, Joseph E., and Steven J. Cuvelier. "Sexual Violence in *Playboy* Magazine: A Longitudinal Content Analysis." *Journal of Sex Research* 23, no. 4 (November 1987): 534–39.

Scott, Kathryn Lee. *The Bunny Years*. New York: Pomegranate Press, 1999.

Segal, Lynne. *Slow Motion: Changing Masculinities, Changing Men*. New Brunswick: Rutgers University Press, 1990.

Seidenbaum, Art. "Minister in the Street and the Girl in the Center-Fold." *Los Angeles Times*, October 20, 1965.

Smith, Neal. "Odd Fact: Women Biggest Viewers of 'Girls Next Door.'" *Denver Post*, December 25, 2007.

Snitow, Ann, et al., eds. *Powers of Desire: The Politics of Sexuality*. New York: Monthly Review Press, 1983.

Spoto, Donald. *Marilyn Monroe: The Biography*. New York: Harper Collins Publishers, 1993.

Stansell, Christine. *City of Women: Sex and Class in New York, 1789–1860*. Urbana: University of Illinois Press, 1987.

Star, J. "Growing Tragedy of Illegal Abortion." *Look*, October 19, 1965.

Steinem, Gloria. "I Was a Playboy Bunny." In *Outrageous Acts and Everyday Rebellions*. New York: Henry Holt and Company, 1995.

———. "What *Playboy* Doesn't Know about Women Could Fill a Book." *McCall's*, October 1970.

Strossen, Nadine. *Defending Pornography: Free Speech, Sex and the Fight for Women's Rights*. New York: NYU Press, 2000.

Strub, Whitney. "Black and White and Banned All Over: Race, Censorship and Obscenity in Postwar Memphis," *Journal of Social History* 40, no. 3 (Spring 2007): 685–715.

———. "The Clearly Obscene and the Queerly Obscene: Heteronormativity and Obscenity in Cold War Los Angeles," *American Quarterly* 60, no. 2 (June 2008): 373–98.

———. "Perversion for Profit: Citizens for Decent Literature and the Arousal of an Antiporn Public in the 1960s," *Journal of the History of Sexuality* 15, no. 2 (May 2006): 258–91.

Swiencicki, Mark A. "Consuming Brotherhood: Men's Culture, Style and Recreation as Consumer Culture, 1880–1930." In *Consumer Society in American History: A Reader*, edited by Lawrence B. Glickman. Ithaca: Cornell University Press, 1999.

Talese,Gay. *Thy Neighbor's Wife*. New York: Dell Publishing, 1980,

Tebbel, John, and Mary Ellen Zuckerman. *The Magazine in America, 1741–1990*. New York: Oxford University Press, 1991.

Time. "Adventures in the Skin Trade." July 30, 1973.

———. "The Boss of Taste City." March 24, 1961.

———. "Coming to Terms." October 24, 1969.

———. "The Desperate Dilemma of Abortion." October 13, 1967.

———. "Disease of Unwanted Pregnancy." September 15, 1967.

———. "Hefner's Grandchild." August 28, 1972.

———. "Hugh Hefner Faces Middle Age." February 14, 1969.

———. "A Letter from the Publisher." March 3, 1967.

———. "More Abortions: Reasons Why." September 17, 1965.

———. "The New Feminists: Revolt against 'Sexism.'" November 21, 1969.

———. "Proof of Abortion's Value." May 26, 1967.

———. "Sassy Newcomer." September 24, 1956.

———. "Think Clean." March 3, 1967.

Tomkins, Calvin. "Mr. Playboy of the Western World." *Saturday Evening Post*, April 23, 1966.

U.S. Bureau of the Census. "Current Population Reports: Income in 1967 of Persons in the United States." Series P-60, no. 60, U.S. Department of Commerce, 1969.

Washington Speakers Bureau. Biography of Christie Hefner, www.washingtonspeakers bureau.com.

Watts, Steven. *Mr. Playboy: Hugh Hefner and the American Dream*. Hoboken: Wiley, 2008.

Weymouth, Lally. "The Princess of Playboy." *New York Magazine*, June 21, 1982.

Weyr, Thomas. *Reaching for Paradise: The Playboy Vision of America*. New York: New York Times Books, 1978.

White, Kevin. *The First Sexual Revolution: The Emergence of Male Heterosexuality in Modern America*. New York: New York University Press, 1993.

Whyte, Jr., William H. *The Organization Man*. New York: Anchor Books, 1957.

Williams, Linda. *Hard Core: Power, Pleasure, and the "Frenzy of the Visible."* Berkeley: University of California Press, 1989.

———. *Porn Studies*. Durham: Duke University Press, 2004.

Williams, Megan E. "The *Crisis* Cover Girl: Lena Horne, the NAACP, and Representations of African-American Femininity, 1941–1945," *American Periodicals* 16, no. 2 (2006): 200–218.

Wilson, Christopher P. "The Rhetoric of Consumption: Mass-Market Magazines and the Demise of the Gentle Reader, 1880–1920." In *The Culture of Consumption: Critical Essays in American History, 1880–1980*, edited by Richard Wightman Fox and T. J. Jackson Lears. New York: Pantheon Books, 1983.

Winerip, Michael. "No Silk Jammies for Her." *New York Times*, September 27, 2009.

Witt, Linda. "Women Do Matter at *Playboy*." *Chicago Daily News*, July 10, 1973.

wowOwow: The Women on the Web. "Ex-Playboy CEO Christie Hefner on Lilly Ledbetter, Women in the Workforce and Political Aspirations." 2009. http://www.wowowow.com/pov/ex-playboy-ceo-christie-hefner-ledbetter-equal-pay-and-obama-242949.

Yalom, Marilyn. *A History of the Breast*. New York: Ballantine Books, 1997.

Index